RHAPSODY IN BLUE

RHAPSODY IN BLUE

An RAF Fighter Pilot's Life During the Cold War

GRAHAM WILLIAMS

FONTHILL

Learn more about Fonthill Media. Join our mailing list to
find out about our latest titles and special offers at:
www.fonthillmedia.com

Fonthill Media Limited
Fonthill Media LLC
www.fonthillmedia.com

office@fonthillmedia.com

First published in the United Kingdom
and the United States of America 2016

This paperback edition published 2017

British Library Cataloguing in Publication Data:
A catalogue record for this book is available from the British Library

Copyright © Graham Williams 2016, 2017

ISBN 978-1-78155-665-8

The right of Graham Williams to be identified as the author of this work has been
asserted by him in accordance with the Copyright, Designs and Patents Act 1988.

All rights reserved. No part of this publication may be reproduced, stored in a
retrieval system or transmitted in any form or by any means, electronic, mechanical,
photocopying, recording or otherwise, without prior permission in writing from
Fonthill Media Limited

Typeset in 10.5pt on 13pt Sabon
Printed and bound by CPI Group (UK) Ltd, Croydon, CR0 4YY

Contents

	Foreword	7
	Prologue	9
1	*Per Ardua Ad Astra*	13
2	*Audax Omnia Perpeti*	23
3	The Ambulance Brigade	39
4	Hither and Thither	61
5	Test to Learn, Learn to Test	84
6	'A' (Fighter Test) Squadron, Boscombe Down	89
7	*Tertius Primus Erit*	128
8	*Concordia Artus Roborat*	160
9	Seek and Strike	167
10	Keeper of the Peace	188
11	Cody's Tree	195
12	*Probe Probare*	204
	Epilogue	220
	Glossary of Terms and Acronyms	232
	Appendix—List of Aircraft Flown	236

Foreword

By
Air Chief Marshal Sir Richard Johns GCB, KCVO,
CBE, FRAeS

Graham Williams's narrative of his career in the Royal Air Force is a fighter pilot's story of his association with military aviation during the Nation's final withdrawal from Empire and the commitment to NATO during the darkest days of the Cold War. A career that started as a Flight Cadet at the RAF College Cranwell ended with retirement 37 years later in the rank of Air Vice-Marshal; Graham was twice decorated with the Air Force Cross. No mention of the awards and how they were won will be found in this fascinating and most readable book.

Its fascination lies in the evocative accounts of some risky ventures and hair raising incidents within a variety of circumstances, and as seen from the cockpits of aircraft ranging from a refurbished SE5 of First World War vintage to the genuinely rapid such as the Lightning. Graham makes no secret of his abiding love for the Hunter—shared with many others—but his tour as a Test Pilot at Farnborough and Boscombe Down coincided with the introduction of three new fighter aircraft, the Harrier, Phantom and Jaguar all of which are the subject of his analytical comment. While it is worth noting that his earlier attendance at The Empire Test Pilot's School was more the consequence of serendipity than career ambition, Graham's involvement in the operational development of these aircraft made a unique contribution to a most welcome expansion of the RAF's offensive air power.

Fifteen or so years later, while serving in the Directorate of Operational Requirements, and having completed a second tour at Boscombe Down as the Commandant, Graham was deeply involved in the procurement of the Boeing E3 AWACS aircraft following the long overdue demise of Nimrod AEW. Thereafter his energy was focused on the European Fighter Aircraft project which evolved into the aeroplane now named as Typhoon. The inside story of associated political and industrial wrangling concerned with Nimrod AEW and Typhoon provides a handy reference for historians and laymen alike.

Away from the esoteric world of test flying Graham served in Fighter Command, Middle East Air Force and RAF Germany. He thus accumulated a wealth of operational flying experience in his ascent from Pilot Officer on No. 54 Squadron to Station Commander at RAF Brüggen in Germany with the nuclear armed Jaguar Wing under command. During this ascent Graham was one of the first generation of Harrier squadron commanders and alone in having previous experience of the aircraft at Boscombe Down which included participation in the Trans-Atlantic air race flown in 1969—a story of a hazardous enterprise he recalls in cool detail. Although the fast jet perspective of squadron and station life predominates this book presents an authentic portrayal of RAF life—warts and all—in the second half of the twentieth century. As a premier division fighter pilot he does not allow anecdotes to suffer obfuscation of the truth and I can vouch for this from personal experience.

Graham's final tour at the end of his career was in the appointment of Commandant General of the Royal Air Force Regiment. He records that he was reminded 'of the merits of loyalty, commitment and duty'. I do not think Graham needed reminding because these attributes illuminate the pages of this compelling autobiography; a 'must' read for all with an interest in aviation, military and civilian alike.

Prologue

The Hawker Hunter
'You are old Hawker Hunter,'
The young man said,
'And your paintwork is no longer bright,
Yet I see you constantly stagger aloft,
Do you think that at your age it's right?'
'Yes, I'm old,' smiled the Hunter,
As you observe,
Yet you're missing the pertinent thought,
Were it not for its age no antique would deserve
All the money for which it is bought.'
'But you're old AND outdated,'
The young man frowned,
'And your instruments ancient and plain.
Tell me, how can you navigate so close to the ground
Without using a digital brain?'
'In my youth,' yawned the Hunter,
Pilots could fly
Using stopwatch, compass and map.
And I'm teaching them still to be Kings of the Sky,
Now be off … while I'm taking a nap.'
Anonymous, Wittering Review, *July 1976*

The Hunter is perhaps one of the few aircraft that engendered such a strong feeling of loyalty and enthusiasm, almost to the same level as the Spitfire had done for the previous generation. It was conceived in the late 1940s and first flew on 20 July 1951. It is interesting to note that the aircraft that flew then is very little different in outline to the last Mk 9. I remember whilst still at school, it must have been 1952 or 53, going to the Farnborough Air Show with my father when the Hunter and the Swift were having a competition as to who could make the loudest supersonic bang over the airfield. Somehow, he had arranged for us to have lunch with Mike Lithgow—I think he knew his father—in the Test Pilots' Tent, and a very sumptuous lunch it was. Mike Lithgow was, of course, an ex-Fleet Air Arm Pilot and a Supermarine Test Pilot for the Swift. Neville Duke was flying the Hunter. I have no recollection of who made the loudest supersonic bang and, despite being in the company of Mike Lithgow, I know which aircraft I preferred—it was the Hunter. Little did I realise then that I would subsequently spend a substantial amount of my time in the cockpit of that aircraft.

There is a saying that 'if it looks right, it flies right'. Even today, in the second decade of the twenty-first century, the Hunter still 'looks right'. Indeed its subsonic performance still matches or even exceeds that of many more modern aircraft. In its infancy, it had one or two foibles. The Mk 1s and 4s, with the Avon engine, had considerable problems with engine surging, especially when gun gases were ingested during gun firing, and you always had to take care with throttle handling. Fortunately, even if they flamed out, one could usually manage to relight them. The Mk 2s and 5s, with their Sapphire engines, suffered from something called 'centre line closure' which caused the engine to seize. This was not usually recoverable and the squadrons so equipped were generally known as the 'Glider Squadrons'. But gun firing did not affect the Sapphire engine in any way and it was somewhat ironic that Rolls Royce took some design features off the Sapphire to solve their problem with the Avon.

My Hunter experience started in 1958 with the Mk 4 and the 100 series engine with about 7000 lbs of thrust, which was subsequently replaced by the Mk 6 with the 200 series Avon with 10,000 lbs of thrust, a significant increase in performance. The Mk 6 Hunter became the standard aircraft of Fighter Command and 2 ATAF. It was not over-endowed with either fuel or avionics. Most of our fighter aircraft had been built to a requirement of the point defence of the UK; and that was not seen to need particularly long range for such a small island. The only navigation aid was DME which would give a distance only reading to a beacon. To get any sort idea of where you were, you had to get readings from two beacons and then plot a fix. This was a time consuming activity, not always successful as the reliability of the beacons was never good, and you never had enough hands and eyes to fly the aircraft and plot positions on a map. It was another peculiarity of the British that any form of autopilot was seen as being quite unnecessary, unmanly and unprofessional for fighter pilots. So our fighter aircraft were never equipped with such a device. The Americans on the other hand had fuel, space in the cockpit, and autopilots (and even ashtrays) in most if not all of their aircraft—one of the results no doubt of living in a large continental land mass where long distances were the norm.

The sole armament of the Hunter consisted of 4 × 30 mm Aden canons with 120 rounds in each gun. They were effective weapons and the recoil when you fired them was such that it felt as though it practically stopped the aircraft in mid-air. In fact it would knock about 20 kts off the airspeed. Aiming was achieved with a gyro gun-sight combined with radar ranging, the latter being notoriously unreliable. But it was a beautiful aircraft to fly. It had just one nasty habit of pitching up if you pulled too hard in a turn; but this was cured later on by the addition of saw tooth leading edges on the wing.

It cruised with ease at low level at 420 kts and at 0.9M at high level. It could climb to 50,000 ft with relative ease. With its hydraulically assisted controls, it was a delight to handle and, once the pitch up had been cured, totally vice free. It was also stronger than it looked. It went through trees (David Brook), bounced off mountains (Henry Ploszek), went through 5 ft high dry stone walls (Ching Fuller) and cut through many a high tension cable, in one instance returning without the fin (Ray Offord).

The final versions of the Hunter were the Mk 9, which became in effect a ground attack aircraft and the FR10 which was a fighter reconnaissance aircraft equipped with cameras. They both had big 230 gallon drop-tanks, a tail chute, and a radio compass as an additional navigation aid. The Mk 9 could also fire rockets, the 3 inch 'drainpipe', so called because that was what it looked like. They had a variety of heads, the most usual being the 60 lb HE and the aircraft could carry eight on each wing. This was latterly replaced by the SNEB rocket pod, which carried 19 rockets on each wing, smaller than the 3 inch but much higher velocity and hence easier to aim. But they could not equal the damage done by 16 × 60 lb HE 3 inch drainpipes which you could feel go off underneath you in no uncertain terms.

I was to spend about half of my flying career in the Hunter, mainly Mk 4s, 6s and 9s and the best part of 2000 hours in the cockpit. In all that time it never let me down. I had one flameout in a Mk 4, totally my own fault because of ham-fisted throttle handling, and one instance in a Mk 6 when one main undercarriage leg failed to come down. Even in that latter case the aircraft was barely damaged, just needing a new drop tank and a new wingtip, and was back serviceable on the line the following day.

My first trip in a Hunter 4 took place on 20 February 1958 at Chivenor in Devon and my last in a Hunter 9, XE601, on 12 December 1985 from Boscombe Down. It was my last solo flight in the Royal Air Force and XE601 was the last single seat Hunter remaining in service. This is the story of how it all came to pass and what occurred along the way. And should my memory sometimes be at fault in relation to time, place and even names, please forgive me. It all happened a long time ago!

1

Per Ardua Ad Astra

Why did I join the RAF? It is not a question I find easy to answer. During the first interviews, they always asked that question and I always had difficulty in finding an exact response, or at least finding the response that I thought they wanted to hear. Obviously I wanted to fly; but that seemed rather a trite and unimaginative answer. Nevertheless it was true and it proved to be adequate.

At school I had never been quite sure what it was that I wanted to do. In those days it was not assumed that everyone wanted to go to university and I had no particular aspirations in that direction. My Father had hinted that he wanted me to follow in his footsteps into the family business but that had no attractions. I had not exactly shone academically, not so much through lack of ability but rather from being inclined to be somewhat idle. After completing the O Level syllabus, I had joined the modern languages stream for two reasons. Firstly I thought that speaking French and German would be a useful asset whatever I did; and secondly it was seen as the easy solution with regard to workload. The problem was that it turned out that I had no great aptitude or feeling for languages. In addition, when you combined that with no real desire to learn, it was a disastrous decision. Oddly enough I did have a natural ability for mathematics, and indeed I enjoyed the subject to the extent that I did a GCE paper called Additional Maths in my spare time just for fun. I never realised at the time how useful this would be.

As a small lad, I had, of course, had all the usual interests in building and flying model aircraft. Like many at the time I had nearly lost several fingers trying to start model aircraft engines. However, my first real introduction to aircraft was when a very close family friend, Maurice Smith, took me to the Farnborough Air display in about 1950. He had been a bomber pilot in the war, flying Hampdens, Manchesters and Lancasters completing two tours in Bomber Command ending up on the staff of No. 8 Group which dealt mainly with Pathfinders. He also collected a DFC and bar on the way and left at the end of the war as a squadron leader having started off as a sergeant pilot. All I can remember was that the new aircraft at Farnborough at the time included the Athena and the Balliol—both advanced training machines—and Maurice commented that they seemed to be more powerful than anything he had flown—which viewed in retrospect was patently untrue. Then, as I mentioned in the Prologue, my father took me to Farnborough a few years later. Somehow he knew Mike Lithgow's father who arranged for us to attend the show and have lunch in the test pilot's tent with Mike Lithgow who was the test pilot for Supermarine. It was the time when there was a great battle taking place between the Hunter and the Swift and breaking the sound barrier and Mike Lithgow was flying the Swift. As you can imagine, I was almost totally speechless to be surrounded by all these men who were, to us ordinary mortals, the heroes of the day. So I decided that I would rather like to follow in their footsteps and start by joining the RAF; little did I imagine that I would just about fulfil my dreams.

The first step was to take a new direction at school. I had been a somewhat indifferent drummer in the school CCF band, it being another easy option. Now I transferred immediately to the RAF section and applied for a Flying Scholarship. The RAF had just introduced this scheme which, if your application was successful, gave you 30 hours of flying at a civil flying school and a Private Pilot's Licence (PPL) at the end of it. It did not commit you to joining the RAF. Then I looked at the various routes open for joining the RAF. You could join as a National Serviceman and, if you were lucky, be selected for pilot training. You could join for an 8 or 12 year Short Service Commission, which had its attractions. Alternatively, you could go to the RAF College at Cranwell, assuming you could pass the entry exams. It seemed to me that the only route to go was the latter just in case you decided that you wanted to make a complete career of it. You could always resign if it turned out to be a drastic mistake. Entry into Cranwell required 2 A Level GCEs or passing the Civil Service exam which was halfway between O and A Levels. I was due to take my A Levels in French and German during the summer of 1954 but had no great confidence that I would pass. So I covered the options by taking the Civil Service exam as well. In the event I passed just one A Level; but fortunately I passed the Civil Service exam. So I had the entry requirements for Cranwell.

The first interviews I attended were for the flying scholarship and the first 'hiccup' was failing the medical exam because I had suffered quite badly from sinus trouble as a child. My father stepped into the breach and arranged for me to go to some Harley Street ENT specialist who examined me and said that it would not be a problem. In fact, he was quite wrong as it turned out. However, I passed the medical on the say-so of the ENT specialist, was awarded the Flying Scholarship and I was sent to the Wiltshire School of Flying at Thruxton. The deal was that I would learn to fly at weekends, which involved leaving school on a Friday evening, catching a bus to Andover where someone from the flying club would pick me up. Thruxton had been a wartime airfield which had runways, a couple of hangars, a control tower and Nissen huts for accommodation. The bar and the restaurant, such as it was, were in the control tower. They had a Chief Flying Instructor and a couple of other resident instructors and, occasionally, an RAF instructor from Boscombe Down would come across at weekends to help out. The Tiger Moth was the aircraft on which students were taught to fly. They did have a few other types such as an Auster and a Proctor. The whole outfit seemed to be run on a very casual basis. Indeed when I look back at it now, I am surprised that we did not have any major accidents. To give a flavour of the atmosphere, we never used to use chocks when swinging a Tiger to start it; which was foolhardy to say the least. There was just one petrol pump opposite the control tower and the favourite sport was to see how close you could get your aircraft to it by taxying up and cutting the engine so that you could refuel it without having to manhandle the aircraft closer—remember a Tiger did not have any brakes. That game came to an end when the inevitable happened and someone (not me) knocked the petrol pump over.

I started flying at Thruxton in October 1954 and shortly after went to Cranwell for two days of selection tests which really have not changed much to this day. It was not long before I heard that I had been accepted for a cadetship at Cranwell starting in January 1955. Meanwhile I carried on with the Flying Scholarship. It took me 8 hours to go solo and I suspect that every pilot remembers the time when he first ventured into the sky on his own. I certainly do and it is not very far from the truth when I say that I was terrified. The thought that there was no longer anyone in the front who could take over if I got it all wrong was a great concern. But then again it was also a moment of great joy and a feeling of freedom. Twenty minutes later I was back on the ground and pretty secure in the knowledge and confident that I had made the right decision to fly as a career. By the end of December I had got halfway through the PPL course but at the beginning of January I was due to present myself at Cranwell.

Theoretically I had to forego the remainder of the Flying Scholarship, as it was only valid whilst I was at school. I do not know how it was managed, but I suspect the books were cooked so that I could come back after my first term at Cranwell and complete my PPL. I have a number of fond memories of Thruxton. Quite apart from the flying, I had my first real introduction to beer (and a surfeit thereof). Cross countries in the Tiger were an adventure. I remember going to Portsmouth, Sandown on the Isle of Wight, and Shoreham. They might have only been 50 miles away at most, but it seemed a long way to me. The Wiltshire School of Flying was owned by the Doran Webb family who did not appear to take any active part in running the place. And the instructors were characters. Wade Palmer was the CFI and claimed to have flown Spitfires from the very beginning of the war. As far as he was concerned, rules were made to be broken and he did not exactly set a good example to the students. John Heaton was a 'gentle giant' and had also flown Spitfires but mainly in the Far East; and he was a steadier character. At the end of the war he had been parachuted into POW camps in Java to bring relief to the inmates. Jumbo Jennings had, I think, been an instructor all his life and provided some stability to the organisation. They were all memorable people and Thruxton was an experience I would not have missed for the world.

On 5 January 1955 I travelled by train to Grantham and thence by bus to Cranwell to join the RAF as a cadet. I shared a compartment with Chuck Coulcher who was to be in same Entry and Squadron as me. I was 17½ years old to the day. There were 36 of us on our particular entry, No. 71, 12 to each squadron named, imaginatively, A, B and C Squadrons. Our first two terms were to be as Junior Entries in the Nissen Huts just south of the Junior Parade Square and north of the Hangars on the South airfield. The officer in charge of junior entries was Flt Lt Des Hall with a Flight Sergeant Mitchell as his deputy and chief drill instructor. Of Flight Sergeant Mitchell, his little Geordie National Service clerk said, 'Och, he's no Flight Sergeant, he's a gentleman'. And it was true, but you still listened very carefully to what he said and followed his directions to the letter. You also knew that you could go to him with a problem if you had one and he would do his best to sort you out. He was a father figure to most cadets.

The first term in Junior Entries was all about getting to know about the RAF, drill and spit and polish of every description. Drill really dominated our lives; that and the fact that it was the task of the entry above you to make life hell if not completely unbearable. We were in 12-man huts which had to be maintained at the highest standard. Floors polished till they shone, coke stoves blacked to perfection, bedding and clothing immaculately folded and presented in a set pattern. And at about ten o'clock at night, just as you had everything prepared for the next day's activities, your hut would be raided and trashed. By midnight you would be wading ankle deep through water and mud with just about everything ruined. You then spent the next 6 hours repairing the damage as best you could and more often than not, by the time the morning inspection was due, you would never have known that anything had occurred. This mindless activity became somewhat tedious after a time; but it was all said to be 'character forming' and part of being a cadet. It was a part that most if not all of us could have done without. We did rebel at one stage, ambushing the senior entry as they were about to raid one night. That seemed to have an effect and a sort of armed truce followed. There were other various activities which were designed, so it was said, to find out what you were made of. One of those was the 'First Term Boxing Competition'. You were paired up roughly by size and weight and then invited to slug it out in front of the whole College. I do not remember too much about it except that I faced Derek Gibson and lost the bout rather painfully. I have always thought boxing to be a somewhat barbaric sport and the experience did nothing to change my views.

Those first two terms in Junior Entries were pretty tedious. You never got near an airplane except for the odd trip in an Anson as air experience. And most of the activities were of a mind-numbingly boring nature. You did get to know your fellow cadets and they emanated from a variety of sources, public schools, grammar schools, ex-National Servicemen, ex Halton cadets, Commonwealth and Foreign Nationals, although we had none of the latter on our entry. We made friendships which last to this day. Apart from the Junior Entries regime, Cranwell operated very much like a university in that you had three terms in the year with an Easter and Christmas break and a long summer vacation. Thus it was that I was able to break the monotony between the first two terms and go and finish my flying at Thruxton. So it was that in May 1955 I passed the flying and ground exams and was awarded my Private Pilot's Licence with a grand total of 30 hours on the Tiger Moth. It was to be another year before I passed my driving test! There was one other aspect that made my life a little easier. The family firm had provided all the children of the directors an allowance of £5 a week whilst they underwent National Service. They decided to extend that courtesy to me while I was a cadet at Cranwell. Since my RAF pay was only £2 9s a week, I was, comparatively speaking, a 'rich baron'. Unfortunately, it was not long before my father had an argument with the rest of the family and resigned from the Board and I lost the allowance.

Our last experience in 'Junior Entries' was the Survival Exercise in the Harz Mountains in Germany led by the College's Senior RAF Regiment Office, Sqn Ldr 'Dad' Roberts, who had a pretty fearsome reputation. This was two weeks under canvas with a number of survival exercises thrown in, forced marches by day and night, and so on. All I can really remember was that it was an enjoyable experience and we gave our mentors a good run for their money. Roberts' comment after the event was that we were the fittest Entry he had ever taken on survival exercise, which surprised us, and did not say too much about our predecessors.

In September we moved out of Junior Entries at last and our living conditions improved to the extent that we had our own rooms in barrack blocks. On 8 September 1955 my RAF flying training commenced. By then the Piston Provost had replaced the Prentice and we started our flying from the North Airfield at Cranwell which was solely grass. To me the Provost seemed extremely large and very complex after the Tiger Moth. To begin with it had a radio which was definitely a step up on the Gosport tube of the Tiger; it had a 550 hp Alvis Leonides radial engine and a variable-pitch three bladed propeller as opposed to the 110 hp of the Tiger and its two bladed fixed propeller. My new flying instructor, Flt Lt Bernie Thrussel, let me know in no uncertain terms that I had wasted my time at Thruxton and I should forget everything I had learned as it only made his life more difficult. It was, of course, absolute rubbish. Basic flying skills are the same the world over and, in any case, it gave me confidence to know that I had already been solo. Nevertheless it served to bring me down to earth and listen very carefully to what he said. It was about another eight hours of instruction before I went solo in the Provost on 9 September 1955 and strange to relate I have no clear memory of the event unlike that at Thruxton. Flying from the North Airfield ceased at the end of December and all the Provosts were moved to Barkston Heath, some six miles south of Cranwell replacing the Balliols which were being phased out as the advanced trainers. The Vampire was introduced and flew exclusively from the South Airfield at Cranwell.

I can remember that my chief concern at Barkston was the fact that we had to fly off a runway. Flying and particularly landing on the North airfield at Cranwell was easy as you had a large expanse of grass to aim at and it did not matter too much which bit you landed on or if you were a few degrees off directionally. Now we had to be rather more precise and land on the runway which seemed to be exceedingly narrow to me. Fortunately, it did not take too long to get used to it and life moved on. Bernie Thrussel was replaced by Flt Lt Phil Cox as my instructor. Phil always had a smile and a twinkle in his eye—and he was a joy to fly with. He had been on a Meteor squadron and he once proudly showed me a press clipping in which some old lady claimed that she had nearly been blown off a south coast pier by a low flying Meteor. He claimed it was quite unjustified but I'm not so sure myself. With Phil Cox every trip was fun but the bonus was that he was an excellent instructor and he certainly taught me to fly.

Life did not only consist of flying. There were some fairly intensive ground school lectures—aerodynamics, thermodynamics, air power, navigation, English, history, mathematics and so on. We were kept busy, but we also had time to enjoy ourselves. We made quite a few friends amongst the local populace, we formed a skiffle group (which was all the rage at the time) called 'The Gorillas' (what an awful name!), and we had a fairly gregarious social life. We also lost the first few of our entry, one because of a 'Lack of OQs' (Officer Qualities) and one because, although he had also completed a flying scholarship, he was unable to cope with the Provost. He proved it one night by planting the aircraft in a field next to the airfield at Spitalgate, a grass airfield close to Barkston that we used to use for circuits and bumps. It was quite a sad sight to see on the following morning, and even sadder for the individual concerned. Other little 'unofficial' competitions also used to take place, such as how high could you get a Provost, and how low could you go. The latter competition came to an end when someone came back with half a hedge trailing from the aircraft. He had some difficulty explaining it away, and we decided it was time to call a halt to that particular game.

Finally on 6 July 1956 I took my Basic Handling Test with Flt Lt Cyril Peters, one of the Flight Commanders, and passed. My Basic Flying training had ended and after a long summer vacation we then moved on to advanced training in the Vampire from the South airfield at Cranwell. Not only did we change aircraft but we finally moved out of our barrack blocks and into the Main Building of the RAF College. The rooms were more spacious, and we even had a batman to look after us although our ceremonial drill kit was ever our own responsibility. Drill was always a part of our lives under the eagle eyes of Sqn Ldr 'Dad' Roberts and, for us in B Squadron, Flt Sgt Chandler who could make the word 'sir' sound like one of the biggest insults in the world. The College Drill team under

Roberts consisted of WO Gallacher, the College Warrant Officer; Flt Sgt Legge (A Sqn), Flt Sgt Chandler (B Sqn) and Flt Sgt Holt (C Sqn) a.k.a. 'Bogbrush' on account of his moustache which resembled said object. Chiefy Chandler's favourite expression when you were presenting arms and he thought that you were not hitting the rifle hard enough was, 'come on, sir, come on, I can make more noise rattlin' me testicles in a jam jar' usually shouted at a range of two inches from your ear. Holt now has a trophy at the College named after him. They were all unforgettable characters whose bark, generally speaking, was far worse than their bite. And it was this team that ensured that the Cranwell drill standard was as good as anywhere in the world and was a skill you never forgot. It was Roberts who, one morning during a drill session, was determined to make an example of someone and he was hanging on to every word of command, just waiting for some poor cadet to twitch. Unfortunately that poor cadet was me and I was doubled off the main parade square to drill with the juniors on the junior parade square for two weeks—the height of ignominy! It was Ken Hayr (69 Entry and later ACM Sir Kenneth Hayr) who one morning decided to take the mickey out of his senior under officer who had a Coronation Medal from his time as a Halton apprentice. So he turned up on parade with this enormous medal on his chest and when the inspecting officer, his squadron commander, got to him he asked what he thought that was, Ken replied 'That, sir, is the dishonourable order of the irretractable digit'. He was dispatched straight off the parade ground as well.

By now, as senior cadets, we were allowed to have cars and generally act like human beings. My first car was a pre-war 1937 1½ litre Jaguar saloon which lasted about a week before it expired on the A1. Apart from that, I remember I had it just long enough for it to get me seven days restrictions (the normal punishment for cadets) for failing to wear a hat whilst driving. My claim that the roof was too low to wear a hat was deemed as irrelevant. With the help of my father who one Sunday morning—I think he must have been a little bored—decided to take me to 'Raymond Way of Kilburn', who was renowned as one of the sharpest car dealers in London, I finally bought an old Jeep which served me pretty well for the remainder of my time at Cranwell. I don't think I shall ever forget my Father and Raymond Way, with an enormous cigar, haggling over the last £5 on a Sunday morning and finally tossing a coin for it (my Father won). In fact my Father wanted me to buy a 1937 4½ Litre Lagonda and I have always regretted not following his advice. The Jeep cost me £100 and it was fairly reliable except that it was always difficult to start, the 6 Volt electrical system not being man enough for the job, especially in winter. The Lagonda was the same price and I dread to think what it would be worth today.

Flying the Vampire was a completely different kettle of fish to the Provost. To begin with, everything seemed to happen rather too quickly for my liking and I can remember to this day the difficulty I had initially with circuits in the aircraft. There was the slight feeling of insecurity because, unlike piston-engined aircraft, there was absolutely nothing in front of you. Fortunately it did not last very long and my instructor, Fg Off Clive Williams (no relation), sent me solo after eight hours dual; in fact we had two first solos because our first solo was in the Vampire T11, the side-by-side two seat trainer. But we also had a whole bunch of single seat Vampire Mk 9s on which most of our solo flying was done. So, as soon as we had soloed in the T11, we were then sat in a Mk 9 and a whole load of cadets would sit on the tail boom and lift up the cockpit so that you could see what the landing attitude should look like, and ten days later I went solo in a Mk 9. Our first Flight Commander was Clive Francis who was succeeded by Chunky Ball who had flown with 77 Sqn (RAAF) on Meteors in Korea and had a DFC to prove it. Clive Francis subsequently found fame by flying a Turbulent through a hangar when he was CO of 54 Sqn, an act that got him the sack.

It was in March 1957 that we had our first fatal accident. I was sitting in the crew-room with Tony Clayton, who apart from being on our entry was also a lay preacher and an excellent gymnast, when Clive Francis walked in and said that there was a spare Vampire Mk 9 sitting out front and did either of us want to fly it. Both of us said yes and so in the end we tossed for it. Clayton won and took the aircraft. The next thing we heard was that he was orbiting over the coast with a jammed elevator and could only keep in the sky by executing a continual steep turn. He tried everything but could not free it and was told to bail out. In those days we did not wear immersion suits and the Mk 9, which did not have an ejection seat, did not even have a dinghy as it was deemed too bulky for baling out of the aircraft manually. And because it was March, the North Sea was at just about its coldest temperature. Being a gymnast, Tony bailed out by crawling over the nose to avoid the twin boom tail and landed in the sea by Skegness. A chopper was sent to haul him out and nearly succeeded but the winchman lost two fingers in the attempt and the helo, having also lost its radio, had to return to base. An Anson circling the area mistakenly identified the crewman being pulled up as Tony and called off the search. A second helo was therefore not launched until the first one got back to base. By the time the second helo got to Tony, he had just about succumbed to exposure and in fact died on the way back in the helo. Not so long after, Dick Thomas had to bail out of a T11 with his instructor. Fortunately this was not a fatal accident but it took so long for Dick to recover that he ended up being put back a term and graduated with the entry after us. Fatal accidents were a fairly regular event in those days and it was not something that you dwelt on or worried about. As far as most of us were concerned it was something that happened to someone else—you yourself were immortal.

Life really was enjoyable, the flying was great, the academic studies bearable and the social life excellent; we often used to go down to London for the weekend and we also had a number of friends in the local area amongst the farming community. The only bad moment came when the authorities decided that a course of two years and eight months was not long enough and that it was to be extended to three years; that meant that instead of graduating in the summer of 1957, it was put back until December. But our final term just consisted of flying with very little ground school so it was not too bad. On 2 November I passed my Final Navigation Test and on the 18th my Final Handling Test. Our only concern from then on was whether we would go to fighters or bombers. Of the 36 of us who started in January 1955, 25 graduated on 17 December 1957. The Graduation Parade is something I shall always remember. Peter Martin won the Sword of Honour, Jerry Cohu the Queen's Medal (for Academics) and Bill Stoker the Flying Prize. Peter Martin had been predicted to win the Sword on our entry almost from the moment we arrived. He was a superb sportsman and athlete, a natural leader and always stood out from the crowd without really trying although, it has to be said, academics were not his strong point. The postings were split 50/50 between fighters and the V force (bombers). Fortunately, from my point of view, I ended up on fighters and was posted to 229 OCU Chivenor to fly the Hunter. Life in the Air Force at large was about to begin. And at the same time the Duncan Sandys White Paper on Defence was issued which predicted the demise of the manned fighter and that all air defence in the future would be carried out by Surface to Air Missiles (SAMs). As far as I could see there were two problems with that. Firstly practical technology had not caught up with the theory and, secondly, SAMs had a habit of always being in the wrong place at the wrong time. They did not have the flexibility of fighters or the capability of identifying the target in those days. But what did I know.

2

Audax Omnia Perpeti

My course at 229 OCU, Chivenor in North Devon was to consist of Jock Heron, Ted Nance, Bill Stoker and myself from our Entry at Cranwell plus Dave Cowley from 70 Entry who had been delayed for some reason. However our course did not begin until the beginning of February so they sent us to RAF Valley in Anglesey, to hold for a month or so. First of all the drive to Valley was something of an adventure in the cars that we had in those days. I had a British Salmson and I lost first and second gear on the way there, which made the drive even more interesting. Salmson gearboxes did not exactly grow on trees and I had to drive like that for some time. Fortunately the engine had a fair amount of torque, so progress with just third and top gear was not impossible.

We had often been told that life at Cranwell was rather more luxurious than you would find on most RAF bases, and Valley proved the point. It was before they built the permanent mess and it consisted of some rather dismal Nissen huts with coke stoves and separate ablutions block about 100 yards away. No matter what you did, it was impossible to keep the stoves alight the whole night. It was mid-winter and I can remember even now waking up on that first morning to find that the snow had come in under the door and settled in the room.

Nor were we exactly welcomed at Valley with open arms. It had been a training base but most of the units had been moved out. There were just a few Vampires left to cope with people like us. However the staff viewed us with a very jaded eye and we were regarded as somewhat of a nuisance and undesirable element as we were the only 'students' on the base and rather interfered with their relaxed lifestyle. Flying was reserved almost exclusively for the staff and we were left to fend for ourselves. Consequently I just managed to fly four trips in January. No doubt the weather did not help, but it was with some relief that we left there to commence the course at Chivenor at the beginning of February.

The accommodation at Chivenor was basically exactly the same as Valley—Nissen huts, coke stoves and remotely located ablutions. However North Devon was infinitely preferable to Anglesey and life took a definite turn for the better. Ground School was only a week or so and we had a quick check out on the Vampire T11 again before going solo in the Hunter Mk 4. This was before the days of the twin seat Hunter T7. After the Vampire, the Hunter seemed to be enormous and it was a sobering thought that you were going to be solely responsible for such a relatively powerful beast. The Hunter Mk 4 was a lovely aircraft although at that stage we did not have any drop tanks so a sortie was never much more than 50 minutes. Neither had the engine in the Mk 4—the Rolls Royce Avon 100 series—reached the levels of reliability that it had in later years. We had a mixture of 113 and 117 Rolls Royce Avons. They only had 7000 lbs of thrust and you still had to be a little careful with throttle handling as you could inadvertently flame it out. Indeed I managed to flameout climbing out one day because of my somewhat clumsy efforts to maintain formation. I also managed to relight it without anyone being any the wiser. The aircraft also had power-assisted controls, unlike the manual ones in the Vampire, which made them comparatively sensitive. Everyone made the error of overcorrecting on the ailerons on their first sortie before you became used to it. First solo in the Hunter took place on 20 February 1958 and progress after that was fairly rapid. Three sorties a day was the norm, learning how to do battle formation, tail chasing, tactics, aerobatics and tracking with the gun-sight. The final part of the course was air-to-air gunnery on the flag towed by a Meteor. One incident involving air-to-air is worth relating. A couple of months before we arrived one of our predecessors from Cranwell, Colin Truman, had had a fire warning light come on when firing on the flag. He had carried out all the correct procedures, flaming out the engine, pressing the fire extinguisher button and, finally, ejecting when the light stayed on. His body was never recovered. Ted Nance had exactly the same thing happen when he was firing on the flag accompanied by Jock Heron in another aircraft. Ted flamed out the engine, pressed the fire extinguisher and the light stayed on, indicating that it was still on fire. Jock was in formation looking the aircraft over as was the Meteor tug who had by now ditched the flag. Both said that they could see no sign of fire whatsoever. It was a pretty blustery day in early April, when the sea is at its coldest. Ted looked down and did not fancy a swim so with one hand on the ejector seat handle, he closed his eyes and hit the relight button. The engine fired up normally and he flew back to Chivenor and landed. I remember the furore this caused with half the staff wanting to throw Ted off the course because he had transgressed by not taking the correct procedure. However there were several redeeming features. Firstly an aircraft that should have been at the bottom of the Atlantic was sitting on the line. Secondly, it turned out that the fault that had set off the fire warning light had also prevented the fire extinguisher from activating; and that same fault was found in a number of other aircraft. And, of course, Ted was alive. Instead of being the villain, he turned out to be the hero.

We graduated in early May 1958 and went off to various squadrons. Jock Heron, as was natural, went to 43 Sqn at Leuchars in Scotland. Ted went to 74 Sqn at Horsham St Faith near Norwich, Bill Stoker went to a squadron in Germany, which was seen as the choice posting, and I ended up on 54 Sqn at RAF Odiham in Hampshire.

Ian Worby had just taken over the squadron from John Stacey (later to be ACM Sir John Stacey) and my first Flight Commander was David Harcourt-Smith (later to be ACM Sir David H-S). David H-S was renowned for his incredible short fuse and lack of tolerance. His neck would go red in just a few milliseconds if someone upset him; but his bark, a bit like that of the drill instructors, was far worse than his bite. The squadron was equipped with Hunter Mk 6s with an Avon 200 series engine which pushed out 10,000 lbs of thrust. We also had 100 gallon drop tanks, normally just one either side on the inboard pylons but with the ability to put two more on the outboard pylons for ferrying. Normal sortie lengths were between an hour and an hour and a half, depending on what you were doing and our primary role was air defence of the UK. But I have to say that the level of professionalism was not quite as high as it became a few years later. I can remember my first debrief by Ian Worby after one of my first simulated combat sorties. As he shrugged off his flying suit he remarked, 'Graham Williams won't last long in any conflict'. I had no idea what I had done wrong or what I should do to rectify the problem; nor was any advice forthcoming.

Odiham had several advantages from my point of view. My parents had a flat in London and a bungalow on the south coast at Ferring. Both were just about equidistant from Odiham, which made for a pretty satisfactory social life especially at the weekends as either could be reached in under an hour. The mess at Odiham was not particularly attractive and the squadron used to virtually live in the Kings Arms in Odiham village. Most of us were bachelors; cars, when they existed, were usually of a somewhat unreliable nature. There were quite a number of Pilot Officers, six as I recall out of a total of 18 pilots, who used to act in the usual irresponsible manner. I well remember Brian Voller crashing his VW Beetle. When he reported the fact to his Flight Commander, he responded, 'so what'. Brian then had to explain that he had actually crashed into the Guardroom demolishing the glass case with all the station trophies in it. The station police were not too pleased or impressed. Crashing cars seemed to be par for the course. It was not a case of 'if' but a case of 'when'. In fact, although predicted to join the club, I managed complete my time in the RAF without joining that elite club—although I have subsequently made up for lost time.

After just two months or so on the squadron, during which I celebrated my 21st birthday, the news came that we were to be sent out to Cyprus. There was one of those recurring Middle East crises in which the stability of Jordan was in question and the UK was going to demonstrate a show of strength in support. I vividly recollect that on one of the last sorties I did in the UK with John Neville leading, he suffered a flameout as we went over a loop in a tail-chase. All of a sudden a dense white trail came out of the tailpipe of his aircraft which was unburnt fuel. He tried relighting but to no avail. It was a beautiful summer evening and we were over the South Coast. We could see Thorney Island airfield although we could not contact them as the place was closed. Nevertheless John elected to land there and completed an immaculate text-book flameout landing. The Tower came up on the radio just as he came to a stop on the runway and asked him to taxi in to dispersal. His reply was not exactly polite or printable.

We went out to Cyprus in July. Being one of the junior pilots and last to join, I had to travel with the ground crew in the transport support, a Beverley, more usually referred to as the Flying Cathedral, which seemed to do everything at one very slow speed and took forever to get out to Nicosia. When we got there it was bedlam. Accommodation was at a premium and we were allocated an eight man tent to live in. There were five Hunter Squadrons, 54, 74, 1, 43 and 208, plus half a Meteor night fighter squadron and sundry transport aircraft. You could say that the Mess was a lively place and that the behaviour was not perhaps quite what one would expect. Quite apart from the fact that we were there to protect Jordan, General Grivas and EOKA were making life quite uncomfortable on the island. We had to go around armed all the time with .38 revolvers in a minimum grouping of four. I was of the opinion that arming pretty irresponsible young pilots in such a fashion was a greater danger to the community at large and to the individuals involved.

As soon as we arrived we had to go on stand-by for the air defence of the island although it was never quite clear to me who we were expecting to attack. We spent hours on stand-by in a little tent on the end of the runway with quite a few scrambles to liven up the proceedings. I remember one such scramble vividly. We were scrambled as a pair against a live target. We climbed up to 40,000 ft and chased after this will o' the wisp. We finally caught sight of it and to our surprise it was above us. We continued climbing almost to 50,000 ft, which was as much as the Hunter could do. Still the target was way above us and we could still see it clearly although it did not resemble any aircraft we could recognise. It looked just like a cross in the sky. Suddenly we were told to break off the intercept—which was just as well because we were never going to get anywhere near it. After we landed we were told to not mention it to anyone and forget we had ever seen it. It was only subsequently that we found out what it was—it was one of our first sightings of a U2, the US reconnaissance aircraft in which Gary Powers was shot down over the USSR in 1960.

Cyprus was a busy and interesting time both in the air and on the ground. There were quite a few incidents. Puddy Catt (54) had a fuel transfer failure and had to land with the port drop tanks full. Unfortunately the brakes caught fire and he veered off the runway into a sandbank and the full tanks disintegrated causing the aircraft to catch fire. Puddy was a rather large gentleman and we had never seen him move so fast out of the cockpit when the aircraft came to a standstill. Despite the fact that the seat was burnt, Puddy did not have a mark on him. Henry Ploszek (43 Sqn and from our entry at Cranwell) managed to bounce a Hunter off the side of a hill and fly it back to Nicosia even though the fuselage was then oval rather than round. Chuck Coulcher (1 Sqn and also from our entry at Cranwell) managed to collect a barbed wire fence as he arrived at Nicosia from UK and taxied in trailing the wire and, as he came to a halt in dispersal with holes in the wing and the flaps, the tyres went flat. He had no idea what had happened. Ray Offord (208 Sqn) while undertaking an exercise with the army up in the mountains, went underneath an electricity cable and chopped off the top of his fin. He was totally unaware what had happened until the army very kindly returned it to Nicosia with their compliments. One of our armourers was servicing the ejection seat and managed to fire it whilst he was still in the cockpit.

The seat went up in the air and landed in the dispersal which had about 40 aircraft in it missing everything. Somehow the armourer had crouched in the cockpit up against the instrument panel so that the seat missed him as it went, when we tried to replicate the incident using a crane to pull the seat out, it just was not possible; he was a lucky man.

And I came close to ending my new career as a fighter pilot. It was a night sortie and I just took off to do a bit of general handling and a few night approaches. The usual approach procedure in those days was to come back overhead the airfield at 20,000 ft. You then headed outbound on a fixed heading which depended on the direction of the runway in use. You were cleared to descend as soon as you were out of the overhead. We did not have airfield radar except for the GCA approach from about ten miles inbound and the controller just had a CRDF bearing to judge your position. At half your height plus 2,000 ft, i.e. 12,000 ft if you started from 20,000, you then turned inbound and the controller would try and position you on the centreline to feed into the GCA. I made the classic error and misread my altimeter, and unbeknown to me started the descent from 10,000 ft instead of 20,000. The problem was exacerbated by the fact that Mount Troodos stood between me and the airfield. But a very sharp air traffic controller saw a variation in the length of the CRDF trace from which he deduced that was not at the correct height. He queried my height and I realised at the last moment that I was extremely low and about to run into Troodos. Needless to say I applied full power and climbed to the correct height and carried on as though nothing had happened. I regret to say that I never confessed to my error and I never thanked the Air Traffic Controller who undoubtedly saved my life that night. Should he ever read these words, please accept my very grateful thanks and apologies for such abysmally poor behaviour.

Life outside of our operational activities was no less hazardous. The bar in the mess was very crowded. Although it was summer, there was no air conditioning and the rooms were cooled by fans. One of the favourite pastimes of some individuals was throwing empty beer cans into the fan and seeing if you could decapitate anyone. This activity came to a halt as some individuals started using full cans of beer which, apart from being a criminal waste, was extremely dangerous. 74 Sqn decided that they would burn their number into the carpet with lighter fluid. This went wrong and one of their members was very badly burnt. Most of the squadrons found themselves banned from the bar at one time or another for some misdemeanour and had to rely on the other squadrons' generosity, passing drinks out of the window. Life outside was not without its hazards either. You always had to keep a careful eye out for EOKA terrorists. We used to go to Kyrenia for R & R. The attractions were the 'Slab' which was a safe place from which to swim, the Harbour Club which was just about the only place you could get a decent meal, Clito's wine-shop—as featured in Lawrence Durrell's book *Bitter Lemons in Cyprus*—for a bottle of wine or two at lunchtime and some chicken, and Ma Newman's Farm from which was the only place you could get fresh milk. Boiled eggs and a pint of milk were *de rigueur* before you climbed on the transport to go back to Nicosia. I do remember Roddy Munday (74 Sqn) clearing the slab in one fell swoop one day. We had been to Clito's for lunch and an argument started up concerning which chamber of the revolver should be left empty to avoid an accidental discharge. Roddy got it wrong and before anyone could stop him he decided to pull the trigger to demonstrate his point. The gun went off and the slab, on which probably thirty or forty people were sunbathing, cleared in a millisecond. Roddy had a difficult time explaining how he was one round short when he handed in his weapon to the armoury on his return to Nicosia. Puddy Catt managed to get himself arrested when, somewhat full of *bonhomie*, he decided to go and have coffee in a Turkish café. The Turks greeted him with open arms. The RAF Police were not amused and accused him of inciting a riot.

For a young pilot it was an exciting detachment: plenty of flying, plenty of fun. At the end of October it all came to an end and we were due to return to UK. Yet again I was sentenced with Dave Scott to fly back to the UK with the Engineering Officer, Dickie Burr, and the ground crew as democracy was not a word that came easily to the squadron hierarchy. The only thing was that our transport was due to be something somewhat upmarket from the journey out, namely a Comet of Transport Command. Come the day we were all due to embark on the aircraft and there was a delay because of some problem with the aircraft's emergency braking system. The main baggage had been loaded and we were all gathered outside the aircraft with the hand baggage in a pile. I was standing and chatting to Dave Scott just by the pile of bags when suddenly there was an enormous explosion. Actually, I remember the smell rather than the noise. And I remember the look of surprise on Dave's face. We both thought that the aircraft was going up and we ran as far as we could from it. Dave beat me by miles over the ground and as he came to a halt, turned round and said 'what the f— was that?' And so saying, he just keeled over. Dave had had his back to the pile of baggage and I had been facing him. He had no uniform on his back whatsoever although the front was pristine. Fortunately, for me, he had taken the brunt of the explosion in his back whilst I was only hit on the parts that had been sticking out, namely my left leg and arm. We spent hours in Station Sick Quarters whilst the medics tried to take all the bits out of our bodies. Dave ended up in Nicosia Hospital as he had more pieces in his backside than most and was having difficulty sitting down. It turned out that the bomb had been in the Engineering Officer's hand baggage in a tin of what had been Milk Tray chocolates. It had been timed to go off at just about the top of climb, 30 minutes after take-off, and it would have been another unexplained Comet disaster. It was the delay caused by the unserviceability which saved us. We were flown home in a replacement charter aircraft the following day and the only thing that upset me was the fact that, because we had served just two days short of the three-month qualifying period for the General Service Medal (GSM), we were not entitled to it even though we had been blown up. Dave Scott got his as he spent the extra few days in hospital in Nicosia. Medals were hard to come by in those days! Some years later I had an x-ray on my leg because I was having cartilage problems. The doctor said that my cartilage was OK but asked me whether I knew that I had pieces of metal in my leg. In fact for some time after the event very small pieces of metal kept coming to the surface of my skin.

So it was back to Odiham and the air defence of the United Kingdom—just in time to start suffering the effects of the 1957 Sandys White Paper; squadrons were disbanded, both in Germany and UK, and existing squadrons were reduced in numbers. Whereas we had had 18 aircraft and 24 pilots, we were cut back to 12 aircraft and 18 pilots. Volunteers were asked to re-role and one of our pilots, Chris Lane, decided to go to helicopters. Others were given no choice and were sent off to be controllers at radar stations or to the CFS course at Little Rissington to be flying instructors. The rest of us just kept a very low profile in the hope that we would not be noticed. And luck remained on my side as I stayed on the squadron.

Air Defence was an esoteric occupation in those days. Of course we had a sophisticated ground radar system but the aircraft had no airborne radar capability. The only aid we had was radar ranging which was not a particularly reliable system and was only any use when you had closed to within 1000 yards on a target; so the main aid to target acquisition was the Mark 1 eyeball. Since Fighter Command had a fairly large number of squadrons there were insufficient controllers to give a pair of fighters, the basic element, detailed interception instructions; so we had a system called 'Broadcast Control'. The North Sea, from which all attacks were presumed to come, was divided up into a series of gates and lanes. The gate would be some 30 to 50 miles off the east coast and each gate had a lane attached to it which projected a hundred miles or so out to the east. When you were scrambled, you were allocated a gate and a broadcast frequency on which you listened to instructions. Your first priority was to make for your gate. The only navigation we had was Distance Measuring Equipment (DME) which could give you a range from a particular ground beacon, mostly positioned on east coast airfields. So you needed a lock on to two beacons to give you a position fix. The theory was good but the practice was something entirely different. When a large number of aircraft were airborne, the beacons would very quickly become saturated and no one could then get a lock on; so most of the time you had to revert to mental dead reckoning navigation, which was fine if the forecast winds were anywhere near correct. Having reached your gate, you waited until you heard the controller tell you that there was a target coming down your lane. You were then released to go down your lane and you had to work out your own interception onto the target. The totally amazing thing was that this system worked quite well. Whilst it involved no end of mental gymnastics by the pilots, the accuracy with which most people reached their gates and went down their lanes was remarkable. We used to look at the radar traces after the event and we even surprised ourselves at how good we were at it. It was actually a challenging task and one which gave a good deal of satisfaction when it was done well.

Fighter Command air defence exercises just added to the fun. When over one hundred aircraft were scrambled in dubious weather conditions the action could become quite interesting and entertaining. People ran short of fuel, got diverted to different airfields, and apparent mayhem existed. But it was rare that these exercises would degrade to a complete shambles. In fact the discipline shown by everyone was impressive and I do not remember any accidents occurring; close calls, yes, but actual accidents, no. And the Broadcast Control system worked extremely well considering its limitations.

Every squadron used to have to take its share of the actual Air Defence of UK and there was always a pair of aircraft on stand-by, as indeed there still is today, to take care of any casual intruders over the UK's airspace. Squadrons based on or near the east coast had the luxury of being able to carry out this duty from home base when their turn came, but being at Odiham meant that we had to detach some aircraft to Wattisham to take over the stand-by duty. It was a pain and extremely tedious as nothing much ever happened in those days. There was one incident that created a little excitement and that occurred to 74 Squadron at Horsham St Faith. For some reason the crew of a USAF B66 had had to bail out of their aircraft, but unfortunately the aircraft had continued to fly on and a pair of aircraft from 74 Sqn were scrambled to shoot it down. This caused not a little excitement in the cockpits of the two aircraft as such an opportunity was a rarity indeed. They were vectored onto the target and closed into firing range and were cleared to fire. In the excitement of the moment they had in fact neglected to identify the target and just as they were about to open fire they realised that it was a RAF Valiant bomber. The crew of the Valiant never knew how close they came to disaster. As for the B66, it was never seen again.

Our social life was really rather pleasant. I had by this time bought a brand-new Morris Minor 1000 at my Father's suggestion. I very quickly tired of that and exchanged it for a maroon TR3 in which I used to commute either to London or Worthing at the weekends. Worthing might have seemed to be an odd destination for a bachelor in those days but there was a lively young bunch of people and a number of very good social gatherings. The 'Blue Peter' at Angmering on a Saturday evening was a must and the 'Ship' in Worthing for Sunday lunchtime. It was after a Sunday lunchtime session that I had a race with another of the group who was driving a modified red Austin A40 along Worthing front. Unfortunately someone got in the way and we overtook him simultaneously on either side. Subsequently I received a letter from the local chief of police and I can remember the wording to this day. It said:

> ... and you proceeded in a manner which could only be described as jockeying for position for the roundabout at the end of King George V Avenue. I would be grateful if you could bring this letter to the attention of the driver of your car.

He knew exactly who it was. I am afraid to say that we did not take as much notice of the various driving regulations then as we do now.

One other highlight of the training year was the detachment to Acklington for air-to-air gunnery. It was always good to get the whole squadron away on detachment and even though Acklington was not one of the more desirable places to be, it could nevertheless be fun. You spent the two weeks doing nothing but firing on the flag towed by a Meteor during the day and out at the local hostelries by night. 66 Sqn were actually based at Acklington, then under the command of a gentleman by the name of Peter Bairstow, commonly known (and still known) throughout the RAF as 'the Bear'. He had taken over 66 when its reputation in Fighter Command was at an all-time low and worked it up into one of the best outfits around (although there were always people who would dispute such a statement). The Squadron crest had a rattlesnake in it and they kept one such beast in a glass cage in the crew-room. It was the Junior Pilot's responsibility to look after it and make sure it was properly fed and watered, not one of the more desirable tasks around. The snake had the most disconcerting habit of striking the glass with a large crack when it saw a stranger approaching and that could make you jump, to put it mildly. The venom would then dribble down the inside of the glass. 43 Sqn had a fighting cock in their crest and they used to take a couple of those around with them on detachment. They had had them in Cyprus when we were there and someone (not us) kidnapped them and they got mightily upset. 54 Sqn's crest had a blue lion with Fleur de Lys on it. Fortunately there were no such animal available, which was just as well because, no doubt, I would have ended up as its keeper. My only real memory of Acklington was the 1959 General Election in which we reduced the mess party to celebrate the event to a complete shambles. Someone got thrown out of the window which, unfortunately, was closed at the time. And two others fell asleep in the fireplace which, fortunately, did not have a fire in it.

For some time we had been having difficulty with Air Traffic Control at Odiham and conflicts with London Airport. In July 1959 the decision was taken to close Odiham and the Squadron was redeployed to Stradishall in Suffolk. We were all a bit disappointed as Odiham was quite a desirable spot with a very pleasant surrounding area. On the other hand Stradishall did not have quite the same attractions. We had shared Odiham with a night fighter squadron of Javelins, 46 Sqn, commanded by Wg Cdr Fred Sowrey (a.k.a. Bent Fred as a result of a car accident which left him with a bent spine). They went off to West Raynham. We had to share Stradishall with 256 Sqn which was renumbered as 1 Sqn. This move also saw a change in the role of the squadron and the accent changed from air defence to ground attack. Ever since the demise of the Venom and the Germany squadrons, the RAF had suffered from a lack of close air support capability and 54 and 1 Sqns were selected to form a new centre of excellence in the art. We still undertook air defence but low level navigation, air-ground gunnery and rocketing became a part of the flying syllabus. Because we were supposedly experts at low level, our air defence priority switched from high level to low level air defence, referred to as 'Rat and Terrier'; which seemed like a licence to terrorise East Anglia as we chased after intruders at 250 ft, but I have to admit that it was great sport and quite challenging.

Mass flypasts were also an order of the day whether it be the Queen's Birthday or Battle of Britain Day; with five or six squadrons with nine aircraft each, led by the lone Spitfire. We would form up over East Anglia, always an exciting event and fraught with difficulties. 111 Sqn, who were at the time the official formation aerobatic squadron, used to insist on joining up in a somewhat flamboyant manner in diamond 9, frightening the rest of us to death, and I well remember the incident over south London, having flown across the Palace, when a plaintive voice came up over the R/T announcing that he had suffered an engine failure. Unfortunately, he did not give a call sign and everyone naturally moved out of formation to see who it was. It turned out to be the Spitfire who managed to force-land on a sports field thus saving the day from any tragedy.

Life at Stradishall was really better than we expected; it still only took us an hour to get to London assuming you drove like a maniac—as we were wont to do. By then I had a Morgan +4 in which you could carry very little else except one passenger and an overnight bag, but it was pretty strongly built as I proved one night by bouncing it off a roadside bank.

In March 1960 we were given new aircraft, Hunter Mk 9s replacing the old Mk 6s. The differences were not enormous as they were basically the same aircraft as the Mk 6 with the addition of a Radio Compass navigation aid, 230 gallon tanks on the inboard pylons instead of 100 gallon tanks, thus vastly improving the range and/or radius of action and a drag chute was grafted on to the rear for a short landing. You could still carry 100 gallon tanks on the outboard pylons but they did not add a lot to your range because of the additional drag. Weapons—60 lb HE Rockets and 4 × 30 mm Aden cannon remained the same. Dave Harcourt-Smith was replaced by Chris Bruce as 'A' Flight commander and many of the original pilots had moved on. Having received our new aircraft we then deployed to El Adem in Libya for an exercise for ten days. Subsequent to the exercise four of our aircraft undertook the first 'Gulf Ranger' to Aden going out by the northern route and returning via the southern route. For some reason, which now escapes me, I was selected to be part of this exercise which was led by Ian Worby, the boss, with the Wing Commander Flying, Bennett, as his number 2, and Chris Bruce and me as 3 and 4 respectively. We had been living in tents at El Adem and I had managed to trip over a guy rope late one night and had impaled the palm of my hand on a metal tent peg and I was concerned that the injury might stop me going. However I got the medical section to bind it up tightly and all was well. We left El Adem on 28 March and went via Nicosia, Teheran, Bahrein, Sharjah and Khormaksar and arrived in Aden on 1 April, leaving on 4 April. The Boss and the Wg Cdr did a couple of operational sorties with the resident squadron (No. 8) which had just exchanged its Venoms for Hunters. Chris Bruce and I were left to do some sight-seeing around the place. I did not realise it then, but 8 Sqn was to become a part of my life somewhat later on.

The return route was via Khartoum, El Adem, Orange (South of France) and thence back to Stradishall. On the first leg one aircraft went unserviceable and we had to wait two days to get it fixed. Needless to say, as the two junior guys, Chris Bruce and I were left to gather up the pieces. I found it all relatively exciting as I had never ventured on to the African continent and, to me, Khartoum was an exotic kind of place in which to be stuck. The first disaster was the fact that the bottles of whisky that Chris was carrying in his bag had both been smashed when he accidentally dropped his bags. So we had nothing to drink although Chris smelt like a walking distillery. We were put up at the Sudan Club which really was like something out of the Raj. There was not a bar as such. You sat in an armchair and clapped your hands for service and a waiter (bearer) would appear as if by magic. The local beer was aptly named 'Camel Beer' and tasted vaguely like a product of the same animal and because of the locals' tendency to use the bottles for storing paraffin it had a most peculiar aftertaste. My most vivid memory of the whole stay was that the first night's entertainment in the Sudan Club was Scottish country dancing—so much for the exotic African continent.

Having rectified the aircraft, we got back to UK without further incident although there was an amusing after event. It turned out that the ground crew, who had followed us around in a transport aircraft, had taken the leading edges off my aircraft and filled them with cigarettes. But they had not reckoned on the aircraft being delayed for two days or so in Khartoum and being left in the open in the searing heat. When they finally got to the cigarettes on our return, they were so dry as to be unsmokeable except by the Squadron Flight Sergeant who would smoke anything. Little did I realise then how familiar I would become with both the northern and the southern route to and from Aden.

June 1960 and Dicky Dickinson replaced Ian Worby as the boss and we continued to hone our skills in the close air support role. The squadron was assigned a Ground Liaison Officer (GLO), a major who came from the Black Watch Regiment whose life style was somewhat better than we could afford. He owned a large part of a mansion by the Thames somewhere near Kingston and used to invite us to drop in at weekends. His wife was superb at whipping up meals at no notice and out of virtually nothing.

Shortly after we were tasked with undertaking a trial on behalf of the Central Fighter Establishment (CFE); basically it was to investigate the capabilities of the Hunter as a 'bomber'. We were to look at three basic modes, level, 30° and 60° bombing. The level mode was releasing the bomb at 50 ft and 500 kts with wings level. 30° was from a 5000 ft turn in and 60° got really interesting. You ran in at 15,000 ft and, when you were aligned with the target you pulled up to 20,000 ft rolled over inverted and pulled until you achieved a 60° dive, rolled upright, and released the bomb at 10,000 ft. All you had to judge the dive angle was a chinagraph 'protractor' on the side of the canopy with 30° and 60° on it. As you went down the dive, you had to glance out the side to make sure you were at roughly the right angle. Four pilots were selected for the dive bombing: Chris Bruce was in charge, Peter Philips, myself and Terry Carlton. The Trials Officer from the Central Fighter Establishment was a lovely man by the name of Hoagy (what else) Carmichael. He was actually a Fleet Air Arm pilot of some renown. He had shot down a MiG 15 in Korea with a Sea Fury, the only recorded incident of a piston aircraft shooting down a jet, I believe. When you heard him describe the incident, it was not quite as it initially seemed. It appeared that he had been flying along leading a section of 4 Sea Furies on patrol when the MiG just passed in front of them. 'Everybody fire', he shouted over the R/T. They did and the MiG just blew up. Hoagy Carmichael was credited with the kill. One of the aspects of the trial was to see how good we were at achieving the correct dive angles; the sight of Hoagy sitting on the target, which was a raft in the sea, with his shirt off and a theodolite in hand, was one I shall not forget.

The trial started off from Stradishall using the Holbeach Range in the Wash. We could not carry bombs on the outboard pylons so we had to carry the 1000 lb bombs on the inboard and put the fuel tanks on the outboard; which was, in fact, an illegal configuration as the CG was out of limits. However, we were given dispensation to fly like that and a warning that the aircraft could pitch up if mishandled, but once you knew about it, it was not a problem. The low level 50 ft and 500 kts release was not difficult and proved to be pretty accurate. The only problems were that on the mud flats at Holbeach the bombs would play ducks and drakes for miles and if they were going to be live bombs you would need a pretty sophisticated and reliable time delay fuse otherwise they would detonate right beneath you. My everlasting memory of that part of the trial was looking in the mirror just after release and seeing a couple of 1000 lb (inert) bombs flying formation on my tailplane having bounced off the target.

The dive-bombing caused us many more problems. We needed at least 5000 ft for the 30° bombing profile and 20,000 ft for the 60°. Even in June and July, which it was, it was difficult to achieve the right weather conditions, so we deployed out to Cyprus where the weather was more reliable. The whole squadron deployed for this detachment and one of the pilots who shall be nameless suffered the ultimate ignominy; he got halfway to Malta and was just about over the south of France when he was suddenly and completely overcome by an attack of 'the runs'. He then had to sit in the resultant mess for the next hour which was bad enough, but worse was to come. He got overhead Malta and they diverted him to Halfar, the Fleet Air Arm base, where he was greeted by a Wren as he taxied in. He was extremely embarrassed and had to wave her away while he tried to sort it out. In fact he was delayed for some time as they had to find another parachute and dinghy pack before he could continue (they were an integral part of the seat).

The remainder of the squadron carried on with their APC and, meanwhile, we got permission to use the bombing target in Episcopi Bay which was normally used by the Canberras. This was quite an expensive device as it was not an insignificant piece of kit fitted with radar reflectors and lights and an electronic scoring device. But the staff at the Headquarters had reckoned that we would not be able to hit it and, in any case, we were only using 25 lb practice bombs. So when we sank it in the first week, they got a little upset!

The technique for bomb aiming was interesting and quite challenging. We only had a fixed sight and it was necessary to drop the bomb with wings level otherwise you could throw it off by a large margin. So you started off by getting the forecast wind and working out the sight picture you would need to have when you released the bomb. You then worked backwards and worked out where you would have to place the sight at the top of the dive, called the Pushover Aiming Area, so that it would drift with wings level to the correct release point. You could make some coarse corrections in the dive especially early on, but you needed to have settled in to a smooth drift 10 or 15 seconds before release. It was the first bomb that was really significant as that would reflect real conditions in that you would not be able to correct for errors. We carried four bombs so that, being human, we could correct for the forecast wind errors with the second and subsequent bombs. What with checking the chinagraph dive markers, achieving the correct Pushover Aiming Area and subsequently the correct release picture and then remembering to release the bomb at the correct release height, it was quite an exercise in coordination and the amazing thing was that we became pretty accurate at 30° dive bombing. The 60° dive bombing technique was similar but achieving the correct release parameters was a little more unpredictable. It was not so accurate with a release height of 10,000 ft. Nevertheless we even surprised ourselves at how accurate we could be.

We came back from Cyprus at the end of November and I found that I had been posted. I had spoken to Dennis Caldwell who had been on 54 Sqn when I first arrived but had subsequently been posted to Fighter Command to look after postings to and from the squadrons. He had advised me that my best option was to volunteer for CFS but there was an outside opportunity of a slot becoming available at Chivenor as an instructor. I decided to put my money on the long shot and, in the event, it came up. December saw me journeying down to Devon with all my worldly belongings packed in my TR2, my current mode of transport. On the way, the generator gave up the ghost and my headlights were getting dimmer and dimmer until finally I was stopped by the police. I explained the dilemma and they very kindly stuck me behind them in convoy and left me on the outskirts of London so that I could at least get home and get the car fixed before going on to Devon.

3

The Ambulance Brigade

The beginning of December 1960 and I arrived at Chivenor, just outside of Barnstaple. It did not seem so very long ago that I had left there and now I had returned to be a tactical instructor on 145 Sqn commanded by Martin Chandler. 145 Sqn was commonly known as the Ambulance Brigade because its crest included a red cross. I was the youngest pilot on the squadron and, indeed, the only bachelor. The rest had already completed at least two or three tours on fighters and some of them even more. And it was back to the Nissen huts with their coke stoves. However there was one major difference. As permanent staff you were allocated a room in one of the 'luxury' huts that actually had a bathroom 'en suite' (to the hut not the room!), so you did not have the morning 50 yard stroll to the ablutions in the freezing cold.

There are two abiding memories of my first week as an instructor at Chivenor. Firstly my instrument rating had lapsed and on the first morning we were standing about in the crew room chatting as flying was suspended because of appalling weather. Somehow, the Boss found out that I was 'unrated' and came rushing in to tell the squadron Instrument Rating Examiner (IRE), Trevor Copleston (a.k.a. The Old Grey Fox), and me to get airborne as the weather was entirely suitable for an IRT; indeed that was all it was suitable for. Trevor was as unwilling as I was, but faced with a determined boss, we had no alternative; the fact that I managed to climb up and then do an approach and land was sufficient for Trevor to renew my Instrument Rating—it was one of the quickest IRTs that I have ever done. Somewhat later in life Trevor left the RAF and became the captain of a HS125 executive jet and was arrested and thrown into jail when transporting President Tshombe of the Congo around Africa. I do not know what happened to him after that.

The second abiding memory was the Boss's Christmas Party. It was one of those deals in which a name was pinned to your back and you had to guess what it was before you could get a drink. It took me ages but it really should not have done. It was 'The Lone Ranger'.

We still had Hunter Mk 4s at Chivenor although they now had a much better engine but still with only 7000 lbs of thrust. And we now had the two-seat Hunter T7 which also had the small engine. There had been a proposal to build a two seater with the big engine and, indeed, one was built but, it turned out, it was only to be destined for the export market. The RAF had to make do with the lesser variant as it was a way of using up some of the surplus Mk 4s. They just chopped off the front cockpit and replaced it with a two seat version. We had only just taken delivery of them and the performance of the students was such that the QFIs were amazed that we had got away with converting people to the Hunter previously without any accidents.

Only a few weeks passed by and I was recalled to 54 Sqn to complete the bombing trial. We had been unable to do enough 30° and 60° bombing and CFE still wanted to fill in some of the gaps especially with 1000 lb bombs instead of 25 lb practice bombs. So mid-January 1961 and I was back at Stradishall briefly before ferrying a Hunter Mk 9 out to El Adem for a month of dive bombing on the ranges in the Libyan desert. There were just the four of us with four aircraft and it was a very enjoyable month. El Adem was not exactly an epicurean centre of delight and, despite being on a major RAF trunk route, things like fresh vegetables, milk and meat were rarities if not non-existent. At the time we were there, there was a US Army mapping outfit as well. They had a small helicopter and a Cessna L19 Birddog with two pilots, a Lieutenant called 'Rupe' and a warrant officer. Whilst their main camp was about thirty miles away in the desert, they used El Adem quite extensively. Quite apart from the facilities of a main base, in particular the bar in the mess, Rupe was courting the station commander's daughter. He was using his helicopter to take her to the beach for the day, which I do not suppose for a moment was in line with US Army regulations. However he gave us all trips in his L19 and, unfortunately, introduced us to a game called liar dice, which proved to be an expensive experience at the bar. He also invited us out to his camp site and we drove out there one evening in a Land Rover and were treated to T-Bone steaks, fresh salad and milk—and the inevitable game of poker. How they could supply their troops in the desert with all this fresh produce yet we could not do so on the main base was beyond my understanding. Around midnight we decided to go home only to find that the Land Rover had a flat tyre. As was the wont of RAF MT in those days, the Land Rover had no tools, no jack, but it did have a spare wheel. We borrowed a wrench off the Americans and one of the American soldiers, built somewhat like Mike Tyson, lifted up the Land Rover manually while we changed the wheel, and so ended a very pleasant evening. Rupe came to a somewhat sad end. Whilst he was down on the beach with the station commander's daughter and his helo, the warrant officer had a bad crash in the desert with the L19. Rupe was nowhere to be found for the rescue attempt and when his authorities found out what he had been up to, I believe he was court martialled.

Early February 1961 and we successfully completed the bombing trial, to what end I am not quite sure. There was no doubt that we could successfully use the Hunter for dive bombing but it never ever came to pass in all the years that I flew Hunters. We awarded ourselves a weekend break in Nicosia, El Adem not being the centre of action on the social front, before flying back to Stradishall. I said my final farewell to 54 Sqn and returned to Chivenor and the comparative tedium of instructing. By June we were re-equipping with Mk 6 Hunters as they were released as a result of the reduction of the frontline and the introduction of the Lightning. Quite what happened to Duncan Sandys predictions I am not sure but it certainly did not prevent the Lightening coming in to service. Being the lone bachelor, I was allowed to take an aircraft away for the weekend whenever I wished. The parents of my girlfriend, soon to be my wife, lived in Broadstairs which had the disadvantage of being on the other side of the country and the advantage of being very close to the RAF base at Manston which was an RAF Master Diversion airfield open all hours. Friday night and I would leave Chivenor at about 4 o'clock in a Hunter or a Meteor and land at Manston. The staff at Manston would always find someone to drop me down in Broadstairs. Sunday night and I would stay in the mess at Manston so that I could get away at 7 o'clock and be back at Chivenor for the 8 a.m. morning briefing. It usually worked well except for one weekend when the south east of England was obliterated by a very large snow storm. It only affected the south east corner of UK and when I rang back to base on the Monday morning to say that I could not move, I could hear the disbelief in their voices. It got worse and it was not until Wednesday afternoon that I was able to get out of Manston and then only by getting the ground crew to tow the aircraft out to the runway, still covered in ice and snow, point it in the right direction before I started up and blasted off. Manston was one of two airfields that had a double width runway which made the task a bit easier. I decided to take the risk of doing that because firstly my girlfriend had had to go back on Monday to London where she worked and secondly I was finding the drinking habits of my future father-in-law somewhat of a trial. We used to go down to the Albion Hotel in Broadstairs and drink until closing time after which we moved next door to Marchesi's restaurant, owned also by members of the family, and continue until the early hours of the morning. It was a matter of honour amongst them to try and get this brash young fighter pilot somewhat the worse for wear. Sad to say, they frequently succeeded. Quite apart from that, I was on this occasion getting more than a little flak from my Boss at Chivenor who thought I was trying to beat the system.

Throughout the remainder of 1961 life rolled on with the succession of course after course of students. There were a variety of courses, primarily students straight out of training, some refresher courses and senior officers' courses. It was one of the latter that caused a certain amount of amusement. We used to have a 'squawk box' in the ops room linked directly to the coffee bar. Dave Todd, a South African, flipped the button and asked if there were any students in the coffee bar. 'Yes' came back a voice. 'Good,' says Dave Todd, 'I want four NATO standard coffees up here on the double'. 'Right,' says the voice. And five minutes later a very senior air marshal comes into the ops room with four coffees. It was one of the rare occasions that I have seen Dave Todd lost for words.

For June and July 1961 Chivenor was closed to resurface the runway and we redeployed for a couple of months to Stradishall. This suited me as the only bachelor but the rest of the squadron were not so pleased. Also, the format of the course started to change. Whereas up to then we had carried on very much as before with a syllabus that reflected the needs of an air defence force, the Hunter front line squadrons had become almost exclusively ground attack, so low level navigation, air-ground gunnery and rocketing became part of the syllabus and it certainly helped to break some of the tedium. Another course still concentrated on the air defence business as it was designed for those pilots destined for the Lightning.

I managed to amuse myself by flying ATC cadets in the Chipmunk, and converting on to the Meteor to do some target towing for a bit of variation. Martin Chandler was replaced by Bunny Warren later in the year, and one morning at the end of September at the morning briefing in the squadron ops room the Boss asked if anyone was interested in ferrying a Hunter to the Far East. As the only bachelor on the squadron, I was the obvious first choice. It was a case of who was going to volunteer to go with me. After some hesitation Tony Park said he would, somewhat reluctantly, accompany me to make sure I did not get into too much trouble. The task was to take the last two aircraft of 20 Sqn, who were in the process of reforming in the Far East, to Singapore as the squadron did not have enough pilots to ferry all of their aircraft. One was a single seat Mk 9 aircraft and the other was a Mk T7, their two seat trainer. There were a couple of extra twists to this arrangement. Firstly the right hand seat of the T7 was to be filled by a staff officer from Fighter Command who 'wanted to come along for the experience'—which was code for a good wheeze to escape the office for a couple of weeks and get in a few rounds of golf in Singapore—and the other twist was that the Fleet Air Arm wanted to take advantage of the flight and add a Hunter T8 to the formation. The T7 and the T8 were virtually identical except for cockpit instrumentation and they had no navigation aids except DME, a device which gave you the range to a beacon assuming that there was such a thing *en route* and that you could actually get it to lock on. With 4 × 100 gallon drop tanks, they had a range of about 1000 nautical miles at best. The Mk 9 had DME and a radio compass, and came with 2 × 230 gallon and 2 × 100 gallon drop tanks giving it a range of about 1400 nautical miles.

Tony and I moved to St Athan in South Wales to prepare for this epic journey and started to collect all the necessary maps and get the various diplomatic clearances. St Athan was a maintenance unit where new aircraft were stored and prepared although I had to go and collect the Mk 7 from Kemble. I remember it well because when the day dawned it was blowing a gale, 40 knots straight across the runway at Kemble which was way outside the crosswind limit of the Vampire T11 in which the St Athan resident MU test pilot, a Polish officer called Yank Jankiewicz, was going to take me. I demurred but Yank insisted that it was not a problem and that limits were not written for pilots of his ability. So we went; and he carried out one of the hairiest landings I have ever experienced in a Vampire, about 20 knots faster than normal and on one wheel for half of the landing run, but he kept it on the runway and I collected our T7, XF310.

Then there was the question of who was going to fly the T8. In those days all the FAA delivery and ferry flights were done by a bunch of civilian contract pilots based at Rochester. The problem was that they were all quite aged and used to delivering aircraft as singletons; hence they had not flown in formation for years—nor it seemed did they want to. So their chief pilot turned up with this somewhat reluctant volunteer in tow who was the youngest guy on the outfit and the one who had the most recent experience of formation. His name was Keith. He was, I was led to believe, ex-RAF and had been at Chivenor himself, albeit on Spitfires. He certainly had a fairly chequered flying career which included delivering Spitfires to a nascent Israeli Air Force in 1948 under the leadership of a lady by the name of Jackie Moggridge. From what little he said, it was a fairly hair raising trip, but it did not alter the fact that it was a good many years since he had flown formation.

We had the aircraft all safely gathered at St Athan and the pilots, including our passenger from Fighter Command. We were already a few days behind schedule, a fact that was going to colour some of my subsequent decisions. Nevertheless I decided that it was necessary to test Keith's prowess at close formation even though that would put us further behind. We did a couple of trips and we were encouraged and surprised to find that he coped fairly well. We had all the maps and charts we needed and, we thought, the diplomatic clearances and the aircraft were ready. The route was planned to be UK—Orange—Luqa—El Adem—Nicosia—Diyarbakir—Teheran—Sharjah—Karachi—Delhi—Calcutta—Rangoon—Bangkok—Butterworth—Tengah; a testing little trip. For some bureaucratic reason, H. M. Customs would not allow us to depart the UK from St Athan, so we had to go to Lyneham on 23 October 1961 and spend the night there before finally launching off on the following day. On the 24th, the weather was abysmal at Lyneham although it was said to be clear at Orange, our first destination in the South of France. I was still a little concerned about Keith but decided to go anyway. We had to climb through 35,000 ft of cloud and I was relieved to find him still on my wing when we lurched out of the cloud at 35,000 ft and we made Orange all in one piece and in time for leisurely dinner.

I decided that we would try and get to Nicosia the following day. The first leg to Malta was uneventful and normally the shorter range of the two seat Hunters meant that we would have to stop and refuel at El Adem. However, when we looked at the forecast winds and did all our calculations, I reckoned that we could make Nicosia in one hop. If it looked as though we were going to be short of fuel, we could always divert from abeam El Adem. And for once the forecast winds met our expectations and we made Nicosia in one hop, but not exactly flush with fuel.

It was at Nicosia that we had our first very negative experience. In those days—and it's probably still the same now—the Transport

Command crews (a.k.a. 'Truckies or Trash Haulers') had absolute priority on all accommodation *en route*. 'Captain Speaking', having travelled down the route in his very shiny Britannia or Comet, dressed immaculately in his best blue, having food delivered to him on demand and being served coffee on the hour every hour, was so exhausted when he arrived at his destination that he had to have air conditioned accommodation so that he could get his eight hours beauty sleep. On the other hand, single seat ferry crews, who had been on the go all day, had done all their own servicing and refuelling, would have been lucky if they had even one cup of coffee and probably had not had anything to eat, arrived at their destination absolutely knackered having done two or three legs in one day only to find that the transport crews had taken all the decent accommodation. And such was the situation when we arrived at Nicosia, for the movements officer regretted to tell us that there was nothing available for us and offered us a tent for the night. At which stage I decided to employ our secret weapon. I had had my doubts about the virtue of having a wing commander as a passenger; however, when I told the movements officer that he would have to explain the situation to our VIP passenger and then introduced him to the wing commander, suddenly accommodation became available. I just knew there was a reason for having him along.

That night in the bar someone told us that we could make some easy money by selling whisky in Teheran; they even told us that if we went to the back door of the German Hotel in Teheran, they would give us a good price for it. So, without really thinking about it, we bought ten bottles of whisky to take with us. We had planned to night stop in Teheran in any case, but first we had to go to Diyarbakir in Turkey which, in those days, was not exactly in the centre of the universe. On the following morning the weather looked pretty fair although there was extensive cloud cover forecast over Turkey. There was a rule that said you could not go if there was more than 50 per cent cloud cover because the Russians had a habit of bending the radio compass beacon so that you ended up over their territory, but I was beginning to get concerned that we were getting even further behind schedule so I decided to go. The forecast was correct, and almost as soon as we got over Turkey we lost complete sight of the ground and we had to rely on dead reckoning navigation as we knew the beacons were unreliable—almost as unreliable as our navigation. I let down on the estimated time and, fortunately, the cloud base was quite high as there are some significant mountains in that area, but there was no sign of Diyarbakir. After some time, we did manage to make contact with the ATC but the controller could not understand our problem, i.e. that we were at least uncertain of position if not actually lost. The two seat Hunters were running very short of fuel although Tony in his Mk 9 with an extra 260 gallons helpfully mentioned that he did not have a problem. I was just about to climb out and head for Adana when suddenly I saw the airfield in the next valley. To say that I was somewhat relieved was probably a slight understatement, but our problems did not end there; the ATC suddenly informed us that the runway was closed as there were sheep (goats?) all over the place and we ended up landing on the taxiway.

I left Tony and Keith to do the refuelling and was taken off to some hut in the middle of the airfield where I understood that I could put in a flight plan for the next leg to Teheran. No one seemed to speak English and when, in a fit of pique, I tried to leave, it was made very clear to me that I was not going anywhere. Even I understood the threat of a couple of rifles in my chest. After a short wait a USAF exchange officer arrived with an interpreter in tow and explained that we had arrived in Turkey without the benefit of diplomatic clearance. This appeared to be regarded as an original sin and there was a weight of opinion that seemed to want to put us in the slammer. Fortunately the USAF officer managed to persuade them out of this and somehow we were allowed to continue. I have never thanked that man but I was extremely grateful to him. He appeared to have the mother and father of punishment postings. He was the sole USAF representative on a wing of Turkish Air Force F84s who were at the time grounded for lack of spares (so he told me). No one spoke English, there were few facilities and Diyarbakir was in the middle of nowhere. I have no idea what he had done to deserve it, but it must have been pretty serious. Without further ado, we got the hell out of Diyarbakir and had a pretty uneventful trip to Teheran.

Teheran was a fairly lively city in those days, even though there appeared to be a surfeit of the military on the streets keeping control and we were accommodated in a hotel down town. The first requirement was to find the German Hotel and offload the ten bottles of Scotch. Wandering around the city with the Scotch wrapped in a map was not something to be recommended when there seemed to be a distinct possibility of being stopped by one of the many patrols and asked to explain what we were doing. In fact it almost turned into high farce as, when trying to avoid such a patrol, we managed to drop a bottle in the street just as we had located the hotel. Fortunately they did not take any notice and after some discussion the hotel took the remaining nine bottles of Scotch off our hands. We concluded that the life of a smuggler was not for us and vowed never to get suckered in ever again. The following morning we left Teheran with some sense of relief and headed for Sharjah in what was then the Trucial States and is now the UAE. Political sensitivities demanded that we flight planned to Bahrein and then diverted in midflight to Sharjah because Iran had some sort of conflicting territorial claim. We arrived at Sharjah and had intended to go on to Karachi but suddenly the canopy of my T7 started playing up and would not close. We had a copy of what was referred to as the 'Vol 1', a sort of Haynes technical manual for the aircraft, but that did not throw much light on the problem.

Sharjah in those days was very different to the modern city of today; it just consisted of a fort, an airfield and a few buildings for the RAF facilities. The accommodation for transients was once again tents. The base was commanded by a squadron leader with about 30 men. So we were stuck and not quite sure how we were going to rectify the problem. That was until an electrician on the base heard of our plight and volunteered to take a look. He knew something about Hunters, having served on a Hunter squadron, and within a very short time identified the problem as a blown fuse, which he replaced, and once again we were ready to go, but we had lost another day on our schedule.

Sharjah to Karachi was not a particularly long leg but we had a major unserviceability *en route*. Keith lost a fuel pump in the T8 and we had to talk him through the necessary procedure to deal with it. It had become increasingly clear as we had progressed that he did not have a great knowledge of, or familiarity with his aircraft and that we would have to nurse him along. At that stage we only knew half of the story as will become evident later on, however we landed at Karachi without any further problem. But there was one procedure that we had to carry out which has been for ever a source of mystery to me. We had to keep the canopies closed taxying in and then under the watchful eye of some official discharge an insecticide aerosol inside the cockpit and sit there for a minute or two just to ensure that we had not imported any nasty bugs. Apart from the fact that we nearly suffocated, I could not for the life of me imagine what bug we could bring with us that they had not already got. We were finally cleared to open the canopies and we then went to clear customs. We had refreshed our store of Scotch by this time—but only for personal consumption—and I declared it to the customs official and, taking no chances, told him that I would be happy to leave it in bond and collect it on the way out. His only comment was 'Why? Don't you want to drink while you're in Karachi?' So I took it with me, which was just as well because we were about to fall even further behind our schedule.

We were accommodated in the Speedbird Hotel just outside the airfield. This was run by BOAC and was primarily for the benefit of slip crews of BOAC and Qantas. It could also take a full load of passengers as well when necessary. It was a pretty high standard hotel, but they were not particularly familiar with RAF crews of single seat jets, and as we were aircraft captains, we were treated as a BOAC captain—an individual just about akin to God—and signed all our bar chits as such. It certainly got wonderful service. That first night, as were having a drink on the veranda, we were treated to a locust storm which was an impressive sight, particularly if you have never before experienced it. We also met a whole bunch of Qantas crews who seemed determined to enjoy themselves. But our more immediate problem was what to do about the fuel pump on the Hunter T8. Out came the 'Vol 1' again and, miracle of miracles, it did describe roughly what we had to do to change the pump. So first thing on the following morning Tony and I decided to examine the problem, as Keith seemed to have opted out. The first thing we had to do was defuel the aircraft. We borrowed a fuel bowser and successfully completed that operation. Then we had to take out the unserviceable fuel pump from the bottom of the front fuel tank, which we did. I found the reference number of the pump and sent off signals to Aden and to Singapore (the nearest RAF bases likely to have Hunter spares) asking for a spare pump. Then we sat back to wait. That evening the Qantas crews took pity on us and invited us to a party. My main memory of this was at breakfast at 6 o'clock the following morning with one of the 707 Qantas crews, having not been to bed, when first of all the co-pilot had an argument with the flight engineer and went out on the balcony to settle it in the old fashioned way. Then, just as we said that it was time to go to bed, the 707 Captain appeared, immaculate in his uniform, and announced that the crew coach was picking them up in five minutes to take them out to the aircraft.

To our surprise, not just one pump but two fuel pumps appeared within 24 hours. The next exercise was to fit it to the aircraft; but when I compared the new one with the item that I had taken off the aircraft, it was only half the size. The reason very quickly became apparent. I had taken the pump out of the fuel tank, but I had also taken the base plate off the bottom of the tank, an item that is normally never touched from the time the aircraft is built to its demise. What I really needed was a new seal before I put it back. We gave the problem some thought and decided that we just could not afford to wait for a new seal. I went to the BOAC hangar and borrowed a large tube of Bostik, put the new pump in the base plate, coated the old seal liberally with the Bostik and reassembled the whole thing, tightening all the nuts up as hard as possible. Having connected everything, we then refuelled the aircraft and sat for some time underneath to see whether it was going to leak. Amazingly enough it did not and we were once again ready to get on the road.

2 November and we were on the way once again. It was a fairly uneventful leg to Delhi and the only notable fact was that we arrived at the airfield at the same time as Nehru, the prime minister of India, which meant that we had to sit sweltering for some time in cockpit whilst we waited for him to clear. A quick turn-round and we set off for Dum Dum Airport, Calcutta. It was here that we were meant to join up with a Canberra weather escort to help us negotiate the ITCZ (Intertropical Convergence Zone) which could, at times, have some pretty unpleasant weather on it. The crew of the Canberra had been waiting for nearly a week as we were so far behind schedule. We were accommodated in one of the finest hotels in Calcutta which was not exactly cheap. The Canberra crew had been restricted to the set menu in the main restaurant and no alcohol; but for some reason on that evening the hotel allowed us free rein. I was invited to sign the check at the end of the evening and I did so in the almost certain knowledge that it would catch up with me at some time and that I would have some difficulty explaining it; and even more difficulty paying it. In the event I never did hear any more about it.

We set off fairly early the next morning, the Canberra leaving half an hour before us. I was trying to catch up some time by this stage so I decided to try and make Bangkok in one hop, and not stop at Rangoon. It was going to leave us very tight on fuel at our destination but since we had to go almost overhead Rangoon, I could make the decision at that point assuming there was good weather at Bangkok and favourable winds. For this I was relying on the Canberra; however we never caught sight nor sound of him ever again—so much for providing them with a decent meal the evening before. However a BOAC 707 heard my calls and came to the rescue. He used his HF to get the actual weather at Bangkok and his navigator—these were the days in which they carried such a crew member—gave us actual winds and we were able to work out that we could just make it, and so we did, but with very little fuel remaining.

Bangkok in those days was a fascinating place. It was not nearly as crowded as it is now and the Vietnam War had not reached the stage such that the city was overrun with Americans. However there was an American influence in that just about every restaurant served T-bone steaks, and very good steaks they were. The British Air Attaché met us, I think because he knew Alan Jenkins, our VIP passenger. But since we were only going to be there one night, he had not arranged anything for us except the hotel accommodation which was on the outskirts of the city. The restaurant in the hotel also did duty as a night club and half way through dinner, it went almost pitch black and we had to finish our meal by feel rather than by sight. The cabaret was everything you would have expected in Bangkok and we went to bed around midnight as we had an early start.

Five a.m. on Saturday morning and we are all in the crew coach waiting for Keith. There was no sign of him and I asked Tony to go back to his room and check. He came back to say that Keith was on his way. He also mentioned that he found him drinking neat Scotch out of a tumbler in his bathroom. It was only at this stage that I realised we had an alcoholic on our hands. He had hidden it very well; or I had been particularly unobservant. In my defence so had the other two, Tony and Alan Jenkins. On the basis that he obviously needed the alcohol to function and that he had functioned reasonably so far, I decided to continue. The intention was to stage via Butterworth and get to Singapore that evening. Once again, if we had the fuel and the weather was kind we would overfly Butterworth and go direct to Tengah. We got to the airport and prepared the aircraft.

At this stage we were getting short of starter cartridges for the two two-seat aircraft and someone had neglected to pre-position any at Bangkok although there was plenty of starter fuel for the Mk 9 which had a different system. We had just three cartridges which meant that one aircraft would have only one and the other two. If the one with one cartridge failed to start, I (as Keith would not have known what to do—it was a tricky job at the best of times), would have to climb out and switch cartridges. So it was essential that we did not start until we had the clearance from air traffic. We checked in on the radio before start but Keith was unable to transmit or receive because, we understood, of heavy static. I got out of my aircraft and went across to see what was wrong. It turned out that Keith could not use the radio because, without the engine running, there was a non-stop audio warning for low hydraulic pressure. All he had to do was hit the audio cut-out switch and all would have been well. It was obvious to me that he really was in no state to go flying, so I called the trip off and decided to stay the weekend in Bangkok (a very difficult decision!) so that Keith could at least, temporarily, dry out.

Alan Jenkins was not best pleased about this as he had a date to play golf in Singapore that weekend. However the decision was fortuitous in more ways than one. It turned out that our staging post of Butterworth was closed on Saturdays and Sundays so that in the event of any problems we would have been in trouble.

The Air Attaché came to our rescue. He made it his mission to show us around the city. He took us to some restaurant in the middle of a lake, which served the most magnificent prawns. He introduced us to couple of guys who had come into town to celebrate the birth of a son; and, ironically enough, I understood that the proud father was in fact a nephew of Duncan Sandys. So I did not feel any guilt at drinking at his expense. Unfortunately they wanted to go on longer and later than my body permitted and my last abiding memory was drinking Saki at a great rate just so as we could finish it and go back to the hotel and go to bed.

Sunday morning and the Air Attaché was on our doorstep again saying that he would now take us to the Number 2 RAF Mess for beer and a curry, we had no idea what he was talking about but just did as we were told. We arrived at this house where his entire staff of three NCOs lived. Two of them manned the office and the third was a crew chief for his own aircraft, a Devon which he used for commuting to the other countries to which he was accredited which included Laos, Cambodia and, I think, Vietnam. His wife used to act as the air-hostess as he piloted himself around South East Asia. It sounded to me just like the perfect job for superannuated fighter pilots.

Monday morning came round and Keith was in a somewhat better state than previously and we climbed aboard our aircraft. Everything went as advertised, all the aircraft started and we took off and flew direct to Tengah. The only incident occurred when I looked round half way and could see no sign of Keith. I could see Tony and I asked him and he could not see him either. We kept calling him on the radio and there was no answer. Knowing what I did, I feared the worst and was just beginning to wonder how I was going to explain losing someone, when Keith came up on the radio. 'Sorry,' he said, 'I fell asleep and nearly lost you'. I was so relieved that I did not even get angry—well maybe just a little bit. This time we had plenty of fuel in hand. When we landed, we handed over all the documentation for the three airplanes and I took the engineer officer aside and told him what I had done to the fuel tank in Karachi. He was horrified. I left the problem with him and I have no idea what he did.

We had a very enjoyable evening in Tengah, ending up in a Chinese restaurant which specialised in crab and I do not think I have ever had the equal of that meal anywhere. The only problem was that the movements officials were at their efficient best (worst). There was a rule that ferry pilots had an absolute priority when it came to air transport home. They had bumped two people off the Britannia due to return to UK the following morning and despite our protests refused to change their minds. Alan Jenkins was of course nowhere to be seen when we really needed him—no doubt on a golf course somewhere.

So a very pleasant interlude and a trip on which I learnt a number of lessons—not least of which was be very careful with whom you fly, especially if they are alcoholics. Never assume anything and always check, and always be careful when you are undertaking engineering tasks of which you know nothing; but it was a magnificent experience and one that remains fixed in my memory to this day. Sadly, I believe Keith committed suicide some years later.

It was with a certain amount of relief that I returned to the somewhat more mundane existence at Chivenor and life resumed its somewhat more regular rhythm. Chivenor has always had a reputation of being one of the more desirable postings in the Royal Air Force despite its somewhat Spartan living conditions and even now people speak of it with pleasurable memories. The mess was just two or three Nissen huts joined together, but it always had a homely and welcoming atmosphere with, in the winter, a very large coke fire burning in the anteroom. At the weekends I would either borrow an airplane or drive up to London, the latter being a somewhat lengthy journey in those days. I do remember that the time we usually tried to beat *en route* was one hour from the centre of Barnstaple to the Clock Tower in Taunton. You had to be very lucky with the traffic or a complete lunatic to achieve it. Regrettably there were quite a few of the latter around. It was after one of my trips to London that my sinus problems came back to haunt me. I was halfway back to Chivenor in my TR2 driving down the hill on the A303 which leads into Amesbury when blood started pouring from my nose. The drive to Chivenor became a little more hazardous than usual as I was trying to stem the flow with one hand and drive with the other. I went straight to the MO when I got back and he confirmed what I already knew—a bad bout of sinus trouble. I went in to hospital for an operation to enlarge the drains. This is not one of the most pleasant procedures that I have endured at the hands of the medics. It is done under a local anaesthetic with a blindfold and basically they use a file to enlarge the drain holes in the bone. It is not so much the discomfort of the procedure which is bad enough but the noise of the file in your head which was horrendous! However the operation was successful and seemed to cure the problem although I was afflicted by sinus problems from time to time during the rest of my flying career.

I had become a little bored with life at Chivenor; I think it was the repetitive nature of the flying which tended to add to the dissatisfaction. That had led me to volunteer for the post of Pilot to the Antarctic Expedition; it was a year's posting to the Arctic to fly the UK team's Beaver around. It would have certainly been a challenge, probably more than I could have coped with. Fortunately they declined my services, which was just as well because I had just become engaged to be married.

By 1962 the novelty of the Nissen huts was beginning to wear thin and I got married—despite gaining a father-in-law whose main aim in life seemed to be putting me under the table. Judy and I were married at St Clement Danes on 3 March 1962, and a wonderful occasion it was. The reception was at the Waldorf Hotel and my father also gave a family party in the Presscala Club in Fleet Street. Judy and I went off on our honeymoon by car and *en route* to the hotel we very nearly turned back to join the party. It has been one of our everlasting regrets that we did not. I think our parents would have been horrified, but we were told subsequently that we missed a very good evening. We had intended to go to Paris for our honeymoon but the OAS put paid to that as they started throwing bombs around and there was also a smallpox scare, so we went to Dorset instead. One of Judy's abiding memories is that I decided to take her flying and, as Thruxton was pretty near at hand, I naturally went there to hire an airplane. All the instructors had changed by then but after a quick check out, they let me have a 'Thruxton Jackaroo' which was essentially a Tiger Moth converted to carry four people. Whilst I was having my check out, Judy had to wait with three or four of the students who were hanging around the coffee bar. They managed to terrify her with tales of how decrepit, ancient and unreliable the aircraft were. Actually I do not think that it was that far from the truth, but by the time she strapped in with me, all she wanted to do was get back in the car and return to the hotel. Having taken off, I gently motored around the local area and then turned to head back to the airfield. The application of just twenty degrees of bank initiated a terrorised scream and a request not to do that again. I explained that I had to turn to get back to Thruxton; and as soon as we did get back, I landed. That was the last time that I took my wife flying until many years later, and that time it was in a somewhat more substantial and more comfortable aircraft—a Basset. But she is definitely not very keen on flying—especially in small aircraft.

In 1962, the Blue Diamonds, 92 Sqn, were the official aerobatic team of the RAF. They had taken over from 111 Sqn, the Black Arrows, who had managed to achieve a 22 aircraft loop. To do that, they had borrowed aircraft and pilots from all over the RAF and it was in 1958 that they achieved the feat in public at the Farnborough Air Display. I remember watching it and being very impressed at how smooth it appeared, but I am told it was not quite like that from the inside. Anyway, Fighter Command always had a 'reserve' formation aerobatic team and this was provided by 229 OCU, Chivenor. In 1961 234 Sqn at the other end of the airfield had provided the team. 1962 and it was 145 Sqn's turn. The Boss, Bunny Warren, naturally led the team. I was No. 2; Pete Stowell was No. 3 and Tony Park No. 4. Although we only normally flew as a four ship, Geoff Timms was No. 5 and spare pilot.

Bunny Warren used to like practising over the sea for some reason. We all hated it because there was not always a well-defined horizon and because sometimes sea merged into sky and vice versa, thus it was often very difficult to know which way was up. It could be quite disorientating but, despite our protests, Bunny continued to do it. Just occasionally we would be allowed to do a display over the airfield and one of those occasions was nearly my last. Our display finished with a downward bomb burst with the four aircraft heading off the four points of the compass. Just after we had pulled out, the leader would call 'rolling, rolling, go' and we would all execute three rapid rolls as we departed the airfield. On this particular practice, either I was slow or Bunny Warren was a bit quick, but the rolling order came before I had completely pulled out of the dive. The bomb burst had left me heading straight towards Barnstaple along the railway line. Without even thinking I executed the roll as ordered and all I know is that as I went inverted, the railway sleepers were extremely large and close to hand. I could not say what my minimum height was, but I would be surprised if it was much more than 20 ft. According to those who were watching, they were convinced that I was going straight into the ground—and they were not alone!

We did not carry out that many displays and our main activity occurred on Battle of Britain Day. We did three displays that day, one at Acklington and one at Middleton St George on the same trip and a final one at Aldergrove where we stayed the night. The two displays in one sortie meant that we had to do the first one with full tanks; something we had not done before and for the second at Middleton, the weather was marginal for a full display. The decision for 'full' or 'flat' was taken by the Boss as we ran in. We had all assumed that it would be a flat show and we were somewhat taken aback when he said 'full'. The first manoeuvre was a line abreast loop with a formation change to box as we came down the other side. But we pulled up straight into one of the biggest black clouds you had ever seen and during the manoeuvre everyone lost everyone at some stage. The miracle was that somehow we came out of the cloud in a perfect box formation and I have never been sure how we achieved that to this day. After that, anything was an anti-climax and the weather at Aldergrove was perfect. But it had been a challenging variation to the normal routine.

1962 was also the year that Bunny Warren decided that his mission in life was to get as many of us as he could through the 'C' exam. In those days there were two examinations that you had to pass before you could be promoted. The B exam was to qualify you to be promoted from flying officer to flight lieutenant and the C from flight lieutenant to squadron leader. The former was automatic on time and passing the exam; the latter also required selection. I had already lost six months seniority because I had not passed the B exam when I should have done and it looked as though the same thing would happen with the C exam. It was really a mixture of idleness and the fact that there were too many other distractions, but Bunny was not going to let us get away with it. Most of the staff at Chivenor were fairly senior flight lieutenants and he was determined that we were going to pass, so he insisted that we all put our names down for the exam. He then proceeded to take over the ground school most evenings and lecture on every aspect, administration and organisation, Air Force law and air power, thus making sure that we revised adequately for the exam. By some means he also ensured that he was the invigilator at the exam. I can see him now strolling up and down the room, pausing behind me every now and again, shaking his head sadly if I had got it wrong. No one failed the exam, although some only got a 'partial pass', which meant that they did not have to retake the whole exam but just the subject in which they had failed. Without his insistence on revising, I doubt whether any of us would ever have passed.

The content of the conversion course at Chivenor had now changed and concentrated far more on ground attack than it did on air defence as most of the Hunter squadrons had now taken on that role and the Lightnings were doing air defence. This led to more variation in the flying and to me at least more satisfaction. Gp Capt. Billy Drake, a well-known Battle of Britain pilot, had taken over as station commander and he occasionally came and flew with us. Normally station commanders in those days rarely flew; and one was always a little concerned if they did as they were never in really current practice. However Billy Drake once flew as my number 2 on a fairly complex sortie and I have to say that his performance as a wingman was quite remarkable. Sadly he fell by the wayside as station commander and was, I understand, relieved of his command for reasons which passed me by.

There were a couple of other memorable, to me at least, events which occurred in 1962. The first was when the Fleet Air Arm decided to put the Seahawk out to grass. They ran a similar course with Seahawks at Lossiemouth as we did with Hunters at Chivenor. One morning, after the demise of the Seahawk was announced, they rang us up asking if anyone wanted to fly the aircraft before they finally went to the breakers yard. Trevor Copleston and I said yes and motored up there quickly in a Hunter T7, did two trips each and came back the same day. It was remarkable in that the Fleet Air Arm had a far more relaxed attitude to flying other aircraft than the RAF and that we never could have reciprocated such an offer without incurring someone's wrath. I especially remember it as on my first trip in the Seahawk I tried to take off with the wing unlocked and, fortunately, the caravan controller on the end of the runway noticed it. It was a very pleasant aircraft to fly and its relation to the Hunter, designed and built by the same manufacturer, Hawkers, was obvious. It had much less thrust and did not have the same performance and only had power assisted ailerons—the Hunter having power assisted ailerons and elevators.

The second incident that sticks in my memory was a trip in a Meteor 7. Dickie Barraclough, one of my fellow instructors, had been promoted and posted as a squadron commander at the college at Cranwell and he wanted to go up there to see what was entailed. I said that I would take him up there but unfortunately no two-seat Hunter was available, so I took a two-seat Meteor 7. I had not flown the Meteor 7 in some time; in fact I had only flown it on my initial conversion the year before, so most of my Meteor flying had been done in the single seat Meteor 8. This was substantially the same as the 7 with one or two important differences mainly to do with the fuel system, specifically the ventral tank. On the Meteor 8 the ventral tank fed automatically; on the 7 you had to select it. You had to rotate the selector to get the ventral to feed and you pulled the same selector to jettison the ventral. Only the UK could design a fuel system so spring-loaded for disaster. I checked before we got airborne and I knew that the ventral was full so when we had got halfway to Cranwell and we were running very short of fuel, being quick on the uptake, I worked out that something was wrong. I concluded that I must have been mistaken and that the ventral had never been filled.

We got down to such a low fuel state that a diversion became inevitable; and I have to say that Dickie in the backseat was absolutely no help whatsoever. He had never flown a Meteor and was highly amused at my discomfort, which was only increased when it turned out that the nearest available diversion was Little Rissington, the home of the Central Flying School. The runway was a little shorter than I was used to so I made sure that I approached at the right speed and when the aircraft dropped out of my hands, fortuitously over the runway, and landed heavily, I realised that the tank was full but not feeding. After I had taxied in and shut down, I double checked and it was still most definitely full. At this stage it occurred to me to look at the tank selector. I was wary of touching it as I knew that it also jettisoned the tank. I certainly did not want to ask anyone for fear of showing my ignorance. Fortunately there were a couple of other Meteor 7s in the dispersal, so I surreptitiously snuck over and checked the position of the fuel cock. They were both different to mine. So I changed mine and refuelled and carried on with the journey. When I got back to Chivenor that evening all hell had broken loose. It appeared that a new mechanic had mistakenly switched the fuel cock. And he had also pulled the jettison. Quite why the tank had not fallen off, no one knew. But I was somewhat relieved by the fact that it had not and that the day had not ended up in disaster.

We did one more formation display after Battle of Britain Day for the Royal Observer Corps' open day and our formation aerobatic season came to an end. For some reason, which now eludes me, we had all given up smoking at the beginning of the season and agreed that it would cost the first one to light up £50. The relief at completing the season without any mishap was such that we all agreed to light up simultaneously.

1962 came to a close and I was somewhat hoist by my own petard. Before I got married I had been asked if I would consider an exchange posting with the Fleet Air Arm. I thought that it would at least be something different and I had said yes. However that was then; and now I was married and Judy was expecting our first child. Being that Sod's Law reigns supreme, I got a telephone call to say that I was probably going to go to 801 squadron flying Scimitars which, of course, would mean a substantial time at sea. I did not know quite how to break the news to my wife but, before I could, I got another call to say that it had been cancelled. It appeared that the Navy was running short of Scimitars and their need for pilots thus diminished.

Instead, at the beginning of 1963, I found myself on the Day Fighter Leaders' Course at the Central Fighter Establishment at Binbrook.

The mission of the Day Fighter Leaders' School was to inject a level of professionalism at the senior level of the front line squadrons. It had not always succeeded in its aims as exemplified in the incident when they lost six out of eight aircraft on a training sortie due to combination of bad weather and, dare I say it, poor leadership! It had always been a course that pushed you to the limit with regards weather and tended to ignore the normal rules of safety, but you certainly learned about flying and leading. February at Binbrook is not a laughing matter. The airfield is on the top of a hill—it must be one of the few hills in Lincolnshire—and the weather factor abysmal. I will never forget one of the early flying decisions. At the morning briefing the air traffic man said that the runway 01 was 100 per cent snow and ice. The Boss of DFLS then immediately stood up and said that we would fly off Runway 19. I could not work out how taking off in the other direction on the same runway was going to ameliorate the ice and snow conditions, but fly we did, and we were pushed to the limit. I came back off one sortie with almost no fuel when I was faced with the fact that the port main wheel would not come down. I tried just about everything including bouncing the aircraft on the runway on the other main wheel to see if I could jolt it down. All to no avail and the fuel gauges were now indicating empty so, because I could not afford to make another circuit, I was forced to land downwind. The port wing dropped towards the runway and the tank held it for a time but unfortunately exploded and I careered off the runway onto the grass and mud just missing the GCA hut. Despite that, the aircraft was rectified overnight with a new wingtip and sequence valve and was on the line serviceable the following morning.

For light relief in the evenings or the weekends, if we could not be found in the bar at the mess, we could always be found at the Humberston Country Club, a gambling casino with a peculiar mix of customers. There were people dressed in dinner jackets and others in dungarees—the latter usually being straight off the trawlers with large wads of cash. They all seemed to take a great delight in looking after us in those days and we had a most enjoyable time and made several very good friends.

The culmination of the DFLS course was a 12 ship high low simulated strike into Germany. The staff had ensured that we were going to be bounced by all sorts of aircraft from take-off. As we got to the top of climb Javelins from the UK were the first 'enemy' that we had to contend with. Having beaten them off and just about regained our track, Dutch aircraft came up at us as we approached the Continent. Then it all became very quiet and we were left alone. The reason very quickly became obvious. The weather was so appalling that no one else was able to fly in West Germany. We let down into the target area and all we could see was the occasional church spire and radio mast sticking above the fog. I was leading the back 4 and we did manage to get to the target area but that was all we could do and I decided to abort and concentrate on recovering all four aircraft in one piece at Gütersloh. That we did and the weather prevented us from any more flying in Germany and we returned to Binbrook a couple of days later. I do remember being criticised, not just me personally, but the whole course, for lack of 'press on spirit'. I thought that we did more than enough in the weather conditions prevailing.

Then it was back to Chivenor and a never ending sequence of students. We moved house across the estuary to Bickington and, as usual, I spent a large amount of my leisure time in the summer playing cricket for North Devon. They had the most magnificent ground at Instow sticking out into the estuary with a large thatched barn for a pavilion. Judy used to come down and watch and also take the dog for a walk along the adjacent beach. It was idyllic. Although North Devon was in reality a village cricket club, it did play cricket to a higher standard than most. One of the mainstays of the team was a gentleman by the name of David Sheppard who subsequently played for Gloucestershire and became a well-known test cricket umpire. There were a couple of ex-Yorkshire league players, and also a couple of guys who had played for the RAF. As well as the normal weekend fixtures, we had all the touring teams come to play two day matches in the summer, the Free Foresters, the Eton Ramblers and so on. And because life at Chivenor was fairly relaxed, I was able to play in many of these games; it was a very happy and enjoyable time.

Although we had changed roles to ground attack, we still had a responsibility for air defence as a reserve squadron in Fighter Command. The two squadrons, 145 and 234 would amalgamate as one and we called ourselves 12345 Sqn. Every year Fighter Command would hold its annual exercise to test the whole system and we would be called upon to participate. We were never told exactly when it was going to occur but we were given some idea of the period. Because Judy was about to give birth to our firstborn, I had been told that, should the callout occur, I would not be required.

The 1963 Chivenor Summer Ball was held on 9 July and a very good party it was. Pete Stowell, Tony Park, Glyn Chapman and I with our wives, were the last to leave the mess at about 3 in the morning. The doors were locked so we had to bail out of the window in the bar which, due to Judy's condition, was not the easiest of exercises. We got her out and just as Pete Stowell was about to be the last to leave, the telephone in the mess rang. We persuaded Pete to go back and answer it whilst we legged it home; 30 minutes later he was on my doorstep, in uniform, saying that it was the alert for the Fighter Command Annual Exercise. I told him that I was excused from the exercise, but I thought that I had better turn up just in case. It was 4 a.m. and I arrived at the squadron to be asked by the Boss what I thought I was doing and that I should be at home. We had enough pilots to fill our requirement and I was about to go home when 234 Sqn rang and asked if we had any spare pilots down our end as their callout system had completely failed. I found myself airborne in the first pair 30 minutes later on the wing of 234 Sqn's boss, Ron Wood, in the dark with my eyes out on organ stops having never done night formation, wishing that I had never bothered to react to the callout. But it was a beautiful morning and we intercepted a couple USAF B66s over the North Sea and landed at Coltishall in Norfolk for breakfast, and a very welcome meal it was as well. We returned to Chivenor in a somewhat more leisurely fashion later in the morning.

My son, Mark, was born on 25 July 1963 at a nursing home in Barnstaple and a very proud moment it was, and at just about the same time came news of a posting. I was to go to 8 Sqn in Aden as a flight commander. I said my farewells to Chivenor in September with a certain amount of sadness and reluctance as I had a very happy time there and made many good friends.

4

Hither and Thither
(*Uspiam et Passim*)

8 Squadron were flying Hunters mainly in the ground attack role and had managed to suffer one of the largest number of fatal accidents of any squadron in what was basically a peacetime air force. I believe one loss had been attributed to 'enemy' action in that period as they were conducting sporadic operations against rebel tribesmen up country. Families were very much a secondary consideration and I was warned that it would be at least a year before my family would be able to join me because of the scarcity of accommodation. Judy packed up the house at Bickington and went to stay with her parents in Broadstairs and I set off on my own to join 8 Sqn.

8 Sqn had been reinforced by two more Hunter squadrons, 43 (with their wretched Fighting Cocks) and 208 Sqn which had come up to Aden from Nairobi and were not very pleased about it. Strike Wing, as it was then called, also had a Shackleton squadron and the whole was commanded by Wg Cdr J. T. Jennings. Khormaksar was a very large base and there was also a squadron of Beverleys, another of Argosies and a helicopter squadron equipped with Belvederes, one of the first twin rotor helicopters. The base was commanded by Gp Capt. Alex Blythe and the Command headquarters was just down the road at Steamer Point, just a little too close for comfort.

I was not quite sure what to expect although I had had a brief glance of the place a few years previously. I had thought of it at the time as not one of the most attractive places in the world but I thought that the flying would be interesting; quite how interesting I was to find out later. I took over from Jock McVie as 'A' Flight commander in October 1963.

The Boss of the squadron was Tammy Syme who had just taken over from Laurie Jones. Tam had the reputation of being a hard man. He had started off life in the RAF as a PT Instructor before he became a pilot and had come to 8 Sqn on promotion having been a flight commander on 65 Sqn at Duxford. The other flight commander was Gordon Talbot who was to be replaced a few months later by Graham Hounsell, a tall New Zealander. We had a Royal Navy exchange officer, Tim Notley, and the engineer was a man called Owen Truelove, a young flying officer who did not understand the word 'impossible'. Inexperienced he might have been, but he turned out to be one of the finest squadron engineering officers I have ever known. This was important because we were at the end of a very long supply line and spares were not always available. And young he might have been, but the ground crew thought he was the greatest thing since sliced bread. Every squadron should have one! For the rest we had a good mix of experienced and first tour pilots who mixed well together both professionally and socially. During the previous two years the squadron had suffered quite a number of aircraft losses, some thought to be due to runaway tail trims. Other accidents were more of the self-inflicted variety although one, which occurred during a leaflet drop, was suspected to be the result of ground fire.

8 Squadron had been based in Aden since 1927 and, apart from a brief period during the Second World War when they became a maritime squadron, they had basically undertaken the same role for the last 40 years, namely what was called 'Air Policing'. The British administration had needed a mechanism to patrol this huge wilderness area. Armoured car detachments were freely available but the difficulty of terrain and the provision of supplies along hostile routes proved difficult to achieve. What was needed was a highly mobile method of policing the desert strongholds of the belligerent tribesmen, and the answer was found by the use of air power. If a village rebelled then that village was bombed—the methodology was as simple as that. Often as not they would be warned to behave themselves with a leaflet drop. Or if they continued to cause trouble an area would be pronounced as 'proscribed' and anything that moved would be a target. Thus the Hunters were used in exactly the same way as their DH9s had been used in the 1920s in Iraq. They did, of course, also undertake air defence duties as well, as there was a significant air threat from the Yemen who were equipped with MiG 15s, 17s and IL 28s but it did not seem to be particularly active when I arrived. The previous couple of years had been relatively quiet apart from a Yemeni air attack on Beihan which led to the squadron

having to fly many intensive air defence patrols in the area some 200 miles north of Khormaksar. Rebels, such as they were, were supported by the then state of Yemen to the North who were, of course, supported by the Soviet Union; and they did their best to foment unrest.

In the air, the first thing one learned was that the maps of the area were not to be trusted and sometimes had significant errors, all of which made navigation an art rather than a skill. The old hands knew the area like the back of their hands and could always be relied upon to guide you home when one became slightly uncertain of position (more usually referred to as 'lost'). And for some parts of the Arabian Peninsula such as the Empty Quarter, maps were of very little use in any case as there was nothing to show except sand, and lots of it. There were other hazards to contend with such as sandstorms which could restrict the visibility down to zero and go up to heights above 10,000 ft. It would be just like flying in a murky goldfish bowl with absolutely no horizon. Low flying could be hazardous because the lack of any features could make it very difficult to judge your height above the ground. You could think that you were safely up at 250 ft or so to find that you had been down at 25 ft. More than one person very nearly hit a sand dune under such conditions.

One of our tasks in those days was to undertake a two month detachment to Bahrein in rotation with the other two squadrons so that basically you ended up doing two months out of every six in the Persian (or Arabian, depending on your persuasion) Gulf. The reason was to show our support for Kuwait and be prepared in case anyone should show aggressive tendencies. Even in those days, Iraq had been casting covetous eyes on Kuwait and making threatening noises, so one of the Aden squadrons had to be at Bahrein all the time. I had been in Aden for less than two weeks when I was faced with my first Bahrein detachment. We flew there via Masirah and were based at Muharraq which was the main base in Bahrein. It was also a civil airfield with an airport manager by the name of Ken Rasdall whom we had taken the precaution of making an honorary squadron member. In fact he and his wife, Ann, were very good friends to the squadron and went out of their way to make us welcome. Bahrein was not as sophisticated then as it is now. The only respectable restaurant on the island was in the airport building although it was quite expensive. If you drove down the other end of the island to the Shell base at Awali you could get a reasonably good steak at a reasonable price but it was quite a trek. And that was about it. The Qatar peninsula had virtually nothing except one long runway which had just been built—and we were not allowed to go anywhere near it.

Saudi Arabia was a definite 'no-go' area. Sharjah had a small RAF base which we could use and a weapons range just down the coast where we could do rocketing and strafing.

Although there was enough activity to keep us out of trouble most of the time, it was fairly restrictive in the main. The Royal Navy always had a frigate based in Bahrein for similar reasons and we used to socialise quite frequently with them—which only goes to show how desperate things were! The station commander was Sandy Sanderson, generally referred to as 'Big Daddy', but not to his face, a man who was definitely larger than life and a man whom you definitely did not cross, as quite a few found to their cost. Most of our flying took place around Bahrein or carrying out simulated high-low-high strikes in the Sharjah area. And we also carried out a fair amount of weapons practice on the Sharjah Range. We had drawn the short straw for this particular detachment in that we had to stay there over Christmas although we were due to get back to Aden for the New Year. The Boss decided that he was going to go back to Aden for Christmas with a few of the others who had their families in Aden whilst he left the bachelors and those whose families were still in UK to hold the fort. Thus I was left in command of the squadron.

It did not take long before we were in trouble. If Aden was at the end of a long supply line for spares, Bahrein was even worse. You depended on Aden for spares and, unfortunately, the other two squadrons back at base would get their hands on the goodies first. So we often ended up flying our aircraft with some deficiencies, commonly referred to as 'Red Lines', as a warning was always written in the F700 (the servicing document) in red for the pilot to see before accepting the aircraft. Some of these deficiencies you would never have accepted in the normal course of events. One morning, the officer commanding engineering wing at Bahrein, Wg Cdr Charles Sloper (who subsequently became the chief engineer of the RAF), decided to wander around the squadron and have a look at what we were doing. It should be said that, although he had no direct control over the squadron as such, he was responsible for the professional engineering practices as a whole. He looked at all our F700s for all the aircraft, said nothing and went back to his office. Half an hour later there was a telephone call requesting the squadron commander and the engineering officer to appear in his office. So I, in company with Owen Truelove, duly complied with his request. It immediately was obvious that this was an engineering spat and that I was only there as a courtesy, being the acting squadron commander. The wing commander stated his dissatisfaction with our engineering standards and a discussion between Truelove and him commenced and I was left distinctly as just an interested bystander. It slowly got more and more heated until, to my dismay, I heard Owen say to the wing commander, 'Look Sir, why don't you fuck off and mind your own business.' I suppose I should have been grateful that he remembered to say 'Sir'. But at that stage I would have been quite happy to have been elsewhere and I was convinced that my first, albeit very short, tenure as a squadron commander was going to come to an ignominious close. I was just wondering when the court martial would take place; but much to my surprise, the wing commander was so taken aback by Owen's aggressive stance that the argument fizzled out and we were dismissed with a warning to watch what we were doing. I could barely believe that we had got away with it.

Christmas in Bahrein was celebrated in what was the traditional RAF way overseas. Every unit on the base had its billet bar and the officers were invited to sample their wares. A prize was awarded for the best decorated bar and that involved the station commander, (Big Daddy!), having to visit each one in turn. And that meant having a drink in each one. Since there were at least twenty bars, the station commander's inspection was a *tour de force*; how he remained standing I'll never know. But he did and he never showed the slightest signs of intoxication, even though each billet bar tried to doctor his drink. It was an outstanding performance.

And further to that, we were sitting in the bar just after dinner on Christmas Eve when the station commander marched in and announced that he was closing the bar. There were some vociferous protests as he marched out of the back door which was a short cut to his house, leaving a sign on the door saying 'This way to the bar'. It was another memorable evening which lasted well into Christmas Day.

We flew back to Aden in time for the New Year's celebrations and life returned to normal—for a day or two when what became known as the Radfan campaign began. The British involvement in Radfan began during the Aden Crisis, with rebels using the Dhala road to bring down supplies for the terrorists in Aden. The British Army took the decision to deploy a garrison into the Radfan to limit the rebels' supplies and thus the Radfan tribesmen's ability to blackmail the traders. The Radfan tribesmen were aided and supplied by the Yemenis, who themselves had received aid and supplies from the Egyptians, and soon had Dhala under daily attack.

According to the commanding officer of 45 Commando the tribesmen of the Radfan were 'a xenophobic lot, equipped from boyhood with rifles, who regarded the British arrival in their mountains as an opportunity for target practice'. The tribesmen mined the road from Aden and ambushed Army convoys, they made the position of the British and Federal garrison as difficult as possible. The usual method of aerial leaflet drops and bombings could not be employed following worldwide critical reaction against similar Egyptian tactics in the Yemen, so the task of counter-attacks was left to the infantry. A large number of so-called dissident tribesmen had attacked the Federal Fort at Thumier and it was decided that a ground force consisting of the FRA, British Army units and the Royal Marines would move into the area to display the Federal Government's determination to maintain law and order. Thus began Operation Nutcracker.

We had only been back in Aden for a few days and we always had a pair of aircraft on standby for both air defence duties and close air support. It was our first weekend back and since my family was still in UK—we were awaiting the allocation of a married quarter, a wait which in the end lasted for nearly a year—I said that I would take the weekend duty. I was joined by Martin Johnson as my Number 2. Stand-by was generally carried out from the crew room on a 15 minute alert as it was far too hot to undertake cockpit readiness. Martin had been on 8 Sqn for some time and was familiar with the local area, a fact which was to turn out to be quite fortuitous, as, although I had now been on the squadron for three months, most of that time had been spent in Bahrein. My memory may be at fault but I do not think that we were particularly well briefed as we did not expect anything to happen. How wrong could we be?

In the early afternoon we got a call to scramble to provide air support in the Radfan. As we got airborne I realised that I had no idea where this was so I handed over the lead to Martin who said quite confidently that he knew where it was. We contacted the Forward Air Controller who seemed to be quite excited. Every time he pressed the button to transmit you could hear the bullets passing him by; so he had good reason. It took us some time but we finally got the message that he wanted us to open fire. It had been some time since 8 Squadron had been involved in active operations and we were having difficulty in believing what we were hearing. At this stage, Martin elected to hand the lead back to me. And having got to the stage where the FAC was pleading with us to open fire on the targets he had designated, we set to with a will. We did have some difficulty in acquiring the targets because the FAC, being under a certain amount of pressure, was somewhat over excited. Like us, it was probably the first time that he had been involved in a shooting war. This was to have some unfortunate consequences.

It was obvious to me, at least, that we were going to be kept quite busy and that we needed some backup. Unfortunately the rest of the squadron was down on Tarshine Beach with their families and girlfriends and, it being after lunch, in no fit state to participate. As soon as we landed we got another two aircraft prepared and off we went again. By this time it was getting towards dusk and I shall never forget flying over the area trying to make sense of exactly who was where and doing what to whom. It was very rugged and mountainous country; spectacular but not so if you were trying to move around on the ground, especially when the enemy knew the area like the back of their hand. There was an incredible amount of tracer flying around and I have to say that I remain convinced to this day that some of our own units were firing at each other. However it was certainly a very exciting day and it continued over Sunday. The rest of the squadron were somewhat displeased with us as we had had all the 'fun.'

The following day I tried to speak to the Royal Marines' FAC to clarify why we had had problems identifying the target. I wanted to explain that he needed to speak calmly and clearly and designate the target with more specific instructions than he had used. When you are flying at 420 kts over such rugged terrain, identifying a specific target, especially dissident tribesmen hidden in the rocks, is no easy task. I could not speak to him personally but spoke to someone who said he would pass the message on. The next thing I know is that I am asked to go up country and brief them personally. When I turned up, it was as though the poor FAC was going through a field court martial, or the RM variant of such an event. I was forced to backtrack on some of the things I had said but, even so, there was little doubt that the young subaltern (or the RM equivalent) was in deep trouble. I have no idea what the outcome was but I do know that I regretted ever opening my mouth—and all I was trying to do was provide some constructive criticism.

I did another sortie to the Radfan on the Sunday and then, quite apart from the fact that the rest of the squadron heard that we were having 'fun' and wanted their share, things went quiet for a time. And it was not until later in the month that air support was required and again in February. Sometimes we were flying in the Radfan and sometimes in other areas.

However in February 1964 I got the opportunity to go home and see my family, for every month or so we used to take a pair of Hunters back to the UK for refurbishment and then bring back a couple of shiny new aircraft. The desert was not particularly kind to aircraft. The sand got in everywhere, and after a fairly short time the external paint would begin to look very sad and the sand used to gather in large quantities in the fuselage of the aircraft adding considerably to the weight. The wiring would be affected although the Avon engine seemed to thrive on it. I took an aircraft back to the UK going via Khartoum, El Adem (Libya), Luqa (Malta) and then direct to the maintenance unit at Kemble in Gloucestershire. We quite often used to have an argument with H. M. Customs who wanted us to clear through a customs airfield—which Kemble was not. However, the aircraft that we were bringing back were often in such a parlous state that the last thing we wanted to do was add another unnecessary leg to the journey. They usually, but not always, accommodated us. The trip usually took two days and 8 to 9 hours of flying, as long as nothing went wrong. The worst leg was from Khartoum to El Adem as it was over desert the whole way. We had to dog leg around Egypt and the only landmark on the whole route was a set of black rocks just on the south west corner of Egypt, affectionately known as 'Nasser's Corner'. There were no radio aids to navigation until you got to within a hundred miles or so of your destination. The voice of the controller at El Adem always afforded a certain amount of relief, especially when you were close enough for him to give you a bearing. So the ferry to UK gave me an excuse for a week's leave with my family.

Back in Aden, there were some slight changes. We were still flying close air support sorties for the ground forces but the Yemen Air Force had been making a particular nuisance of themselves in the area around Beihan again, some 200 miles north east of Khormaksar. There had been a number of overflights by MiG 15s and IL 28s and also some incursions by Yemeni ground forces. It had happened in the past from time to time and the Hunter squadrons were tasked to provide a standing patrol in the area from dawn to dusk. There was in fact a small airstrip at Beihan but it was deemed too short for the Hunter to operate from. March 1964 saw a recurrence of the problem and we found ourselves doing these 'Beihan Patrols'. We flew in pairs and it took approximately 30 minutes to get there. We would then alternate between medium and low level. One aircraft would spend twenty minutes at low level with the other one at about 15,000 ft and then we would swap over to balance the fuel consumption, as low flying used more fuel. It was extremely tedious and considering the amount of time that all three squadrons spent on patrol, we never caught an intruder.

The only time that we nearly caught an aircraft was during the AOC's annual inspection. This latter event involved the whole airbase.

Everything that moved was saluted and, if it did not, it was painted. The air officer commanding, who was Air Vice-Marshal Johnnie Johnson (of Battle of Britain fame), came and inspected the whole base, the day starting off with a full parade on the main aircraft parking area. As the man who was in charge of the flying programme, I had naturally put myself on the stand-by roster so that I could legitimately avoid the parade and any of the other sundry unattractive activities that went on throughout the day. Much to my astonishment we got a scramble right in the middle of the parade. And it appeared that our local radar station had a positive identification on an IL 28 in the Beihan area. We were told to make all haste. That I did, using the taxi track for my take-off which interfered somewhat with the parade. When we contacted the controller after take-off he was absolutely positive that he had a lock on the IL 28 and I decided to cut the corner to Beihan which involved flying straight across the south east of the Yemen. We were actually given a precise controlled interception on to the supposed intruder but when we got there he was not to be seen despite searching high and low. He had disappeared back to his own airspace. It was a great disappointment; but it was infinitely preferable to and more fun than participating in the AOC's parade. In fact we used to get quite a few air defence scrambles but we never actually caught anything.

It was only some ten days later on 27 March 1964 that, having retired to bed after a session in the Jungle Bar in the mess, I was almost immediately woken by a banging on the door. Who should appear in the room but the Boss telling me that he needed four pilots for a dawn sortie. Since it was already well past midnight, there was a question as to whether we could find four pilots sober enough to participate in whatever the task was. We all lived in a bungalow with eight bedrooms in the grounds of the mess which had belonged to 8 Sqn from time immemorial. Indeed it was the only accommodation in the officers' mess which had air conditioning, contributed by some grateful soul from the past. It has to be said that the only air conditioning unit that seemed to work was that belonging to the squadron engineer by some quirk of 'fate' or that was what he claimed. The Boss was unavailable for the task as he had somewhat carelessly managed to break his arm; so the two of us went down the bungalow, turning on the lights of each bedroom, to check on the sobriety and availability of each living-in officer. We scraped up two more besides myself and I do not think I will ever forget the reaction of Martin Johnson. As we turned the light on and asked the question, he was already standing at attention drinking a pint of water to persuade us of his fitness to fly—even though he did not know what the task was. Nor, indeed, did I. Fortunately we did not need any more than three pilots as the wing commander, John Jennings, decided that he was going to lead the sortie, with the three 8 Sqn pilots in his four ship, followed by Phil Champniss, the CO of 43 Sqn, with another four ship.

It is probably worth saying something at this stage about the armament of the Hunter, the 3" 60 lb Rocket, known affectionately by all as the '3 inch Drain', because of its rather obvious similarity to a drain pipe. It had started life in the Second World War on Tempests and Typhoons and had not been altered since its inception. It had a horrendous gravity drop when you fired it and aiming the thing was not so much a question of skill but more of an art form. If the fins had been in any way damaged or bent, you got what was euphemistically called a 'twirler' when the rocket could go anywhere but usually managed to give the pilot quite a fright by appearing straight in front of the cockpit instead of dropping away. And if you had a hang-up on one of the bottom rows the two rockets would then fall woefully short; which was fine for most of the time unless you were firing in close proximity to your own troops. The rocket had three alternative heads, a 60 lb HE head, a 60 lb SAP head and a concrete head which we used on the range. From the cockpit you could select whether you wanted to fire in salvos or ripple of 2, 4 or 8 rockets. When you carried 16 rockets and fired them off at a ripple 8 setting it made a fairly large 'bang' which you felt in the cockpit as you went over the target. Despite its age, it was in fact quite an effective weapon with the kinetic energy adding substantially to the explosive effect. I certainly would not have fancied being on the receiving end. And despite the difficulty in aiming the thing it was more accurate than a bomb. You could generally get it closer than 20 feet to the target. The Hunter with a full load of 16 rockets had the flying qualities of a brick!

Then you always had the option of 4 × 30 mm Aden cannons with 120 rounds of ammunition per gun. There was a switch in the cockpit which allowed you to select 2 or 4 guns. Firing all four at once was quite arresting in more ways than one. Quite apart from the horrendous vibration, it would knock 20 or 30 knots off your speed which was usually around 400 knots. The rockets and the cannon were a pretty effective combination especially in the circumstances.

We briefed at some ridiculous hour in the morning whilst the ground crew were preparing the aircraft with sixteen HE rockets and a full load of HE 30 mm for the cannons. The plot was for a Hunter FR10 of 1417 Flight to go off on its own and take a pre-strike picture of the target and drop warning leaflets just five minutes before we arrived, for us then to strike the target with rockets and canon and then for the FR10 to take a post-strike photo. The target was to be the Yemeni fort at Harib just over the border from Beihan. I flew as No. 3 to the wing commander with Martin Johnson on my wing. To get a full load of rockets on the aircraft you had to take the outboard pylons off and replace them with a rocket rail. If you left the pylons on you could only load 12 rockets. 43 Sqn made the sensible decision to leave the pylons on and just carry the 12 rockets, whilst we decided to do it the hard way and replace the pylons with rails so that we could carry all 16. It was not a particularly easy or quick job but the ground crew did the first three aircraft with ease.

Unfortunately for Martin, the fourth aircraft proved to be somewhat recalcitrant and as we started up and checked in, the armourers were still struggling with his aircraft. So we taxied out without him, telling him to catch up if he could. I do not think I have ever seen such an anxious face, sitting in the aircraft, terrified that he was going to miss out. We took off just as dawn was beginning to break and the seven aircraft made their way up country. It was about a 30 minute transit to the target, and after ten minutes we were treated to the sight of Martin approaching us at a high rate of knots and joining up with the formation.

It was a beautiful morning as we pulled up and tipped in on Harib Fort. All appeared to be quiet and John Jennings let rip with 16 rockets fired in ripple. I had a ringside seat as I went down the dive and I saw his rockets hit the target just as I fired mine. Then the fort just disappeared in smoke and dust. We made a second pass with guns, then the FR10, having waited for the dust and smoke to disperse, took a post-strike picture. We landed back at Khormaksar an hour and a quarter after take-off just as the rest of the squadron were coming in to work. For some reason we were sworn to secrecy with regards to where we had been or what we had done. This was slightly embarrassing as Gordon Talbot, my fellow flight commander who had been on the squadron far longer than me but missed what was undoubtedly a major event, was all over me asking what we had been up to. In the end I gave in and told him under pain of death and he was most put out that he had not been involved. However there had not been time to call in the married people who lived off base. The post-strike target photos were quite interesting. No one had said anything during the briefing about air defences, not that I recollect anyway. But when we looked carefully at the photos, there were quite a few anti-aircraft guns, including ZSU23/2, in emplacements around the fort. The covers had been taken off (or blown off) but no shots had been fired as far as we knew.

A few days later I was tasked to lead another eight ship strike on another fort deeper in the Yemen. However, this was cancelled at the last moment due, I believe, to protests by the Yemen to the UN and the UK incurring the displeasure of the Security Council and so ended the affair of Harib Fort.

Things quietened down after that and not long after that we were back on detachment in Bahrein for our usual two month stint. We also used to ring the changes every now and again by flying out of Sharjah for a day or two. Sharjah had not changed from my first visit in 1960. It was an airfield in the middle of the desert and consisted of a fort, a few huts and tented accommodation. The only recreation (apart from sitting at the bar) was to take a trip to Dubai. The journey took the best part of two hours in a Land Rover going mostly along the beach. Today it takes ten minutes along a modern multi-lane highway. And once you got to Dubai, there was not a lot to see apart from the boatyards where they built Dhows and the Soukh. There were no hotels or restaurants, little electricity and large numbers of Arabs armed to the teeth. The airfield at Sharjah did not have a hard runway. It was oiled sand (murram) which was rolled after each landing. As you churned up one bit you just moved along and used the next bit. Then after a while the airfield staff would roll the used bits and you would start the whole process all over again. It was quite firm; indeed even the Comet used to land on it. The old airfield and fort is now in a built-up area and the old runway, which was given an asphalt surface in later years, is part of the road system.

The only real bit of excitement during this detachment came when we had a rather rowdy Friday night session with the Paras. They were based elsewhere on the island and, as a matter of good manners, we had invited them for a couple of libations to celebrate the end of the week (as you do!). This led to some rowdy behaviour culminating in an argument which basically boiled down to the fact that the Paras believed that we would not have the guts to jump out of the back of a Beverley with them on their next jump. This was naturally like red rag to a bull and the inevitable taking up of the challenge. The following week a stick of eight 8 Sqn pilots followed the Paras out of the back of the Beverley on to an old disused airfield south of Sharjah. This was achieved with no injuries and honour was satisfied. However, our Headquarters at AFME back in Aden somehow got to hear of it, and were less than pleased with our performance. Indeed there was talk of disciplinary action, even court martial for a time, but fortunately it all cooled down and nothing further was done.

At the beginning of June we were back in Aden again and the following day were back in action against the dissident tribesmen who appeared to be becoming more and more dissident as time went by. June was a busy month as far as operations were concerned and there appeared to be quite a number of armed bands operating in the mountains between Aden and the Yemen. Every tribesman in the Protectorate carried a gun. To go out without one would be unthinkable. Shooting each other—and anyone else who offered themselves as a target, especially the British Army—was a national pastime, there being no Eastenders on television to distract them. Shooting at aircraft was an even better sport; fortunately they mostly only had rifles but they did sometimes have machine guns. Nevertheless they occasionally used to put holes in our aircraft. According to one commentator of the time combatants included 'disciplined Marxist murderers, primitive tribal pursuers of the blood feud, teenage tearaways and dedicated nationalists'. The area in which they operated was mountainous, full of caves and sangars, and generally difficult to get access to. From the air it was often difficult to detect where the targets were and you were never sure as to whether you had fired at the right area. We had some pretty intensive operations in June and it was during one of these that I took what was said to be a bullet through the engine whilst operating up in the mountains. I pulled away, jettisoned all my remaining weapons and the external fuel tanks but could still only just make 15,000 ft at full power which, for an aircraft that would normally make well in excess of 40,000 ft, indicated that there was something wrong, and not of a trivial nature. I managed to get back to Aden and landed with a certain amount of relief. When we looked at the compressor blades subsequently, they were a mess and it says something for the robustness of the Rolls Royce Avon engine that it kept going, but as to whether it was a bullet or a ricochet, who knows.

By the end of June, activity in the Radfan had died down to a degree. Instead we had moved on to a system of 'Proscribed Areas'. Basically the tribesmen were warned that anything in certain areas that moved would be shot. I was never certain what this was supposed to achieve apart from a certain amount of discomfort and inconvenience for the tribesmen and their families. It was, of course, aimed at discouraging them from siding with the so-called dissidents; but I doubt that it ever had that effect. It probably achieved exactly the opposite. We used to take off at dawn and patrol these 'proscribed areas' shooting at anything that moved. Very rarely did we see tribesmen; more often than not camels or cattle. And at varying intervals during the day we would repeat the exercise. It was in fact exactly the method of control that had been in use since the early 1920s. *Plus ça change.*

August was the middle of the hot season and the heat must have made the tribesmen liverish as it was a pretty active month and we were kept busy with armed reconnaissance sorties interspersed with four and eight ship strikes on various targets in the Wadi Bana, Mudia and Jebel Khuder. Indeed we were so busy that we had little time for any other flying activity. As the weather cooled in October and November so also did our operational activity decrease, indeed in December there was none at all.

Life in Aden was, despite the heat and the flies, enjoyable. The beach and the bar at Tarshine were always a pleasant way of passing the time. Indeed we spent most of our leisure time down there. The married men would bring their wives and children and the bachelors spent most of their time chasing young ladies, often as not air hostesses from Aden Airways or visiting airlines. It was an ideal setup, a beautiful beach, with a swimming pool and a bar. In the evenings there were plenty of restaurants to go to, mainly Italian. It was during an evening out to an Italian restaurant in Khormaksar Beach that I had an amazing experience. It was a Saturday evening and I had borrowed a Volkswagen Beetle from Sid Bottom, a fellow pilot and a South African. There were five of us in the car and on the way to the restaurant as we were going along the coast road the engine died a natural death. I pulled in to the side of the road and a couple of locals pulled up behind me and asked me if I needed any help. The answer was 'yes' and they offered to take everyone to the restaurant and get the car fixed whilst we were having dinner. It was about 8 p.m. on a Saturday so I was somewhat dubious of the offer to get the car fixed whilst we were having dinner. I had no idea who these guys were and the car was not mine. So I was not inclined to leave the car in the hands of some strangers even though it was not the greatest piece of automobilia that you had ever seen. So we accepted their offer of a lift to the restaurant and I remained with the car whilst they arranged to have it towed in to the back streets of Crater, not an area normally frequented by Europeans. The whole place was a hive of activity and it turned out that the 'garage' undertaking the repair operated in the street. Everyone I met was extremely polite and I was given cold drinks whilst I waited. It took a couple of hours to effect the repair—the petrol pump had given up the ghost—and I have no idea from where they got the spares.

The two locals disappeared and whilst I was waiting, I wandered into the next street and there was some religious ceremony taking place. It was extremely crowded and I was most definitely the only European there. I joined a crowd of locals who were obviously as inquisitive as I was. There was what one could only describe as a tent which looked like something out of Arabian Nights. Outside were a number of young men dancing themselves into a frenzy. According to a local I was standing next to, they were some form of extremists from the Whirling Dervishes, and the culmination of the ceremony involved the dancers putting a sword through their stomach. As far as I could gather, they were regarded with suspicion and a certain amount of fear by most people. The only time that any sort of hostility was shown to me was when I tried to light a cigarette. It was snatched out of my hand by someone and I was told that smoking was strictly forbidden. Unfortunately—or was it fortunately—a young Arab boy turned up and told me that my car was ready, so I left before the climax. It was now after 11 p.m. and the two locals had reappeared. There was a slight snag in that, because it had been a petrol pump problem, the repair had left the car without much petrol in the tank. I was immediately asked to follow the pair in their car and they took me to a petrol station which was closed. They had the keys to the place and unlocked everything and filled up the car. I tried to pay for the repair and the petrol but they declined any money apart from taking the equivalent of ten shillings for the mechanics. I made it back to the restaurant just before midnight as the rest of the squadron were finishing their meal, and so ended a pretty bizarre episode. When I related it the following day to the security people at Khormaksar, they were horrified; but I had been treated with every courtesy, a courtesy which is, of course, an Arab tradition.

At long last, much to the relief of my parents-in-law who had begun to think that I had disappeared for ever, my wife and son joined me in Aden. We had a small top floor flat in a block of flats in the Ma'alla Straight. We also had a Somali girl called Kadega as an ayah who did not think that she had done her job correctly unless my son, Mark, was totally scrubbed and polished—much to his displeasure.

Unfortunately Judy's arrival coincided with a gradual deterioration of the security situation. To begin with, it was not too bad; just the occasional riot and an odd grenade or two, but we still went shopping in the Arab part of town and had some excellent beach parties in Little Aden where we used to take the squadron ski boat, a few crates of beer and a picnic with all of the families for a day out. On the beach that we used, you could pick oysters off the rocks and it really was quite idyllic, but it was not to last for ever.

During October 1964 we were sent on detachment to Masirah for ten days. It was a strange detachment in that, for some reason that escaped me at the time, it was a mixed detachment of 8 Sqn and 43 Sqn although it was led by Tammy Syme and I was the deputy, but there was no supervisory element from 43 Sqn. Despite our protests, which were ignored, the detachment went ahead on that basis and it was a very successful and enjoyable detachment—until the return trip. It had been decided to give the lead of the eight ship return to Khormaksar to one of the 43 Sqn pilots who had never led an eight ship before. It was a clear day although it was hazy and the sea was flat calm which meant that the horizon was not well defined. We had a very extensive brief, in fact more extensive than we would usually have done because it was the leader's first attempt at leading a large formation, which covered all eventualities. The brief was to take off in four pairs, join up in battle formation, fly over the airfield and then climb away for Khormaksar. Tammy Syme was flying in the number 2 position and I was at the back end as number 8, so that we could supervise the sortie. Unfortunately, after take-off, I was unable to fully retract the undercarriage and had to make three or four reselections before it successfully retracted. Whilst I was doing this, my leader who was a junior pilot from 43 Sqn, was passing underneath me to check on the position of the undercarriage, during which time we had climbed to about 3000 feet. Just after I had made the final selection, my leader flashed underneath me and confirmed that it was successful. I still had flaps down and so I cleaned up the aircraft and looked up in time to think that my leader was at an odd angle and no sooner had the thought passed through my mind when he hit the sea doing probably in excess of 400 kts. It was an amazing but sickening sight. The whole aircraft went under the sea and erupted almost immediately out of it, and as it came out of the sea it disintegrated. I knew that there was no chance he had survived. We sent the rest on home to Khormaksar and Tammy Syme and I landed back at Masirah but there was little we could do and later on that day we too returned home.

The inevitable board of inquiry was painful. It was headed by someone who had little idea of the basics of fighter operations and he spent hours questioning us as to the need for 'battle formation and crossover turns'. The outcome was that we were held responsible for 'lack of supervision' which was somewhat ironic in view of the trouble we had taken over the supervision of this very simple sortie. The station commander, a certain Gp Capt. Beetham (later MRAF Sir Michael Beetham), who had recently arrived with a remit to tighten up discipline, recommended that we should face a court martial and we were invited to comment under the relevant QR. Fortunately for us, someone further up the chain of command saw sense and the whole thing was quashed and no blame attached to us. However it was an uncomfortable few weeks.

But life went on and whilst the operational pressure was not quite at the same level as it had been, it did not completely die away. 208 Sqn had by this time disappeared permanently up to Bahrein and we had reverted to an odd arrangement whereby all the aircraft were pooled and the two remaining squadrons worked a system of 24 hours on and 24 hours off. Basically you came in midday on one day and flew through to dusk and then again the following morning to midday. Before we had always tended to work 'tropical hours', 0600 to 1300 and then retire gracefully to avoid the heat of the day unless operational considerations intervened. Naturally we always had aircraft and pilots on stand-by throughout the whole day. The disadvantage of this new system was that you arrived at work to find that the previous squadron had left you very few serviceable aircraft and that you spent your 24 hours trying to recover the situation. No doubt 43 Sqn made the same accusations of us as well. However, judging by the amount of flying we managed to achieve it did not work too badly—but it was, in my view, a retrograde step. You lost that important close relationship with the ground crew and even with the aircraft. In theory it was a more efficient way of operating; but in practice it was not.

Christmas 1964 arrived and it was to be my first Christmas with my family. At least that was the intention. Unfortunately, as was often the case overseas, I had to go in and serve Christmas lunch to our ground crew and, what with one thing and another, I arrived home many hours later than predicted and was greeted with very little enthusiasm. All I can remember was that I demolished the Christmas lunch at about seven in the evening and never even noticed that the vegetables were all totally stewed and, according to my wife, totally inedible. She still reminds me of the occasion.

Whilst the operational activity in the air had definitely declined to two or three sorties a month, the security situation in Aden itself had deteriorated. The daughter of the SMO at Khormaksar had been killed when someone lobbed a grenade into their garden during a teenage party. Restaurants had wire netting over them to prevent grenades being lobbed into them and the terrorists had progressed to using bazookas against buildings. Our flat was elected as the best and safest place for parties as it was on the top floor and generally thought to be well out of harm's way, which had advantages and disadvantages—the latter generally outweighing the former.

In March 1965 the CO, Tammy Syme, and I were tasked to visit the Sultan of Oman's Air Force (SOAF) in Muscat. In those days, SOAF consisted of about a dozen seconded RAF pilots with about eight armed Piston Provosts and four Beavers on their strength. The Provosts were used for close air support and the Beavers for transport support. The CO was Sqn Ldr Brian Entwisle and his deputy was Flt Lt Pat King. The servicing of the aircraft was carried out by Airwork on contract. Ostensibly the visit was to standardise their operational procedures but, as I recollect, it was more in the nature of a social visit. It was an eye opener to me at least; it was, I imagined, like going back forty years or more. The walled city of Muscat was like something from the Middle Ages. When it came to night time you could not move around the city (although I would have hardly described it as such) without a lantern which was issued by the gatekeeper. If you tried to do so and were caught, you would spend the rest of the night in the local gaol—not an experience to be recommended.

SOAF operated a very civilised regime. You arrived at the squadron at 0600 and then flew the first wave, landing at about 0830. Everyone then retired to the mess for a very large traditional English breakfast with all the trimmings. Then back down to the squadron and the second wave took off, landing by about 1300 at which stage everyone retired to the mess for a few beers and a curry lunch before the afternoon siesta. This regime existed as long as they were not involved on operations in which case they flew as long as and hard as they were required. The airfield itself was fairly small and surrounded by hills just outside Muscat (it is now a housing estate) with a short murram runway.

I had a number of trips in the Provost which was a very different animal to the Provost that I had trained on. It was much heavier and equipped with 2×0.303 inch machine guns and the capability of carrying 8×3 inch rockets. Oman is a very beautiful place with many mountains and fertile lush green valleys. Flying a Provost in these mountains was quite a demanding and dangerous business. If you went down a wadi, you could very suddenly come to a dead end. In a high powered jet like a Hunter, you could pull up and out of the mountains. In a heavy and slightly underpowered Piston Provost, you had no such luxury and it was a case of either pulling up into a stall turn, assuming you had room to do so, or hitting the mountain side. You had to know your way around and which wadis were passable and which were not. On one sortie I was flying with one of the young inexperienced SOAF pilots and he frightened me to such an extent with some ham-handed handling of the aircraft that I was forced to take over control from him. My other fond memory was when it was decided that we would do some air-to-ground firing. Puddy Catt was the weapons officer and a more English character you could not imagine. I knew him from the past as he had been on 54 Sqn in my first tour. Puddy was a well-spoken, large rotund officer with an unruly mop of blond hair and a confirmed bachelor. He was not exactly the public image of an RAF officer or, on second thoughts, maybe he was.

But you could be misled by his somewhat pompous approach to life. as he was a very able pilot. I asked him where the firing range was and in reply to my question he walked to a cupboard and pulled out a deck chair. 'What on earth is that for?' I asked. 'That', he said, 'is the range safety officer's chair'. And so saying, he walked out of the crew room and put the chair outside, walked across the adjacent runway and pulled up a 15 ft square hessian target. The 'firing range' was actually on the airfield, something I had never ever seen before (or since). And off we went in one of the aircraft, ran in on the airfield, pulled up applying full boost and fully fine pitch, turned in and opened fire at about 400 yards, ceased fire at 200 yards. It was an eye-opening and exhilarating experience but I am not sure that we actually achieved much when it came to standardising operational procedures. Procedures were so different in a small heavy piston-engined aircraft as against a powerful fast jet fighter that it was like comparing chalk with cheese. I had also had a chance to have a go in a Beaver, which had a slightly surprising consequence a couple of years later.

Back to Aden and life went on much as usual. The Beihan Patrol returned to prominence. Despite the hundreds of patrols carried out with the aim of catching Yemeni aircraft violating the border, only once did we ever catch sight of one. That happened to a 43 Sqn pair of aircraft and the number 2 suddenly saw a MiG 15 pass underneath him. Unfortunately it just so happened that the two aircraft were having communication problems and the leader remained unaware of the sighting. The number 2 did as he was trained to do and stuck with his leader instead of doing what most of the rest of us would have done and ignored the leader and chased the MiG. So a golden opportunity was missed.

May 1965 and 8 Sqn got a new boss, Sqn Ldr Des Melaniphy and a new OC Strike Wing, Wg Cdr Martin Chandler, the latter having been my boss when I first arrived at Chivenor as an instructor. I also took the opportunity to take a couple of weeks leave in Kenya. One of the 'perks', if you could call it that, of being in Aden was that once during the tour, you were given a free return flight for yourself and your family to Kenya. The NAAFI ran a leave centre just outside Mombasa called the Nyali Leave Centre and, unusually for NAAFI, it was one of the nicest and best run facilities I have ever come across. The accommodation was fairly basic, wooden huts with thatched roofs, just cold water and pretty much open to the elements. But they were right on a beautiful beach of white sand—you just walked out of your hut, onto the beach and into the sea. The dining facility was run just like an RAF mess, in fact rather better than an RAF mess. There was a children's dinner at 5 o'clock at which the staff opened the bar. So the fathers usually did the child minding duty whilst consuming a couple of pints and then we would all get together for dinner later on. We went on Safari for a couple of days, staying at the Kiliguni Game Lodge. It was a wonderful two weeks and we had not realised how much we had needed a rest from the tensions of Aden. We got back to Aden fully refreshed and ready to face the remaining months of my tour; that was until just as I was putting the key in the front door of my flat a bazooka hit the flat opposite. The flat belonged to a school teacher and it hit her bedroom whilst she was in bed having an afternoon siesta (at least that is what she claimed). The warhead went underneath her bed, hit the wall opposite and rather rudely woke her up. My wife's reaction was to say that enough was enough and that she was going home with our son, a decision with which I could not really argue. So I was left to my own devices for the last three months of my tour.

The security situation within Aden itself was slowly deteriorating. Grenade throwing and bazooka attacks increased, riots became more frequent and violent. Strangely enough there was little activity up country and throughout June, July and August there were barely any operational sorties, but there was one event that remains strong in my memory.

This is a little tale concerning a ferry trip carried out in August 1965. As was the custom every two months or so, we would take a couple of old aircraft back from Aden to the UK for refurbishment and pick up a couple of new ones. On this particular occasion I had to pick up a new Hunter T7 (XF321) and my number 2, a certain Flt Lt R. E. Johns (now better known as Air Chief Marshal Sir Richard Johns) of 1417 Flt, had a brand new Hunter FR10 as his mount. The T7 had 4 × 100 gallon tanks and the FR10 had the usual 2 × 230 plus 2 × 100 gallon tanks. The discrepancy in performance between the two aircraft was quite marked and the FR 10 on my wing could easily outperform my T7 despite the significantly greater weight.

All went well for the first five legs, Kemble to Lyneham to clear customs, Lyneham to Istres, Istres to Luqa, Luqa to Akrotiri and finally Akrotiri to Diyarbakir. It is a long time since I have been to Diyarbakir but in those days to describe it as a dump was being kind. It was somewhere in the middle of Turkey in the back of beyond with only very basic facilities; not a place that any sane man would schedule a night stop. We refuelled and taxied out for take-off. And that was when I discovered that I could not get the T7 into power controls. Every time I selected ailerons and elevator into power, the dolls-eyes remained white. Flying a Hunter in manual control is an emergency situation although it cannot be said to be that difficult. The controls are extremely heavy and usually require two hands on the stick. We did use to practice manual landings from time to time; but manual take-offs were not in the pilots' notes. So as I taxied out, I was wondering quite what to do. My instinct was to avoid going unserviceable at Diyarbakir, but I did not like to say anything over the radio to Dick Johns, my thoughts tending to anticipate the subsequent Board of Inquiry in case of some mishap. The less anybody knew about what I was about to do, the better.

So I committed myself to a manual take-off, not a recommended practice nor one that I had ever tried before. In fact I do not know of anyone who has tried it, although I am prepared to bet there a few who have done it inadvertently. The only aspect that worried me was where to put the elevator trim, too much tail up and I might not be able to control the pitch-up, too little and I would have trouble getting the nose wheel off the ground. However Diyarbakir's runway was quite long and I guessed that I would have time to get airborne even if I had too little tail up trim. So I erred in that direction so that I would avoid the pitch up which could definitely be embarrassing. Off we went down the runway and, quite apart from the inferior performance of the T7 it became clear to Dick that nothing much seemed to be happening with regard to getting airborne. After a while he gave up any attempt to remain on my wing and accelerated past me into the air. I actually got airborne just at the end of the concrete in a flurry of dust, sorted out the trim, raised the undercarriage and flaps and climbed nonchalantly away.

It was not until we had landed at Tehran that I was able to tell him what the problem was, and because there was no one to rectify the problem at Tehran, I had to do the next leg in manual as well. This time Dick was prepared for the take-off and I had in any case learnt from the first manual take-off what to expect. When we got to Muharraq (Bahrein), I managed to find a knowledgeable technician who took one look at it and diagnosed blown fuses; which indeed it was, so we were able to continue our way on to Khormaksar, via Masirah, in fairly good order. The last leg was not without a few 'moments'. Going direct from Masirah to Khormaksar in the T7 with its restricted fuel load could be marginal with any sort of headwind, and needless to say we had a headwind which meant that the prudent thing to do was to land and refuel at Salalah. However I was keen to get home and as we passed over Salalah I decided to press on. We did make it—but only just. The line chief said that, when he refuelled the aircraft he put more fuel in than the book said was possible. It was not a trip that I shall forget, indeed ferry trips hardly ever failed to test one's ingenuity, resourcefulness and initiative. They were always a challenge and also great fun; and you always learnt a thing or two!

Apart from a brief flurry of activity around Jebel Khuder when the FRA ran into a little local difficulty, my time in Aden was coming to a close. Peter Taylor arrived to take over from me and my thoughts were beginning to focus on what was to happen next. I had decided some months earlier to volunteer for the Empire Test Pilots' School at Farnborough. I had spent a considerable amount of time on detachment, separated from my family and I felt that it would be nice to have a period of stability on a home base. Life as a test pilot, I thought, would provide just that—assuming that I could pass the course. I was due to go back to England for the ETPS interviews in July when I suddenly received a posting notice to CFS. Being of somewhat of an idle inclination, I thought that that would be a simpler and easier path to follow and would provide the 'rest cure' that I thought I craved. So I cancelled my application to ETPS only to get a very strongly worded signal back from the personnel branch telling me in no uncertain terms that my withdrawal was not accepted and that I was to report to them for an interview before going on to Farnborough for the various exams and interviews. I remember flying back to England in a Britannia trying to read AP129, which was the pilot's technical bible, in an attempt to at least not look completely silly in front of the ETPS Board as I had done absolutely zero preparation.

My 'discussion' with the personnel people left me in no doubt that they wanted me to go to ETPS, not particularly for my own good, but because they had insufficient volunteers with the right background and experience of fighter ground attack in the light of the new aircraft due to come into service over the next few years, so off to Farnborough I went not without some misgivings. All I really remember of the exams and interviews was how unsatisfactory they were in that you sat there being grilled by a triumvirate of experienced test pilots and ETPS tutors and, having attempted to answer their esoteric questions, they never told you whether you were right or wrong or just talking absolute nonsense. I never discovered the reason for this until many years later when I found myself on the other side of the room. The truth was that they were not always sure whether you had got it right or wrong! Much to my surprise, I was accepted into ETPS for the course starting in January 1966.

My last few weeks in Aden involved handing over to my successor and saying farewell. The latter was made a little difficult by the fact that a complete curfew on all movement after dark had been enforced, a curfew which we did our best to avoid. Despite the enforced separation from my family, it had been a challenging, enjoyable and satisfying two years. I had completed just under 100 operational sorties, no accidents (apart from the 43 Sqn pilot), and a very professional bunch of aviators who were always willing to enjoy themselves both in the air and on the ground; it was not a tour that I will easily forget.

5

Test to Learn, Learn to Test

Having returned from Aden and being reunited with my family again, there was the tedious business of finding somewhere to live near Farnborough—a task easier said than done. However we finally found a house in Frimley and set up the marital home with some expectation of staying put for a year or so. I had to go off and do two months at the Junior Command and Staff School at Ternhill, more commonly known as the Reading and Writing Course, and then I finished the year being tutored by the ETPS chief ground instructor, Barry Stribling, on mathematics. Fortunately I had always had a mathematical bent, so far from being a bit of a trial I found myself enjoying the time revising.

The ETPS Course itself began in the New Year of 1966. No. 25 ETPS Course was a very mixed bunch of students both in background and nationalities; there were USAF and USN students, Canadian, Israeli, South African, Indian, Australian, French, Dutch, German and Italian, a total of 18 students in all, both rotary and fixed wing. It was interesting to note that the South African student, Paul Bothma, always felt that he was being closely watched by the UK security services and that we were holding back information from him. Despite many reassurances that no one was really that interested, he never managed to fully relax and thought that he was for ever being discriminated against; which was a little ironic to say the least.

ETPS had its own mess at Farnborough and was a totally independent unit commanded by Group Captain Bill Straker. The mess, the classrooms and the hangars with all their facilities were on the south side of the airfield separate from the activities of the Royal Aircraft Establishment.

The chief test flying instructor was Wg Cdr Pete Bardon who was ably assisted by four tutors: Murph Morrison, Ian Keppie, Mike Bruce and Ian Normand plus a couple of QFIs, Bill McAusland and one other who shall be nameless, being an unpleasant and arrogant little man. Sqn Ldr Barry Stribling was the CGI and he had been a tutor at Cranwell when I was a cadet. The first two months were mainly occupied by ground school with just an occasional trip in a Chipmunk or a Piston Provost to remind you that you were actually a pilot. Because my background was almost exclusively on single seat, single engine aircraft, namely the Hunter, it was deemed necessary to get me familiar with twin and four-engined aircraft. So, apart from re-familiarisation with the Meteor, my first real challenge was the Viscount 744, a four-engined turbo-prop. After a couple of very brief duals, I found myself solo in the Viscount with just a flight engineer—a very brave man if I may say so. However I also suspect that, although only a flight engineer, he was far more capable of flying the aircraft than I was especially as it had a very odd flight instrument system. The flight engineer operated the throttles on the instructions of the captain. However, in our case, it did not matter what you said, you always had exactly the correct power setting!

So began the first of many exercises during the year. Ground school would go through the theory at first, and then you would fly a test programme on an aircraft and take all the measurements with what would now be regarded as archaic analogue instrumentation. This was followed by spending hours analysing the readings and calculating the results before writing up the whole exercise. In this manner two or three trips would involve hours of work on the ground and pages of writing, not to mention some very involved calculations. The exercises started off fairly simply and slowly increased in complexity and they usually involved aircraft with which one was unfamiliar. My first few exercises were on the Viscount, the Canberra and the Twin Pioneer with the Piston Provost being the only one on which I had any real experience. I did my twin piston instrument rating on the Twin Pioneer and I can remember the single-engined overshoot to this day; it seemed to go on for ever.

Apart from the normal activities, we were expected also to complete five hours of glider flying at the weekends. It does not sound very much but when each trip is of the order of 15 minutes or so—unless you were very lucky—and you probably spent most of the time dragging gliders around the airfield—it was a pretty time-consuming occupation. You probably only got one trip in a day; and that day was one of your very valuable days of so-called rest. I have never been very keen on gliding and my experience at ETPS did nothing to engender enthusiasm. So I completed my five hours of glider flying as soon as I could and never went anywhere near a glider again.

We had many visits to industry—those were the days when we still had an aircraft industry - and every time we went anywhere, Paul Bothma was convinced that he was being told different things to everyone else. He was a nice guy but I do not think I have ever met anyone so paranoid in my life. Even though our noses were kept pretty much to the grindstone, we still had time to enjoy ourselves. It was after a little outing to one of the local hostelries that Bill Newman (USN) managed to put his very upmarket Ford Mustang through a bridge parapet and land upside down in the river. He had Ollie Sutton (RN) with him as a passenger and Ollie's description of the incident on the following morning was to the effect that he had been in that situation before, upside down in the sea with the cockpit filling with water, so he knew exactly what to do. Bill was outraged a few weeks later to get a bill for the repair to the bridge which turned out to be a listed 'ancient monument'!

Slowly but surely the exercises became more complex and demanding, take-off and landing assessments, stick force per G, stability and control, lift and drag assessments and, not least, spinning. You were also given one sortie in an experimental aircraft mainly for experience and also to undertake a very brief assessment of its characteristics. ETPS had the Short SB5 for this particular exercise. The SB5 was the original low speed research aircraft for the Lightning and sophistication was not its strong point. It had a fixed undercarriage and you could vary the sweep of the wings and the position of the tail-plane although whilst it was at ETPS the tail-plane stayed in the optimum position and the sweep was fixed at somewhere around 70°. It had very basic flight instruments, the ground crew had to bolt down the hood after you had strapped in and its endurance was just over 20 minutes. Once the ground crew had bolted you in, you felt rather like I imagine a Kamikaze pilot must have felt! The aircraft was surprisingly pleasant to handle on the approach and not at all what you expected and not dissimilar to its rather more sophisticated cousin, the Lightning.

My spinning exercise was carried out in the Hunter which had been very briefly cleared for spinning in service; a clearance that was rapidly withdrawn after one of the CFS instructors was killed demonstrating it to the staff at Chivenor. Nevertheless ETPS carried on spinning the Hunter for years without a single incident. My first experience was in a Hunter T7 with Ian Normand, the FAA member of the staff. He had the uncanny knack of falling asleep in the air no matter what sort of manoeuvre you were doing. He also excelled at demonstrating the inverted spin which was one of the most disorientating experiences in an aircraft. Having had the demonstration, we then had half a dozen sorties on our own to carry out all the various tests including mishandling the recovery and so on. My own experience in the Hunter was that if you took your hands off the controls and left it alone, the aircraft would almost invariably recover of its own volition. And as a result of my experience at ETPS, I found it difficult to understand why it had not been cleared for spinning in service. I doubted that the accident at Chivenor had anything to do with the spinning characteristics of the aircraft.

The beginning of September and the (then) annual Farnborough Air Show took place. Everything came to a halt for the annual show. In those days the ETPS mess was a magnet for all the test pilots of industry and the service to get together for a rather noisy reunion. We, as students, had to do duty every day on the door of the ETPS mess to try and keep out interlopers. My main memory of the occasion was that I tried to throw out John Cunningham (of 'Cats eyes' fame), one of the better known and internationally famous test pilots of the time. I had not recognised him and it was not until someone pointed out the error of my ways that I let him pass with many profuse apologies and a rather red face.

The course progressed through mid-term ground school exams and we even had a short summer break. Shortly after we returned, I was scheduled to do a sortie in a Hunter 6 and I walked out to the aircraft, did the pre-flight checks, started up the engine and taxied out to the runway. At which stage I was given a red light from the caravan and told to taxy back in. I was less than pleased at this rather rude interruption of my progress until I climbed out and asked what the problem was. The ground crew pointed at the aircraft and I then saw to my dismay that I had left the starboard intake cover in place. Had I been allowed to attempt the take-off it would no doubt have ended in disaster. I was mortified and had little doubt that my time as an aspiring test pilot had come to an end. That night, 15 September 1966, my daughter was born, and, the following day, I waited in vain for the axe to fall. The only comment that was ever made came from the CTFI as he passed through the crew room and said that it was lucky for me that my daughter had been born on the previous evening. In reality he did not have to say much more. Despite the circumstances, it was a stupid mistake and one that I was unlikely to make again.

The final exercise at ETPS was the Preview. This was where you were given an aircraft that you had never flown before and had to produce a complete report on the suitability of the aircraft for service in whatever role it was designed for. We usually did this in a team of two or three and in my case Don Ward, a USAF pilot, and I drew the Lightning. ETPS had just taken delivery of a Lightning T4 as part of its fleet and this was to be its first official exercise. We spent an evening at Coltishall in the flight simulator before returning to Farnborough and flying five sorties each in the aircraft. The Lightning looks as though it might be somewhat of a handful but in fact it is a very pleasant aircraft to fly. With two very powerful Avon engines, one on top of the other, it certainly goes. After take-off you have to be quick with the undercarriage or you find that you have exceeded the limits and the nose wheel remains stuck down because of the airflow. More than a few pilots have taken off and climbed to 40,000 ft only to find that they still have the nose wheel down. A clean Lightning accelerates very quickly and it is one of the few aircraft that I have ever flown that you have to throttle back when you reach the limiting speed—in this case Mach 1.7. The later Lightnings with a bigger fin can reach Mach 2. But they all have one big drawback—too little fuel and hence a very limited range and endurance. They were also very limited in armament, the earlier aircraft having just two missiles, but they were effective as a very rapid point interceptor. I have not seen Don Ward since that time although I know that he became the head of the USAF Test Pilots' School at Edwards AFB.

Our time at Farnborough came to an end with the McKenna Dinner at which all the awards were presented and the postings were announced. I had flown 120 hours in the year on 12 or so different types of aircraft and had become, although I did not realise it, a rather more experienced and capable aviator. Tom Lecky-Thomson and I were to be posted to 'A' Squadron, the Fighter Test Squadron, at Boscombe Down, together with Andy Jones, an ex-Lightning pilot. The foreigners went back to their own countries, some went to Bedford which was the home of pure research; some went to the RAE at Farnborough which concentrated more on systems, and we arrived at Boscombe in what was to be one of its more challenging and interesting periods.

6

'A' (Fighter Test) Squadron, Boscombe Down

First things first and we found somewhere to live, it was a rather nice chalet bungalow just on the outskirts of Wilton, a very pleasant little town just on the outskirts of Salisbury. Tom Lecky-T and his family found an old house right in the centre of Wilton. Salisbury is a lovely market town with a wonderful cathedral and some very beautiful surrounding countryside; it is England at its very best and we felt privileged to be part of it.

At the beginning of 1967 'A' Squadron was not fantastically busy in terms of test programmes. The CO was Wg Cdr Alan Merriman and the senior pilot was Hugh Rigg, the brother of the rather better known Diana Rigg. For some reason, which always escaped me, we did not follow the usual RAF system of a CO and two flight commanders but we used the Fleet Air Arm system of a CO and his deputy referred to as the senior pilot. We had a total of 10 pilots including the CO and senior pilot. Hugh Rigg, Derek Parry and the CO were just beginning to undertake testing of the Harrier but there were no other really significant programmes in existence at the time. However we did have a pretty eclectic and mixed bunch of aircraft; we had a Kestrel and a P1127—one of the original prototypes from which the Harrier was developed. We had a number of Lightnings, mostly DBs (Development Batch/pre Mk 1), Hunters; a Mk 6, a T7, a Mk 9 and a Mk 10. The Mk 9 was owned by Porton Down (the Chemical Defence Experimental Establishment) and modified so that we could spray various liquids out of the tanks for their peculiar testing requirements. We were also responsible for the testing of light aircraft and single-engined piston aircraft although we did not have any on inventory at the time.

There was a Javelin Mk 2 which had been fitted with engines of a Mk 7 and stripped of its guns and its performance was quite extraordinary—for a Javelin. It could cruise on one engine at M 0.9 at 50,000 ft. It was the master calibrator aircraft for pressure error corrections for the whole of the aircraft industry. It had a side-facing camera so that you could photograph an aircraft as it came past and measure the difference in height to inches. It also had a system whereby you could fill one of the ventral tanks with diesel fuel to trail 'smoke' so that other aircraft could see you and line up on you for the flypast. It was somewhat unnerving to sit there in the Javelin at Mach 0.9 at 40,000 ft whilst a Lightning would line up on you and fly past just a wingspan out at M 1.7. You just had to hope that the Lightning pilot had lined up correctly; but no matter what, it created quite a thump when it came past. Last but not least we had a Jet Provost Mk 3 which was the squadron hack aircraft.

One of the first tasks that Tom and I were given was to try and refresh the remainder of the squadron on the latest tactics and SOPs of the frontline squadrons. For that we used the Hunters—usually creating simulated combat sorties with two aircraft versus one, and one incident which I remember in particular involved Derek Parry in the Hunter Mk 10. Sometime previously Derek had written a critical letter to the RAF flight safety magazine *Airclues* about pilots who overstressed their aircraft (pulled too much G) claiming that to do so was total incompetence. Whilst he had a point, it was something that was quite easy to do inadvertently in the heat of a combat situation and at the time we felt as squadron pilots that he was being unfairly critical. And what happened on one of our first 'refresher' sorties? Derek disappeared into cloud in some combat manoeuvre and managed to overstress the Hunter Mk 10 by some margin. We smiled wryly.

For the first few months we were kept busy getting familiar with all these aircraft. The Javelin was particularly memorable, not because of its traits in the air but because of its very sensitive toe brakes leading to a particularly lurching gait on taxying until you got used to it. Indeed we always used to watch anyone on his first sortie to see if he managed to keep it on the taxiway. In that first year I flew a variety of types including various Marks of Lightning, the Javelin 2/7 and the Mk 9 which we had taken on inventory as the old one was considered to be past it, although most of us thought it was a backward step, the Sea Vixen, Jet Provost Mk3, Meteor NF 14 which we used as a photo chase aircraft, a Chipmunk which we acquired from somewhere—as I recollect it was for testing a special radio fit for the Prince of Wales flying training—

and the Harvard which was also used for photo chase particularly of parachutists. My conversion trip for the Harvard was memorable in that it was done by the Canadian exchange officer, Jamie Sutherland. He had difficulty finding time to do it and he decided that the only way that it could be done was on a trip back from Feltwell where the aircraft had been for some static display. We were taken up to Feltwell and Jamie then proceeded to sit me in the front cockpit and take me through all the switches and controls. He then climbed in the back and after a very short time there came a very loud and long chain of expletives. Someone had taken out the stick, which you could do in a Harvard and it was usually stowed in the rear cockpit. But for some unknown reason it had been left behind at Boscombe. There was a short silence and then came the statement: 'Aw gee, I don't need a f*cking stick, the rudders will suffice'. So we flew back to Boscombe, and that was the sum total of my conversion trip.

Flying many different types of aircraft can have its hazards as, in the RAF at least, we are usually only flying one type of aircraft and you know its systems and its foibles intimately. Many of the aircraft we had on inventory were 'one-offs' and non-standard so that even though you thought you might know about the aircraft, there was often something different to catch you out. We used to make our own check lists for these aircraft and condense it down in to a kneepad note to include checks, major emergency actions, various important limitations and approach and landing speeds. The one thing I always used to make sure I knew about was the fuel system which is often peculiar to each type and even varied between Marks as in the Lightning. Most of the other systems—such as electrics and hydraulics—look after themselves if they go wrong and there is probably not a lot that the pilot can do to rectify a fault other than try a reset. There are, of course, exceptions to prove the rule! However, fuel systems are often different and nothing is more embarrassing than to have to bail out of an aircraft with fuel still on board but not available because of some stupid oversight, so the fuel system was the one thing I always tried to ensure that I fully understood and could manage. Having said that, there are some aircraft, like the Jaguar for instance, which seemed to be designed to mislead the pilot and in which the pilot has ostensibly taken the correct actions in a fuel emergency only to find himself sadly mistaken—more of that later.

One morning in March at the morning briefing in the 'A' Squadron Ops Room, Hugh Rigg asked the assembled gathering if anyone had ever flown a Beaver. There was a total hush and then I remembered that I had actually been in one of SOAF's Beavers a few years before, so I said so; and before I knew it I had been appointed the Beaver project pilot. There was a requirement to put a camera on the wing tip and we had been asked to clear the handling and assess the quality of the photography. Before I actually did so, I spoke to the Army Air Corps and managed to find someone who knew something about the Beaver and who was willing to give me a quick conversion. Coincidentally it was someone with whom I had been at school, John Everett-Heath. He came over to Boscombe, took me back to Middle Wallop for lunch and returned me to Boscombe in the afternoon. I was now a Beaver pilot. Ten days later I was told to go up to Hawarden to pick up the aircraft with its new camera installation. I remember it well. We (I took the squadron adjutant who was a navigator with me) went up there in the Bristol Freighter, more normally referred to as the Bristol Frightener because of its age and general decrepit state. We climbed on board the Beaver and the first problem was starting it. The Beaver has an inertia starting system and for those unpractised in the art it was not the easiest starting system in the world if you were not used to it. So we sat there in a snow storm, reading the manual to try and get it going; which we did, but not before the ground crew, who were freezing in the snow outside, had become very unhappy at the pace of our progress. However, we got it started and flew it back to Boscombe.

For some reason, we kept that aircraft for nearly a year and, as the project pilot, I became a very popular person as everyone wanted to fly it. Not only that, but the F95 camera on the wing came in to great demand for taking pictures in particular of people's houses. The actual handling trial was interesting not for its complexity but for the fact that it was one of the few times that we were able to take a trials engineer on a sortie with us. He had devised a very full and extensive flight trials programme, but it was immediately apparent that the camera on the wingtip had very little effect and that most of the trials programme was superfluous. Normally we would have had difficulty in persuading the trials engineers that this was so, but because he could see it for himself sitting in the right hand seat we were able to abbreviate the trial quite considerably and thus accelerate the clearance. It was not always thus. After a few months we took the original aircraft back and collected another with a slightly modified installation and we undertook some fairly extensive trials of the equipment and of a new VOR system. It was to be nearly a year before we finally got rid of the Beaver; but it made for a very enjoyable and diverting interlude. Meanwhile we had the use a very flexible aircraft that could go to all sorts of airfields that we could not usually use.

Towards the end of the year (1967), I was scheduled to start my conversion to fly the Harrier. We had a Kestrel on strength and this aircraft was one of those which had been used by the Tripartite Evaluation Squadron a couple of years previously. This had been formed by three nations, UK, US and Germany and had been manned by pilots of all three nations. It was primarily going to investigate the possibilities, advantages and disadvantages of a V/STOL capability in a fighter aircraft. After they had finished the trial, the aircraft were split between the three nations and we had one at Boscombe. We used it mainly to convert pilots for the Harrier which had just started its test programme. Unfortunately my conversion was delayed when Derek Parry managed to rather spectacularly write off the aircraft. He was practising a flameout landing pattern when he just misjudged the final roundout and instead of overshooting just at the end of the approach as was the norm, he hit the runway hard, broke off the undercarriage, careered across the airfield and ended up upside down in a ditch. He was incredibly lucky as, although it took the firemen some time to extricate him from the wreckage, he was totally uninjured. However that was the end of my conversion for the time being.

Derek left the squadron at the end of the year and the only two pilots 'V/STOL' qualified were Hugh Rigg, the senior pilot, and Alan Merriman, the CO. The Harrier was deemed to be the most important programme, and Hugh was relieved of his post as senior pilot so that he could concentrate totally on the Harrier programme. One Monday morning I was wheeled in to the CO's office to be told by him that I was to be promoted to acting squadron leader to take over the post of senior pilot. It was a total surprise to me (and probably to a few others as well). I was reluctant to actually put the rank on my uniform as I had yet to see it in writing, but when I came to work the following day still with a flight lieutenant's rank, I was told in no uncertain terms that I was incorrectly dressed. So that evening my wife sewed on the braid and at the end of the week we received a very nasty letter from the CO of the RAF administrative unit at Boscombe asking for an explanation as to why there was an officer walking around masquerading improperly as a squadron leader. Fortunately, before this row could escalate, written confirmation of my appointment arrived, but I spent a few very uncomfortable days before it did.

As senior pilot, I was responsible for running and supervising all the flying carried out on the squadron—be it just continuation training or test flying—plus ensuring that we met all our training commitments.

Just as importantly, I was responsible for vetting all the flight test reports before they went to the CO for his final approval. This could sometimes be a somewhat time consuming activity in busy periods. Indeed I very quickly found out why it had been deemed necessary to free Hugh from these responsibilities so that he could concentrate purely on the Harrier programme which was slowly but surely increasing in importance. He had total responsibility for anything to do with the Harrier and Tom Lecky-T became his nominated deputy.

With no Kestrel to fall back on we reverted to using the old prototype P1127 for our conversion programme and in the middle of January 1968 I carried out my first solo on the aircraft. The first sortie was always flown as a conventional one and I remember it well for two reasons. Firstly the aircraft was not particularly pleasant to fly in conventional flight and, secondly, the weather deteriorated to such an extent that I had to do a full GCA to get back in to Boscombe. All of which was quite a challenge—to me at any rate. The next three sorties, all of five minutes or less duration and on the same day, consisted of VTOs and VLs, then a VTO followed by a transition to normal flight and back for a VL and finally what we chose to call STO hops which were basically short take offs followed by short landings. One more 20 minute sortie a week later and that was my conversion complete. The sorties were necessarily short because the performance of the P1127 was so marginal in terms of thrust that VTOS and VLs could only be made with a minimal amount of fuel—usually no more than 400 lbs aside (800 lbs total) which, when you were using the best part of 200 lbs a minute in the hover, did not give much time to complete the exercise. The only good thing was that this all occurred in January when the temperatures were relatively low and, thus, the margins for hovering better than average, lower temperatures equating to higher thrust.

One of the tasks we had in those days was converting other pilots to the 1127/Harrier, fortunately not too frequently as it was nearly always a very stressful occupation. I remember one incident particularly well although I will desist from naming the individual. If we had had any real say in the proceedings, we would have terminated this individual's conversion after the second trip as it was painfully obvious that he did not have the slightest aptitude for the aircraft. Indeed, if he had had any sense, he would have terminated himself. But he did not and, to our relief, he completed the requisite number of sorties and departed to inflict himself on his own unit, fortunately without any disastrous results—mainly because I believe he saw the light and desisted from flying the aircraft.

There was very little trials activity in the first part of 1968 and I seemed to spend a large amount of my time as the photo chase for Harrier gun-firing trials using either a Meteor NF 14 or a Hunter T7, but I did have the occasional trip in the P1127 just to remind me what it was all about. At the end of June I was flying in a Jet Provost Mk 5 with Graham Andrews who was the 'A' Sqn Jet Provost project pilot doing relighting trials. We were obviously fairly cautious as to how we carried out such trials ensuring that we were over the airfield and in clear weather. We had just flamed out the engine and were at 5000 ft when we heard a frantic Mayday emergency call. It was Hugh Rigg in a Harrier which belonged to Rolls Royce and was the Pegasus engine test bed. He had taken off from Filton to do some engine trials and had had the misfortune to get an engine surge during a slam check at 40,000 ft. Unfortunately he was not able to take the necessary corrective action quickly enough and the turbine blades were burnt out—not that he knew that at the time. He was overhead Boscombe Down, flamed out and intending to carry out a flameout landing, so at that stage we had two aircraft in the pattern flamed out. We very quickly relit the engine in the Jet Provost and cleared out of the way to watch ensuing events.

Sure enough Hugh appeared in his Harrier going down like a lift shaft. However he looked as though he was pretty well positioned to complete the flameout landing. That was until he put the undercarriage down as he was turning finals. It very quickly became evident, both to us and to Hugh, that he was not going to make it and he ejected at about 500 ft, descending rapidly. We thought that he had left it too late as the aircraft exploded on the ground close to the Pains-Wessex firework factory just off the end of the runway and he disappeared. However, suddenly his parachute appeared out of the fireball going upwards as a result of the heat and he landed right by the side of the factory and escaped with just a few minor burns and singed eyebrows. But the crash did set back the test programme for the Harrier over-all as we had to take another aircraft out of the schedule to give to Rolls Royce so that they could continue with the engine testing. One of the more bizarre consequences of this incident was that it led to a unique new local flying order which stated that no more than one aircraft should be flamed out at any time!

One morning just a few weeks later, in July 1968, I had drawn the short straw and was 'on the desk', which meant I was the authorising officer responsible for running the flying programme. I was generally minding my own business, drinking a cup of coffee, when the phone rang. It was ETPS asking if we could help them out with a little problem they had;

it seemed that they had a serviceable Lightning T4 and a student ready to do some particular exercise but they had no one qualified to fly the Lightning as captain. The Lightning had appeared on ETPS in 1966 and whilst students did an exercise in it, they were not allowed to go solo in it. Normally, a tutor would sit in the right hand seat as a qualified captain of the aircraft whilst the student did unspeakable things to the aircraft at ridiculous speeds. In fact, as related earlier, I had done my preview exercise on this aircraft whilst on the course in 1966 when the aircraft first arrived, but that was more than two years before and the last time that I had flown it.

I asked around and there was no one Lightning-qualified and available on 'A' Squadron except me—and I was already employed on the desk. I also had a quick look at my log book and since it was some time since I had flown a Lightning—at that time we had about 6 of them on 'A' squadron—and neither was I a WIWOL merchant (WIWOL = 'When I Was On Lightnings'; if you haven't stood at the bar and been bored to death by WIWOL stories, you haven't lived). So I ruled myself out on a lack of currency. We did have a couple of ex-Lightning pilots but they were not around at the time, so I answered the ETPS query saying that there was no one available and that I was the only one vaguely qualified to do it, but did not feel that I was sufficiently current to go supervising an ETPS student. Half an hour later the phone rang again and it was ETPS on the line begging me to go act as captain of the aircraft as they really needed to complete the exercise and that there was absolutely no one else who could do it. Again I refused. Ten minutes later the phone goes again and I then made a big mistake and succumbed to their pleas; they assured me that the student in question was very capable and that all I would have do was sit there.

The exercise was something to do with stability and control, exactly what I cannot remember; except that it involved doing all sorts of unspeakable things to the aircraft including stick jerks at up to M 1.6 at 36,000ft. This was not something that I would have chosen to do myself, but then the choice was not up to me. The weather was not that good with mandatory GCAs for recovery. However, off we went and the cloud cover meant that we were unable to do the low level part of the exercise so we climbed to 36,000 ft just out of the cloud tops for supersonic runs down the channel. Whilst the student was busy doing whatever it was he was trying to do, I amused myself looking around the cockpit to familiarise myself with where everything was, as I had never flown in the right hand seat. I cannot say that it was one of the most comfortable rides with the activity taking place in the left hand seat, but one thing that I did notice, with some surprise, was that as well as the normal relight switches on the left hand side, there was a duplicate set on the right. Quite why, I never discovered; but presumably it had something to do with the fact that this aircraft was the original two seat prototype and they had been put there for trials purposes. It turned out to be an extremely significant observation.

Now the Lightning is not exactly over-endowed with fuel and by the time we had done two runs down the channel we were down to 800/800 (lbs) at which fuel state you would expect to be in the circuit. Even I realised that we were going to be a little tight on fuel and I got the student to point the aircraft in the direction of Boscombe so that we could be fed directly into the GCA. As we went into the cloud tops at 36,000 ft, I instructed the student to throttle back to idle/idle to conserve fuel. A word of explanation; the Lightning has two engine idle positions, idle/idle and idle/fast idle, the latter so that one engine always remains at sufficiently high RPM to keep the electrics on line. This is only really required somewhere below 20,000 ft as the idle RPM reduces in the descent. Normally you used only the idle/fast idle setting, but if you were really tight on fuel, as we were, you could conserve a little bit by going to idle/idle at high level and then, as the RPM decreased in the descent, setting the engines to idle/fast idle before the generators dropped off-line. However the throttle stops could be a little confusing if you were not used to them, and much to my amazement the student, not being too familiar with the throttle stops, pulled both throttles back through the HP cocks and the engines flamed out.

There was a pregnant silence followed by a number of expletives (from me) and I immediately took control. The instrument panels did their best to impersonate a couple of well-lit Christmas trees and I do not think that I have ever seen so many warning lights in a cockpit in my whole life. We were now in cloud, on emergency instruments and above the relight envelope—but descending rapidly as the Lightning is not one of the best gliders in the world. It was at this stage I remembered seeing the extra relight switches on my side of the cockpit.

I do not know what the Air Traffic Control at Boscombe is like today, but they were extremely good then and the handover from Southern Radar to Boscombe was always very slick. In fact, Boscombe Tower would always keep an eye on you whenever they could, whatever the circumstances, and they were pretty 'switched on' that day as they responded immediately to my 'Mayday' call, and proceeded to give us headings to feed us directly into the GCA. My knowledge of the systems on the T4 was not perhaps as encyclopaedic as it should have been, so I was not certain of the relight envelope, or of how many relight attempts the batteries would give you (no doubt some WIWOL merchant will tell me). So I left it until we got below 20,000 ft and then tried it. One engine immediately wound up, and once we had the electrics on line, we got the other one going as well. Air Traffic fed us straight into the GCA and we landed low on fuel, but not as low as I expected, and all in one piece. Shutting down the engines saves even more fuel than just going to idle/idle; but it is not to be recommended.

So what did I learn from all of that? Firstly, beware of the siren voices of the ETPS tutors and do not believe everything they say; they can get you into situations that you would much rather avoid. It also turned out that the student in question, far from being a capable experienced fast jet man, was a maritime pilot and had never been near a fast jet before arriving at ETPS; so do not allow yourself to be suckered into something you know that you ought not to be doing, check the facts and be prepared for the worst. I find it somewhat ironic that that particular aircraft is now the gate guardian at Boscombe and reminds me forcibly of that incident every time I pass it.

The overall activity of test flying was beginning to increase with the Harrier and then the imminent arrival of the Spey engined Phantom and the Jaguar, the test flying of that latter aircraft being done out of Istres in France by Robin Hargreaves. Robin had completed the French Test Pilots' course at EPNER before his arrival on 'A' Sqn so he was a completely fluent French speaker although he seemed to have taken on a little more than just the language. I was given the job of being the Phantom project pilot. We were not due to take delivery of a Phantom until the following year but I was sent off for a week up at Holme-on-Spalding Moor (HOSM) followed by a week in Germany to fly the F4 simulator with the USAF at Hahn. HOSM was an interesting experience; it was the flight test airfield for Hawker Siddeley Brough and the home of the Buccaneer and had been given responsibility for the F4 in UK. I stayed in the local pub in the village, which was excellent, and the airfield reminded me of the opening shots in the film *Twelve O'clock High*—abandoned Nissen huts, overgrown vegetation everywhere and a general feeling of a deserted airfield. I was convinced that they must have used it as a location for shooting the film; it certainly was not very convincing as one of the UK's premier flight test installations—especially when the Chief Test Pilot, Derek (Block) Whitehead used to turn up for briefing in the morning dressed just like an English country gentleman in jodhpurs having been out for his morning ride. The whole place had a very pleasant atmosphere but it was also somewhat redolent of decay. Nevertheless it was a very enjoyable week, as was the week at Hahn. Hahn is just adjacent to the Mosel valley and we were hosted by a USAF Major who was unusual in that he spoke fluent German and delighted in taking us round all the local hostelries rather than remaining on base as was the normal habit of USAF personnel. But the variant of Phantom simulator was not particularly relevant to the F4K and F4M, the designation of the UK variants. Summertime and the Mosel valley is not a bad place to be, so I had an enjoyable week; but I regret to say that I did not learn very much.

On the last day in July 1968 I was exposed to the delights of the Harrier for the first time, however the sorties were very few and far between—three in August and then one in October. This was not the ideal way in which to achieve familiarity with a new aircraft and, more to the point, a new concept of aviation. I was given the task of running the Operational and Reliability Test Flying (ORTF) programme with one of the first production Harriers, XV 741; an aircraft with which I was to become especially familiar a few years later although I did not know it at the time. The intention was to fly a fairly concentrated programme of representative operational sorties to try and ascertain the overall performance of the aircraft especially with respect to serviceability and reliability of the systems. It started off well enough in November, but by January—and after just half a dozen sorties—it had ground to a halt because of a shortage of Harrier airframes in the overall test programme, mainly due to the demise of the engine test aircraft. As a result priorities were readjusted and the ORTF went out of the window and 1968 ended with a very much increased activity in flight test programmes, especially of the Harrier. With Hugh Rigg now gone, there were only two Harrier qualified pilots apart from the Boss, Alan Merriman, who was about to leave in any case. These two were Tom Lecky-Thomson, who was now the project pilot and myself.

The US Marine Corps had been showing an interest in the Harrier and we had entertained a couple of their high priced help, Colonels Tom Miller and Bud Baker when they came over earlier to fly the Harrier out of Dunsfold with Hawker Siddeley. Their lobbying back in the US had obviously had some success as they then sent over a team from Patuxent River, the US Navy Flight Test Centre, to undertake a formal assessment of the aircraft at Boscombe under the leadership of Major Bill Scheuren of the USMC. They spent a week or so at Boscombe undertaking a preview of the Harrier flying 12 sorties. Either Tom or I had to be present at each briefing to ensure that they were not going to try and do something outrageous with the aircraft—which they did not—and there was just one incident that remains in my mind; they got to the final sortie and this was to cover handling in emergency situations, one of which was flying the approach without autostabilisers engaged.

A word of explanation: the Harrier had autostabilisers that were designed to work only at low speed with the undercarriage down. You switched them on when you did your pre-take-off checks and they automatically switched off when you accelerated past 250 kts. When you came in to land, you had to manually switch them on again when you were below 250 kts. So we stood at the back during the briefing and listened to their plan. They explained that they wanted to do the approach without the benefit of 'SASS'—a word that was complete gobbledegook to us. They then explained that this acronym stood for 'Stability Augmentation Sub System', a somewhat grandiose term for the Harrier's very basic system. They then asked how they could do that. Easy, we replied, just don't switch it on after you have put the undercarriage down. That caused a certain amount of consternation and much whispering in the US team. They then stood up and with straight faces said that they would like to do an approach with 'SASS on'. It turned out that they had not realised exactly how the system worked and they had never done an approach with the autostabilisers on during the whole week.

The year came to an end with an announcement that the *Daily Mail* was going to run an air race between the top of the GPO Tower and the top of the Empire State Building to commemorate the first crossing of the Atlantic by Alcock and Brown in 1919. There were to be a number of categories, supersonic aircraft, subsonic aircraft, light aircraft, using scheduled services and so on. Some bright spark—I believe it was Wg Cdr Phil Champniss who was at that stage the project officer in MoD—suggested that the Harrier should be entered. There were a number of problems to be considered; first the aircraft had not entered service and was still in relatively early days of development. Secondly, there were only two pilots with sufficient experience of the aircraft who could fly the aircraft; one was Sqn Ldr Tom Lecky-Thomson and the other Sqn Ldr Mike Adams who had been Senior Pilot on 'A' Sqn before Hugh Rigg and was now based at Dunsfold with Hawker Siddeley as the Operational Requirements Liaison Officer (ORLO) and now flew with HSA as part of their test team. Mike was the most experienced RAF Harrier pilot, followed by Tom L-T, and then I came a very bad third with about ten hours on the aircraft achieved over a period of nine months or so.

As I understood it, the company were not that enthusiastic about participating; they thought that it was far too early in the aircraft's life and a very high risk venture—an opinion with which I could only concur. However in the end it was decreed that we would participate despite the many unanswered questions that remained, not least the take-off and landing venues. The aircraft would be 'officially' based at RAF Wittering, already nominated as the first Harrier base and the pilots, Tom Lecky-T and Mike Adams, would be 'posted' to Wittering as normal squadron pilots rather than the test pilots they were so that the RAF could claim that the aircraft were flown by ordinary line pilots. I was to be the spare pilot in case anything happened to Tom or Mike.

January 1969 life went on much as usual, although I did start to increase my participation in Harrier trials, namely navigation accuracy and weapon aiming accuracy trials of the Inertial Navigation Attack System (INAS). It would seem that the obvious and best way to do this was to get a complete system together and test all the modes at once but that was not the way it was done. I suspect, but cannot be sure now, that we did not have a system that was capable of switching to all the various modes, so the navigation accuracy trial was done on one aircraft and system whilst the weapon aiming was carried out on another. On this basis one aircraft had the navigation mode tuned to perfection and the other had the weapon aiming tuned to perfection. Whilst the navigation accuracy was never much to write home about—at best about 2 nms/hour error—the weapon aiming both for cannon and rockets was absolutely superb. Tom Lecky-T and I did most of the weapon aiming and it seemed to both of us to be difficult to miss, especially with the SNEB rocket. We were very impressed. Unfortunately, that was the only time the system worked and when the aircraft went into service the following year, it was so bad that the RAF had to revert to firing rockets and guns with a fixed gun-sight and it took years to get it right. I have always believed, rightly or wrongly, that the fault lay in tuning each separate system to a particular mode rather than testing a completely integrated system.

It was at the end of February 1969 that the bombshell dropped. Mike Adams was taxying out at Dunsfold in a Harrier and the nose leg sheared off; not exactly a great disaster but it did completely wreck Mike's back and he was declared unfit to undertake the race. Suddenly I was catapulted into the limelight as the spare pilot although I did not have much experience on the aircraft. It was stipulated by the Air Force Board that I could participate as long as I had 50 hours flying on the aircraft. In fact that was not going to be as difficult to achieve as one might have thought, mainly because we still had to do the flight refuelling trials which involved sorties of seven hours duration to physically check such things as engine oil consumption. Just as crucial was the pilot's oxygen consumption, which was also an unknown quantity at that stage; in fact neither turned out to be critical.

As part of the preparations I was tasked to do some air-to-air refuelling (AAR) trials. In the UK system of AAR, the receiver aircraft is fitted with a probe and the tanker trails a drogue into which you have to engage the probe. The degree of difficulty tends to vary according to the position of the probe on your aircraft. The Lightning can be quite difficult as the probe is quite a long way out on the wing and is not easy to see. You often hear AAR described as trying to ram a red hot poker up a wild cat's arse—and although I have never tried that particular exercise, I can understand the sentiment. I had never undertaken AAR before in any aircraft, so I thought it would be prudent to try it out with some other platform. I looked around for a suitable aircraft. We had a Lightning fitted with a probe on the squadron but that happened to be badly unserviceable and was never going to be repaired in time. There was also a Canberra fitted with a probe, but that was unserviceable as well. At that stage I was beginning to run out of ideas and in desperation I rang the 'C' Sqn, the RN test squadron at Boscombe; I asked if they had an aircraft around that was fitted with an AAR probe. 'Yes', they said.

'What is it?' I asked.

'A Scimitar' they said.

'Is it serviceable?' I asked

'Yes', they said, 'and it is sitting ready to fly on the line and we've got no one interested at the moment.'

I explained the problem I faced but I was slightly dubious about leaping into the air in an aircraft with which I was totally unfamiliar and trying to do air-to-air refuelling.

'No problem,' they said, 'just pop down here and we'll arrange for a tanker and give you a quick brief'.

By the time I arrived at 'C' Squadron Operations about 20 minutes later, they had arranged a Sea Vixen tanker from Yeovilton and 30 minutes after that I was airborne in the Scimitar, rendezvoused with the tanker, did about a dozen AAR engagements and the exercise was completed. But the Scimitar was extremely easy to refuel mainly because the probe is right in front of you, fortunately not unlike the Harrier.

One way and the other we were pretty busy, what with trying to get everything ready for the Transatlantic Air Race, various trials, and just to complicate matters, the arrival of the first Spey-engined Phantom. Alan Merriman left to become the station commander at Wittering and was replaced by Ian Keppie who had been one of the tutors at ETPS. I well remember one of his first appearances on the scene. It was a Sunday morning and I was on the ops desk running the flying programme and just before he walked in someone had burst a tyre in a JP5 closely followed by Andy Jones doing the same thing in a Harrier. I was somewhat stressed trying to sort out the ensuing shambles when the new CO, with immaculate timing, walked into the ops room. 'What the hell is going on here?' he asked, actually rather more forcefully than that, in his strong Scottish accent. The last thing I needed at that stage was more gratuitous advice. I explained what had happened and he just said 'Well, bloody well sort it out!' And so saying he turned round and walked out. My heart warmed to the man and we did, in fact, become very good friends.

We had been working seven days a week for some time which, for Boscombe Down, was virtually unheard of. I was still the Phantom Project pilot with Barry Tonkinson as my deputy and since we were the only ones who had done the simulator and ground-school we were, ostensibly the only ones who could fly the aircraft; although I have to admit that it had all happened so far in the past that it was almost irrelevant. I took time out from the Harrier trials and did a quick couple of conversion trips on the F4M followed by a couple of minor trials sorties before turning back to the Harrier.

The two aircraft for the race had been selected. Tom was going to fly XV741 and I was allocated XV744. 741 had a full Inertial & Navigation Attack System (INAS) fitted but 744 was what was described as a Mod 9 aircraft; it had no INAS and just some temporary basic flight instruments, a small standby artificial horizon, a turn and slip and a GIV compass. The airframe configuration for the transatlantic trip was different to normal. Hawkers had designed wingtip extensions for ferrying which were said to reduce drag and increase range. These tips were meant to be easy to attach to the normal wingtips and increase the wingspan by about 4 feet or so. Since we only had small 100 gallon drop-tanks in those days, any small benefits were gratefully received. Whether or not it did anything for range I do not know, but it did increase the stability of the aircraft and made it easier to fly at high level. We found that we could cruise at M 0.88 at 36,000 ft using just under maximum continuous power. Since the Victor tankers could achieve the same speed, that was what we decided to use. It is of interest to note that when the aircraft went into service, the squadrons elected not to bother with the extended wingtips as they were too fiddly to fit and were not thought to produce sufficient benefit. As far as I am aware the tips were only ever used on the occasion of the air race—although someone will probably tell me differently.

We were now focused totally on the air race and the preparation for it. The aircraft had passed all the necessary tests with flying colours, but the real issues were more of a political nature, finding a place from which to take off and land in New York and London with all the necessary clearances. It is worth mentioning that the whole effort was headed up by the then station commander at Wittering, Gp Capt. Peter Williamson (later to become Air Marshal Sir Peter Williamson and to die rather tragically of cancer shortly after he retired). There is no doubt in my mind that, had it not been for him, the Harrier's participation in the air race would never have happened. He had the innate ability to talk the hind leg off a donkey and his initiative, drive, and powers of persuasion were instrumental in getting all the necessary clearances on both sides of the Atlantic. Strangely enough, I understand that it was a bit easier to get the clearances in the US than it was in UK. Tom L-T was involved in the negotiations in the US and, after a few false trails we ended up with a landing site on a jetty in the East River on Manhattan Island.

As a late-comer to the programme I had only got involved in the selection of a landing site in London. An obvious choice would have been somewhere in Regents Park which was, after all, a large open space; but, for some unknown reason, they would not give us permission. We looked at a couple of building sites which would have been extremely gamey and it was only at the last minute that the landing site at the old coal yard at St Pancras Station was made available. I had a very quick look at it just before I left to go to the US by civil air. It was cobble-stoned and we would have to lay a MEXE landing pad over the top to make sure it was safe to land on. Needless to say that had not been done when I had to leave and I was not sure exactly where they were going to put it.

Tom did a trial run from east to west with XV744 which served to confirm the capability of the aircraft and the concept, and prepositioned my aircraft in the USA. He took off from RAF Northolt, rendezvoused with the tankers and after six refuellings landed at Floyd Bennet Field, a US Navy Air Station on Long Island that was to serve as the base for all UK activities connected with the air race. I left UK by commercial air and arrived just two weeks before the event. The ground crew were in place, led by Sqn Ldr John Manning, although they suffered from the slight disadvantage of no familiarity with the Harrier, but there were enough company reps, both Rolls Royce and Hawker Siddeley Aviation around to ensure that all was well. In fact one of my lasting memories was the reliability of the aircraft throughout our time in the US with the exception of one incident which I shall get to in due course. The plan was that after coming down the lift from the top of the Empire State Building, I would leap into an E-Type Jaguar for the drive to the pad just off Manhattan in the East River. Jaguar in New York offered me an E-Type as personal transport which I declined, taking instead a little Austin America (1300) which I deemed to be less likely to kill me and not quite so ostentatious. Once I had crossed the Atlantic and landed at St Pancras I would get on the pillion of an RAF Police motorcycle for the trip to the GPO Tower, and thence up the lift to the top. Pretty straightforward really!

In the week preceding the race, I carried out a couple of air tests and demos plus a practice rendezvous with the tankers over Boston. The New York Air Traffic Centre was extremely cooperative and helpful at all times and bent over backwards to accommodate our somewhat unusual requirements—unusual to them at least. I managed to cause a six car pile-up on the roads just outside the airfield as a couple of drivers became mesmerised by the sight of this fighter aircraft hovering with no visible means of support. However I have two main memories of this time; one was a press conference with the UK and US press representatives when I managed to get totally blitzed drinking ice-cold gin and tonics. David Bainbridge, Hawker Siddeley Aviation's PRO, finally managed to drag me away when I thought I was doing so well! All I could remember the following morning was that I had been talking to the *Daily Mirror* Defence Correspondent (Ellis Plaice?). However, I had no idea what I had said and was very concerned as to what would be in the paper. I happened to meet him again that day and I asked him. Much to my relief he said he had no idea because he had been totally blitzed as well.

Somewhat more significant was a request that I appear on the Johnny Carson Show. I was escorted by a very attractive lady from the British Embassy to the TV studio for what I thought was to be a briefing on my precise role in the programme. We sat down in an office and started talking informally with some executive of NBC. In the discussion I was asked what I thought of New York and I replied that I was somewhat disappointed as in those days it was a rather untidy and tacky city, Times Square in particular. In fact I was less than impressed with the whole place and said so I thought no more about it until I arrived later that evening for the show and I was handed a script which repeated all my comments word for word. I was aghast. I was in uniform and there was no way I wanted to say what they had in the script on the Johnny Carson Show which was in those days coast to coast. I sat down in make-up next to Ed McMahon who was Carson's well-known winger and, thank goodness, an ex-Marine aviator—in fact he had been a colonel in the US Marine Reserves, served in the Second World War and went on active duty in Korea flying spotter aircraft for the artillery. I explained my predicament to him and he told me not to worry as Carson would not wish to embarrass me in any way. I remember sitting waiting to go on with the other guests—Alan Funk of Candid Camera fame, Mamie Van Doren, a busty blonde film actress (a poor man's Jayne Mansfield), and Sergio Franchi, a film actor/singer. I was last on and apart from being marched on to the tune of Colonel Bogey, Johnny Carson was, as promised by McMahon, very discreet and I never was asked about my views of New York.

All that I had to do now was await Tom's arrival in XV741, fly the aircraft off the Manhattan pad to Floyd Bennet and then complete my part in the air race. On the morning of the 5 May we got notice that Tom was on his way, so we got ourselves down to the pad to await his arrival. The weather was perfect and he duly arrived and landed and rushed off on the back of a motorbike. I climbed in the aircraft to take it back to Floyd Bennet, and I could hardly believe what I found. The cockpit was filthy and everything was covered in a black dust—which I later found out was coal dust from the coal yard at St Pancras. My new white kid leather gloves very quickly became grey kid leather gloves. Nevertheless my job was to take the aircraft away from Manhattan and so I started it up. I cannot remember what the fuel state was but I had less than 1200 lbs, not that I needed very much to get to Floyd Bennet. I wound the engine up and slammed to full power for a vertical take-off; and all I got was the mother and father of a bang surge. I am told that it was quite spectacular, a large sheet of flame coming out of the front of the engine. The normal procedure would have been to shut down and have the aircraft checked to ensure that there was no damage, however the thoughts that ran through my head at that stage was that the last thing we needed to do was to start working on the aircraft in the middle of New York. I was pretty certain that I knew what had caused the surge—namely hot gas re-ingestion, so I cracked the nozzles a few degrees from the vertical, slammed the engine again and ended up doing the most rapid VTO and transition to forward flight that I had ever done. I landed back at Floyd Bennet and told John Manning what had happened. The engineers then went through a series of checks and found that the rod that activated the inlet guide vanes had bent, but other than that all was in good order.

Once all the hullabaloo had died down, we settled down to wait for favourable weather conditions for my west to east trip. We were looking for a good tail wind, preferably a jet stream, to cut down the time *en route*. Then on Tuesday evening Tom and I had decided to go into New York for a bite to eat. We were sitting in a bar—I can even remember that the bar had Watney's Red Barrel on draught—minding our own business, and the television was on. We had, of course, been a newsworthy item for some days but it suddenly seemed that we were about to be up-staged by the *Queen Elizabeth 2* which was due to arrive in New York on her maiden voyage in 36 hours' time. We decided that we were not going to allow that to happen and we hatched up a plan there and then to hover either side of the bridge as it came into New York.

There was, of course, the question of getting local clearance to do it and, more importantly, clearance from the RAF authorities in UK to do it. First thing in the morning we set about getting all the local clearances and, as usual, everyone was very helpful even to the extent of keeping all the helicopters out of the way. The question of getting clearance from the RAF authorities was, I decided, one that was going to be a step too far, so we decided to ignore that problem, fly the sortie and ask for forgiveness after the event. We took off and caught the *Queen Elizabeth 2* after it had come through the Verrazano Narrows. It was blowing a gale, a problem that we had not realised before take-off as the cross-wind limit for hovering was only 15 kts in those days. The *Queen Elizabeth 2* was less than cooperative in that she was travelling cross wind which meant that we had to transition to the hover with a 30 to 40 kt wind across and from slightly behind which made life even more difficult. Nevertheless we managed to hover either side of the bridge as intended as the *Queen Elizabeth 2* came up the Hudson River. Later that day, we were invited to the welcome cocktail party on board but were unable to attend as I was on stand-by to fly my west-east leg the following morning. In the event we could have been there as the trip was delayed another day whilst we waited for the ideal conditions. I never did hear anything from the RAF about our exploit even though it hit the headlines in the UK newspapers. I discovered subsequently that an Air Marshal, who shall be nameless, took the credit for the idea, saying that he told us to do it. I like to think that he did it to cover our backsides—but somehow I don't think so!

By Thursday evening we were beginning to get desperate; the weather was not cooperating and we were running out of time, as Saturday was the last day of the race period, we decided that I would go on Friday come what may. The weather forecast was absolutely horrible for the East Coast of America but not bad for the UK. Come dawn and it was pouring with rain. In fact the weather was so bad that Kennedy Airport was closed although the cloud base over New York was not quite so low because of the heat generated by the city. There were no diversions on the East Coast within range so that if I missed the tankers, I was going to be in deep trouble. Nevertheless we decided to continue as though it was a practical proposition. Tom prepositioned the aircraft for me on the pad in Manhattan and I went to the top of the Empire State Building to check out. We had rehearsed the run from the Empire State Building to the pad but in bright sunshine, but it was a different kettle of fish in the pouring rain. The hood of the E-Type Jag was down and the weather meant that everyone was driving at a snail's pace and we seemed to catch every traffic light in the city; by the time I got to the pad I was soaking wet. I climbed into the aircraft, strapped in and started up. There was an FAA official on the pad who was meant to be controlling the go/no go decision. However Bill Bedford, the former Chief Test Pilot for Hawker Siddeley Aviation, kept him engaged in conversation in a tent and he did not realise what was going on. By the time that he did, my engine was accelerating for the vertical take-off and his protestations became irrelevant.

The take-off was a bit of a struggle. I had 2000 lbs of fuel but the temperature was alarmingly high despite the weather. The aircraft staggered into the air and I accelerated away into the murk. Unfortunately in my haste to get away, I had not allowed enough time for the flight instruments to erect correctly. My aircraft, XV 744, did not have an inertial system in it and it just had a hotchpotch of conventional flight instruments instead. As I accelerated away the artificial horizon toppled and I was left with just a turn and slip and a compass. The cloud tops, I subsequently discovered, were at 38,000 ft and as soon as I checked in with New York Centre they asked to make a procedure turn, a request I turned down as politely as I could as I was having trouble keeping the aircraft the right way up. To make things worse, the air conditioning system could not cope with all the moisture around and everything— the flight instruments and the canopy—started to mist up—so that I was continually having to rub the instruments with my glove to see what was happening. With a certain amount of relief, I shot out of the cloud tops at 38,000 ft just to confront the next and rather immediate problem—finding the tankers. I had air-air Tacan (tactical air navigation) as an aid which would give me a range to the tanker but not a bearing.

I was even more relieved when it immediately locked on and the range was decreasing which indicated to me that the tankers were there and on track; but I was slightly concerned about the cloud tops which were right on the planned refuelling height. Would I be able to pick them up? No sooner had I started to worry about it than I caught sight of them trailing in the cloud tops coming towards me. They immediately turned and with a big sigh of relief I plugged in for my first refuelling bracket with less than 1200 lbs of fuel remaining. Now at least I could reach the first available diversion, which was Gander in Newfoundland.

As we trundled our way to the north-east, I had time to sit back and relax—slightly! There were three Victor tankers in front of me which was, I thought, somewhat overdoing it, but who was I to question it. Two I could understand, one to provide the fuel and a spare in case of some malfunction. But three was belt and braces. As I got towards the middle of the Atlantic, I had to make a number of short refuels to ensure that I had, in theory, enough fuel to make a diversion in the event of a refuelling malfunction, but as we approached Newfoundland the immediate problem was to refuel the tankers. As if by magic three more Victor tankers appeared heading towards us. They performed a 180° turn and slotted in directly in front of the three tankers in front of me which in turn refuelled for the crossing. It was a magnificent sight and a really professional performance; all I could do was sit at the back and admire it.

After all the excitement of the take-off and climb out and finding the tankers, the trip then became relatively humdrum. We were all cruising at M 0.88 at 38,000 ft, I say cruising but my throttle was right up against the maximum continuous setting. The air-to-air refuelling turned out to be relatively easy and once I had plugged in to the drogue, I actually received a bit of a tow, allowing me to reduce my throttle setting for a brief time. Three quick top ups in the middle of the Atlantic and I was then on the home run. I took a sixth refuel about 350 nms off the coast of Ireland and I then got the weather for London and I could hardly believe my ears; 1/8th Cu at 2800 ft with 13 nms visibility and the tailwind had picked up to 90 kts at 25,000 ft. That was all going to make my life considerably easier, so now I had to concentrate on arriving at the far end with the correct fuel state to be able to carry out a vertical landing. I declined the seventh scheduled refuelling and as I passed the east coast of Ireland started a slow descent at maximum speed. Air Traffic were extremely helpful and more or less allowed me to do what I wanted. My aim was to arrive at 2000 ft at Alexandra Palace, a landmark so large that not even I could miss it, then turn right and follow the railway line straight down to St Pancras. The weather was even better than I expected, not a cloud in the sky and you could see almost all the way across London. I was told that there had been a thunderstorm earlier in the day which had settled all the usual dust and crap that you associate with London to leave gin clear skies. I hit Ally Pally doing 550 kts, picked up the railway line and as I followed it down to St Pancras I could see the GPO Tower straight ahead. I was so mesmerised with all the sights that I suddenly realised that if I did not slow down I was going to overshoot St Pancras by miles; I chopped the throttle, threw out the airbrake and managed to slow down just in time to flop straight on to the pad in the coal yard.

I shut everything down, unstrapped and jumped down from the cockpit using the AAR probe. A RAF Police motorbike awaited and I jumped onto the pillion. I expected to be taken directly to the tower but, much to my surprise, I was dumped on to a waiting helicopter which then ferried me directly to a landing platform, called the Moss Site, right outside the entrance to the tower. Having not seen this structure before, for a moment I had no idea where I was, but once I had got my orientation I ran over to the Tower got in the lift and arrived at the check-in desk at the top of the Tower, totally out of breath, in exactly 5 hrs 49 mins and 58.52 secs. Much to my surprise, as it had not been arranged before I left, was that my wife was the first one to greet me, followed closely by several air marshals and a defence minister!

After sundry press and television interviews, I changed in the toilet and then sat down to a celebratory dinner in the revolving restaurant at the top of the Tower hosted by Sir Harry Broadhurst who was then working for Hawker Siddeley. The RAF, with its usual consideration and foresight, had not made any arrangements for me to get home or to stay anywhere; but fortunately my brother lived in Kensington and we retired with a certain amount of relief to his flat, in which my children were also ensconded. All in all, it was a satisfactory ending to a pretty busy day.

I had thought that I would have to move the aircraft away from St Pancras on Monday morning. My brother had arranged a family lunch at Syon Park on Sunday and I was just about to leave for the lunch when I got a call asking me to move the aircraft to Northolt, so I had to forgo the lunch. The family met me at Northolt on Sunday afternoon and there was then a slight disagreement with the duty officer who was unwilling to provide us with transport to get home to Porton (Salisbury). In the end they provided us with a van and driver for a not very comfortable run home; back to reality with a thump! In fact I did not win the west-east race. I was beaten by a few seconds in the subsonic category by a crewman in a SR Victor, and overall the RN Phantom beat me by a somewhat larger measure, but they were in the supersonic category. However, I do not think that that really mattered. The point was that we were given a perfect opportunity to promote the aircraft and it behaved perfectly. Tom won the east-west race and remained in the US. He was joined by John Farley, the HAS test pilot, and they spent a week touring the US with two aircraft demonstrating the unique capability of the Harrier, again very successfully and without a single hiccup. Originally I thought that the whole exercise was madness and extremely risky; I remember saying to Tom beforehand that if we both got away with it, we would be very lucky. As if to prove a point, a few months later we had a considerable amount of engine problems as the aircraft entered service, mainly because of a manufacturing defect in the first stage fan blades. The aircraft was grounded until the problem was rectified.

Back at Boscombe, May turned to June and we were kept pretty busy. We had to clear all the UK weapons on the Phantoms and my time was split, in the main, between the Phantom and the Harrier with occasional light relief with Lightnings. At the beginning of June I had to deliver one of the early DB Lightnings, XG 329, to Cranwell where it was to be used as a ground instructional aid. I remember the trip well because the runway at Cranwell is not over-endowed in length and if the braking chute did not work I was going to be in trouble. As far as I am aware, it was the only time a Lightning went into Cranwell. For sure it never came out—unless it was on a low loader!

Harrier XV 741, after its moment of glory in the air race, reverted to being the Operational Reliability Trials aircraft. Unfortunately, that did not last for long again as we had to give up one of the other aircraft, XV 739, to Rolls Royce to replace the aircraft that Hugh had dumped on the fireworks factory. So the ORTF went by the board and 741 became a part of the overall test programme.

By now I was becoming pretty familiar with the F4, which was just as well as I had been tasked to go to Edwards in August to do the single engine, hot weather performance of the F4. My back seater for the trial was to be a RN Observer, Lt Dick Searles. A Boscombe trials officer from performance division, Dennis Sharpe, completed our team. Of significance was that Dick Searles was an enthusiastic golfer with the same handicap as me and there was a pretty good golf course on the base, which was just as well as it turned out. This trial was to be carried out under the auspices of McDonnell Douglas flying out of Contractors Row at Edwards. The aircraft to be used for the trial was XT595, the original prototype F4K.

Our first trip took place on the 11 August 1969 and my main memory is of being unable to control the aircraft accurately down the approach. It had the most ghastly 'Dutch roll' which I was totally unable to damp out. I thought that it must have been something I was (or was not) doing so I was a little reluctant to make serious criticisms at the debrief in front of all the McDonnell Douglas experts, but finally, on being cross-examined by the McDonnell test pilots, I did admit to having a little difficulty on the approach. There was almost an audible sigh of relief and they then told me that ever since the aircraft first flew it had had this problem and that it had thwarted every attempt to fix it. In consequence they had decided to live with it and they had christened the aircraft 'Wally the Whale', but it certainly made for a very uncomfortable approach.

We got off to a pretty good start, flying three sorties in two days. The profile was pretty much the same for each sortie; we did a measured take-off on each trip to gather performance information followed by a series of single-engined partial climbs to measure the single engine performance. The plan was to slowly increase the weight until we achieved the maximum All Up Weight—or it just became too dangerous to continue, but having completed three sorties we ran into a problem. Every time we taxied out, lined upon the runway and tried to engage reheat for take-off we started to get some horrendously loud bangs from engine surge and more flames out of the front than out of the back. I judged that it was prudent not to proceed any further and taxied back in. This state of affairs went on for two weeks and I lost count of how many times we changed the engines. The relationship between Rolls Royce and McDonnell became very frosty, with Rolls Royce in one corner blaming the intake on the F4 and the McDonnell blaming Rolls Royce for their engine with Dick and me standing in the middle. Personally, I thought that it was the result of over-fuelling by the reheat fuel system caused by the finite time taken for the catalyst igniter system to work. The only good thing was that we were able to play plenty of golf.

I also had a USAF friend, Einar Enevoldsen, who had been on exchange at Boscombe and retired from the USAF to fly for NASA at Edwards. He was kind enough to take us under his wing, lend us a car for sorties into Los Angeles in return for crewing for him at weekends when he was competing in the California Gliding Championships. Most weekends we would follow him around on the ground with his car and trailer for the glider, ready to pick him up wherever he landed as he attempted to complete their cross country task. It was a great way of getting to see the local countryside. He also took me up to NASA Ames at Moffett field in an Aero Commander to look at the superb wind tunnel facilities they had. One was an enormous low speed wind tunnel in which you could put a full size aircraft. To my surprise in the tunnel they had the British Hunting H126 aircraft which had been designed to test the concept of blown flaps. On the way back we were asked to go to Nellis to pick up another crew who had been diverted. As it was now 6 o'clock in the evening, we went to drag our passengers out of Happy Hour at the Officers' Club; and the first person I bumped into was 'Black' Fergy Ferguson who was the RAF exchange pilot at Nellis. By the time we got back to Edwards it was late evening, so we landed the Aero Commander at Lancaster Airport with a promise to pick it up on the following day.

The other memorable event was watching the lifting body trials, the precursor to the space shuttle. It was flown by Gerry Gentry. A B52 flown by an RAF exchange officer, Dusty Miller, carried the lifting body on a wing pylon up to 40,000 ft and then released it so that Gerry Gentry could glide (I use the term loosely) and land it on the salt lake. I was privileged to attend the briefing, witness the whole flight from the roof and attend the debriefing, the latter being quite hilarious. It appeared that the co-pilot had made a horrendous cock-up. On the run in to the drop point he had gone through all the various checks including putting the pylon to 'live' 60 seconds before the drop. The only problem was that he had not checked the position of the actual jettison switch and as soon as he put the pylon live, the lifting body jettisoned. As Gerry Gentry somewhat crudely put it: 'I was sitting there pickin' my nose, mindin' my own business when suddenly I'm airborne!' The drop point was very carefully calculated so that to be dropped seven or eight miles short could have been disastrous, but he managed to correct for it and carried out an immaculate landing on the lake. With some justification, the co-pilot came in for a certain amount of critical banter.

While we were enjoying all these extra-curricular activities, the trial was not proceeding well. In those two weeks we must have taxied out at least half a dozen times only to be greeted by the same engine problems as before. The relationship between Rolls Royce and McDonnell Douglas was getting worse and worse. We were falling so far behind schedule that it was decided to fly during the weekend, a step that was regarded as a last resort because everyone had to be paid overtime. Friday night and, as usual, we attended happy hour in the officers' club and were led astray by the flight surgeon who was determined to demonstrate how hospitable Americans could be, and I have to admit that he succeeded. When we arrived at 6 a.m. for our briefing on Saturday morning (the Americans do tend to insist on ridiculous working hours), we were feeling a little bit on the shabby side. I made the mistake of taking some salt pills just before walking out to the aircraft and that had a predictable deleterious effect. However we taxied out, lined up, and engaged reheat. Much to our astonishment it worked, and off we went; but I fail to understand why it is that it always seems to be the flight surgeon—and it does not seem to depend on nationality—normally tasked with keeping us fit to fly, who is often the instigator of inflicting one with some doom laden alcoholic mix!

In the next ten days we did 15 sorties gradually increasing the weight until we achieved to maximum. Needless to say 'partial climbs' became 'partial descents' as, at the higher weights, the aircraft could not maintain height. The greatest excitement occurred one day when coming back to land and someone had blocked the runway. I was 'diverted' to land on the adjoining salt lake. I had not actually given it much thought but it was not as straightforward as one might think. You have nothing to use as a reference point for judging height and it was a question of feeling for the ground. Fortunately runway length is not a problem, but the ground crew were not too pleased as they had to wash down the aircraft completely. We had no recurrence of the surge problem on take-off and the aircraft ran like clockwork. We successfully completed the trial on 9 September and flew back to the UK courtesy of BOAC.

I was now back at Boscombe having missed most of our children's school holidays, (a fact which my wife still reminds me of), and back to the weapons carriage and release trials. These were mostly uneventful although I do remember a sortie with Pete Desmond which involved carrying 9 × 1000 lb bombs at up to 550 kts and M 1.1 and then dropping them in salvo on the range. Over the next twelve months, we went through the whole selection of weapons, 1000 lb bomb, 540 lb bomb, Lepus Flare, Sneb Rocket and a 'Special Store' and all the various profiles. However the most interesting trials involved the Recce Pod which the F4M carried on the centre line station.

It was originally intended that reconnaissance would become the chief secondary role for the FGR2 and to equip the recce squadrons for this role, EMI was contracted to design, build and deliver a dedicated reconnaissance pod. Using a considerable amount of technology originally developed for the TSR2 reconnaissance systems, EMI eventually created the biggest, most capable and most expensive reconnaissance pod of the

1960s. To ensure the pod could be safely carried underneath the FGR2 on the centreline store, with sufficient ground clearance, the pod was made roughly the same dimensions as a 500 gal external fuel tank.

The EMI pod usually carried forward, vertical and oblique F95 70 mm and one F135 cameras together with an EMI P391 Q band SLAR with mapping and MTI capability and a roll stabilised Texas Instruments RS-700 Infra-Red Linescan. For night photography four F135 cameras could be carried in the pod and electronic flash equipment was carried in a separate pod carried under the wing. For special tasks, a F126 vertical camera and an F95 oblique camera with a 12 in focal lens could also be fitted. It was in fact a very impressive piece of kit—at least I thought it was, but then I am not of the 'killum with fillum' fraternity (i.e. a recce specialist). I am of the belief that if you have managed to fight your way to the target, it is preferable to bomb it than just take a pretty picture.

For the most part of this trial I was just the driver airframe acting under the direction of the back seat man, usually Pete Desmond, Timber Woods or Ted Pearson. I do remember being very impressed at some of the IR imagery we had taken off Spurn Head in a snow-storm. You could see individual cows in the Yorkshire fields to the extent of being able to tell which way they were facing. Overall it was a pretty impressive system although I am led to believe that it did not turn out to be very reliable in service and was ditched after a year or so.

What did I think of the F4? It was a typical naval aircraft—built like a battleship and mostly brute force and ignorance. Its overall performance was very impressive and the aircraft was more sophisticated than anything else we had in service at the time. It was a pity that politics and industrial pressures led us to replace the J79 engines with the Spey. Rolls Royce at the time made some very optimistic claims for the improvements in performance that would accrue, 20 per cent better range, more power and so on. In fact the Spey engined F4 was inferior to the J79 and you did not need to look far to find the reason. The intakes on the F4K/M were twice the size of those on the US variants and whilst it might have been true that the SFC and thrust of the Spey was superior to the J79, it was unable to overcome the increased drag of the intakes, so the outcome was a very expensive variant of the F4 that was not the equal of the US variant. We added to the expense by insisting on putting in a Ferranti inertial navigation system (in the M) which at the then state of technology did not do that much for you. Nevertheless it was a very capable aircraft in which one would have been very happy to go to war, and, of course, many people did so with great success.

1970 was to be my final year at Boscombe and was in many ways one of the busiest, mainly involving the Harrier, although there was also some F4 work and an operational assessment of the Jaguar down at Istres. The two major activities with the Harrier were the Deck Trial and the Hot Weather Trial. In preparation for the Deck Trial, we had a dummy deck painted on the runway at Boscombe from which to practise Short Take Offs. You positioned yourself as far back on the deck as was considered feasible, accelerated down the 'deck' and rotated the nozzles as you hit the forward limit of the angled deck—this was well before the development of the ski jump. The second Boscombe pilot was to be Ian Keppie, the CO of 'A' Sqn and we would also be joined by John Farley from Hawker Siddeley Aviation. We would be taking two aircraft on board HMS *Eagle*, XV 740 and XV 281. Both aircraft would be focused on deck take-off performance but 281 was also going to undertake Inertial Navigation Trials. Ferranti had developed a piece of kit designated FINRAE (ask me not what the acronym stands for) which was designed to permit the Inertial Platform on the aircraft to align whilst at sea. Normally you had to be stationary for 12 minutes or so to do a full alignment on land but being linked up to FINRAE theoretically permitted you to overcome that problem.

After many STOs off the deck painted on the runway, we were ready to go to sea at the beginning of March. I had a discussion with Ian Keppie as to who should lead the trip out to the carrier, HMS *Eagle*, cruising in Luce Bay. I told him that it was only proper that the CO of the squadron should lead the sortie and he responded that the right thing was for the nominated trials pilot to lead. Truth be known, we were both a bit nervous about being able to find the carrier on the first attempt and were keen to shift the responsibility on to the other. However rank had its way and I was told in no uncertain terms that I would be leading. We launched from Boscombe on a cold morning of the 9 March 1970 and in the event had no problem locating and landing on the carrier.

HMS *Eagle* was working up for a commission with a squadron of Buccaneers and a squadron of Sea Vixens on board. The captain was John Treacher, Wings was Ted Anson who had in his former life been a test pilot as well which was helpful, as we were generally regarded by most on board as a nuisance and a bar to progress. We were allocated the forward hangar in which the FINRAE equipment, our ground crew plus all their equipment were located. Having landed we were marshalled to the forward lift and whisked down to the hangar, and as I climbed out of the aircraft I found a full union meeting taking place. All of our ground crew were civilians although most of them were ex-servicemen and, on this occasion, a lot of them ex-RN. It seemed that when they had arrived on board the previous evening, no arrangements had been made for their accommodation on board. As a consequence they had had to sleep wherever they could—on the bar, in armchairs and so on. The dismay must have shown on my face and the 'shop steward' took me aside and said to me, 'Don't worry Graham, we aren't going to let you down but we are just making a point.' Having made their point and after the Navy sorted out the accommodation fiasco, they set to with a will.

We were given 'lift times' to come on deck for a launch and we had to meet those times or miss the sortie. The fact that this was a trials programme was of no interest to the Navy who were conducting a full flying programme for their own work-up. We would fly six sorties a day and, as far as I can remember, we only missed one lift time in 12 days because of an unserviceability.

The main aim of the trial was to define the optimum performance and technique for free deck take-offs, a secondary aim was to look at the performance of the IN. We started off at very light weights and then gradually increased the fuel load and the weapons load until we reached the maximum AUW or achieved a 12 ft sink off the end of the carrier. For those not versed in deck take-offs, any sink seems a long way; a 12ft sink seems horrendous. The first problem I encountered was taxying around the deck; you came up the forward lift, started the engine and then had to taxy to the round down at the far end of the deck. With the ship doing about 30 kts forward and you taxying at 5 kts or less in the opposite direction, it gave you the sensation of rushing at 35 kts to the aft end and very likely to end up in the wake of the carrier. When you finally reached the round down, the marshallers made you go so close to the edge that you could only see the wake of the ship as the cockpit of the Harrier is well ahead of the nose wheel. The petty officer doing the marshalling left you in no doubt as to what he thought of your parentage and the colour of the streak down your back. It was a relief to get lined up and then take-off which by then seemed relatively simple. There was just one other little facet that nearly caught me out. Whilst we had done all those take-offs on the runway deck at Boscombe, you were always still in ground effect when you got airborne which meant that you got a slight pitch down which you countered with a bigger pull back on the stick. Off the carrier, as you left the deck you were immediately out of ground effect with a tendency to pitch up. I had not taken that into account on my first take-off and pulled back as I had done on the runway only to find myself pointing almost vertically at the sky. Having thoroughly frightened myself, I managed to recover the aircraft and climb nonchalantly away. If it had not been for the fact that we were at a very light weight, I am not sure what would have happened.

This trial went on interspersed with 'Press Days' and a demo for the Imperial Defence College. The weight slowly got heavier and heavier until we achieved the 12 ft sink off the end, a sink which certainly got my attention. The idea was that that defined the max AUW for take-off once it had been scaled back to an 8 ft sink for the average squadron pilot. We had a number of VIP visitors, press and government officials and Bill Scheuren, who was by this stage the USMC exchange pilot at Boscombe, and who represented the USMC's interest in the trial. He was meant to witness two days of flying but was sandbagged by various FAA aircrew and their flight surgeon (yes, the flight surgeon, yet again, who seemed hell bent on practising his anaesthesia skills) on his first night on board; so much so that he spent the whole time in his cabin and never saw a single take-off or landing. I have often wondered exactly what he said in his report back to the USMC.

All in all it was a successful trial. The Navy were impressed that we had managed to do exactly what we said we would do with the minimum of fuss. We had also managed to create favourable comment because we had remembered to arrive on board with an 'E' painted on the tail of our aircraft to denote our assignment to HMS *Eagle*. Both aircraft had stayed serviceable and FINRAE was proved to be a feasible piece of equipment for aligning the navigation equipment at sea. The subsequent development of the ski jump would only enhance matters. HMS *Ark Royal* had appeared at one stage and, as far as I am aware, that was the last time that the two Royal Navy carriers, HMS *Eagle* and HMS *Ark Royal* were seen sailing together.

We returned to Boscombe on 20 March 1970 and continued with all our other activities—Phantom weapons, Phantom Recce pod, numerous Harrier trials including a night flying trial mainly to test the efficacy of a certain lighting system for VLs on a pad at night. We had concluded that to test it properly required an airfield without any lighting. At an airfield like Boscombe it is surprising how much peripheral light there is around even if you switch off all the airfield lights, so we decided to try and use Upavon which was in the middle of the Salisbury Plain with little surrounding habitation. Whilst we did conclude that the lighting system was quite usable, we also managed to frighten ourselves on a number of occasions!

The Harrier Hot Weather Trial was to take place at Yuma, Arizona and Cherry Point in North Carolina. The nominated pilots were to be myself as the leader and trials manager and Bill Scheuren the USMC exchange pilot at Boscombe. Normally we would have taken a trials management project officer with us but it was decided to dispense with their services for reasons of economy and leave it to me. I had gone out to Yuma a couple of months previous to the trial to look at the facilities and the accommodation. The USMC could not have been more helpful and we were given whatever we asked for. Being on the border of Mexico, they were not short of Mexican Restaurants, but there was one that seemed to be favoured by the locals and that was called Creteens. The USMC introduced me to this establishment on my first recce visit and I had managed to impress the local Mexicans by eating a full bowl of red and green jalapenos. This was to come back and haunt me when I returned.

We shipped the aircraft, XV 741, out by air and then had to assemble it at Yuma. I flew out by BOAC to Los Angeles and called in to The Douglas Aircraft Company at Long Beach as they were going to provide support if I needed it. I met Stan Hubbard, who was ex-RAF and had been the chief instructor at ETPS in a former life. He surprised me by showing me that he had a full set of technical drawings for the aircraft and that there was nothing they did not know about it; a fact which came in very useful as it happened.

Besides a fairly small team of engineers to service the aircraft, we had a couple of trials engineers and a RAF doctor, Sean Marshall, with us. His job was to monitor the physical aspects of flying the aircraft in high temperatures and to help him he had wired us up with an inner body temperature probe (in the ear, not where you are thinking) with a read-out on our kneepads. We were under strict instructions that we had to abort the sortie if the reading went above a particular level. The aircraft was ready to fly on the 1 July and I duly strapped in to do the air-test. The first thing that happened was the doctor's inner body temperature limit was exceeded before I had even finished strapping in, so we decided to ignore that little problem, and from then on things went well—although the doctor was a bit miffed that we had decided to ignore his advice.

Initially we had decided to live off base in a motel but it quickly became evident that it would be more cost effective and convenient to live on base. The only downside to that was that the base was full of US Navy Reserve squadrons who had taken Admiral Zumwalt at his word and had the longest hair of any units I had ever seen in the military—that was until I came across the Dutch armed services later on. Bill Scheuren, being of the old-fashioned USMC discipline, took personal umbrage at this and wanted to take issue with them all about their appalling lack of personal discipline. I had to remind Bill that he was part of a UK team and that I did not want an international incident on account of the long haired USN aviators. They were not even a part of the USMC but as far as Bill was concerned they were on a USMC base and should therefore conduct themselves appropriately. Bill was persuaded to keep his mouth shut but you could see him seething every time these guys walked into the bar.

I had been told by Air Cdre Eric Burchmore, the Harrier Project Officer in London, that I was not to do anything other than get on with the trial. However from the day of arrival I was continually harassed by the press who wanted to get a good look at the aircraft and see it fly. It finally got to the state that I could not ignore them any more so I rang the Air Cdre and told him that the only way I could satisfy the local interest was to give a Press Day and a demo. His response to me was that I was the man on the spot and whatever decision I made would have his whole-hearted support, so we organised a Press Day at 0630 in the morning. With it being mid-summer, that was the only time of the day that I would be able to guarantee a vertical capability. But the excuse I used was that with a full test programme to complete in the heat of the day, 0630 in the morning was the only time we had available. We got away with it and the Press Day successfully took the pressure off us.

The test programme went on uneventfully until we suddenly discovered a burst air duct in the conditioning system, quite how or why it happened nobody knew, but we suspected that the duct was made of titanium and nowhere in Yuma was there a titanium welding facility. As a result of this we were going to have to rely on the offer of help from the Douglas Aircraft Company. I rang Stan Hubbard and explained the problem; he told me to stand by and wait while they checked up at their end and, having looked at all their drawings, they rang back to say that it was steel and not titanium. We welded up the duct, wrapped it in tape dipped in adhesive and were able to carry on with the trial. The duct never gave us any more trouble.

We were not quite so busy that we did not have time to socialise. At that time we were the first Brits to use Yuma and were very much a novelty. I found myself talking to several breakfast meetings—an experience quite new to me. We were invited out to Sunday lunch at a ranch and it turned out to be one of the biggest disappointments of my life. I had expected to find something like the High Chaparral, see a great many horses and cowboys and be fed an enormous steak for lunch. Instead, what did I find? A ranch house just inhabited by a couple, albeit charming people, and just 20 acres of alfalfa fields that fed cows which never saw the light of day. And what did we get for lunch? A chicken curry—'to make us feel at home'!

We also had a memorable outing to Mexico. The border at San Luis was only a short distance away so we decided to have a day's outing to Mexico. We had a hire car and the rules were such that you were not allowed to take it across the border. So we drove up to the US border post, parked the car and walked across into the town of San Luis. As we arrived, we could see that a dust storm was about to arrive, which it did, closely followed by a violent rain storm. We just had time to duck into a Cantina before the heavens opened, and with its raised wooden sidewalks and earthen streets, it was just like something straight out of a Western film. The streets were reduced to mud in no time flat and became totally unusable. So we availed ourselves of the facilities of the cantina for a couple of hours, by which time the sun had come out again and dried off everything. We then decided to take a taxi to 'Boystown', a euphemism for a somewhat dubious entertainment centre in the desert where anything goes. For some reason which now escapes me, I still had the imprest of a thousand dollars or so on me; and, as we disappeared into the desert for some time, I started to get worried that Pancho Villa or at least his modern equivalent would come hurtling out of the hills and relieve me of all our money, but we finally arrived at 'Boystown' unmolested to find that it consisted of half a dozen cantinas in a horseshoe in the middle of the desert. It was one of the sleaziest operations I have ever experienced, it turned out that most of the so-called girls were men, the places were filthy and it was a relief to escape back to our taxi and back to civilisation—with the imprest still intact.

For some reason obviously connected with PR, I was tasked to take the aircraft to Los Angeles International. The flight is impressed on my memory although the precise reason for it lost in the sands of time. The flight to LA was uneventful but when I arrived the weather, much to my surprise, was pretty awful. Whilst it was clear above 2000 ft, the visibility below 2000 ft was minimal, and I found myself joining the LA approach system in a long queue of commercial aircraft. Sitting at 2000 ft on the way in I could see 707s, 727s, DC8s etc. to the side of me (they used two runways simultaneously at LA), in front of me and behind me. I was vectored on to the final approach with my speed being adjusted to keep the separation between aircraft and as I got to seven miles told to complete the approach with ILS. There was only one little problem and that was I did not have ILS. I have to say that the reaction of the LA controllers was pretty sharp and they converted to giving me a stepdown radar approach which I do not suppose they had done in years. I met a bunch of VIPs (ask me not who) and a couple of my own ground crew, Taff Johns and Derek Dawkins, who usually followed me around by civil air and who made a great show of asking me for the toolkit whenever we went anywhere. The 'toolkit' consisted of two Allen keys welded together which I carried in my flying suit pocket. I departed LA and, without thinking, accelerated to 400 kts plus for the short trip to the Douglas facility at Long Beach. Air Traffic came on the air very quickly and asked me what speed I was doing. I had totally forgotten about the 250 kt restriction below 10,000 ft and quickly decelerated. The voice from Air Traffic said, 'That's better!' I landed at Long Beach where I left the aircraft overnight in a car park with an armed guard. I was entertained in the Yacht Club at Long Beach that night and returned to Yuma the following morning.

Having managed to fight off the press, the next problem was the Commandant of Marine Aviation. The Marines had by this time committed to buy the Harrier and his staff officer, a US Marine Colonel, kept ringing me up and asking me to take the aircraft to El Toro (a very large USMC air base just outside San Diego) to show it to the troops. I kept saying that we did not have the time and that I did not have the authority for such an undertaking. In the end I acceded to the smooth talking son-of-a-bitch, but not before I had extracted a promise from him that, if I was sacked from the RAF, I could have the equivalent rank and seniority in the USMC. It was, he said, a deal. Fortunately I never had to test it. The following day I diverted on a trials flight to El Toro and much to my astonishment found the whole base lined up and was greeted by a couple of generals who thrust a microphone into my hand and said, with their usual persuasive manner, 'Now Squad Leader, talk', and talk I did for 30 minutes or so, and then I escaped back to Yuma. I do not think London ever discovered about that little foray.

We had just about completed our trials sorties at Yuma and it was time to take the aircraft across country to Cherry Point. It was while I was in the planning room planning my route that I heard someone do the most enormous belch. Without even thinking or looking up, I said in my best British accent, 'After you with the trough, old boy.' There was a hushed silence and I turned round to find that the perpetrator was a very large black NCO. The whole room, having held its breath, collapsed with laughter and the NCO grinned feebly with embarrassment. A major international incident was averted!

Having been given the responsibility for the whole trial, it became my responsibility to move the whole outfit from one side of the US to the other. I had hired a truck to take the spare engine to Cherry Point by road and a Lockheed Electra to take all the other equipment by air. I was horrified when a 727 appeared instead of the Electra (which was a far cheaper option) until I discovered that they were only going to charge me the same as they had quoted for the Electra. We had also looked at the possibility of the USMC providing C130 tankers for the trip to Cherry Point, but as I had to go via St Louis to give MacDonnell Douglas their first look at the aircraft they were going to build under licence, it was all going to be under the heading of 'too difficult'. Instead, I decided to refuel at Amarillo—the choice of airfield being largely driven by the availability of a certain type of jet fuel. The trip was uneventful until my arrival at St Louis. For some reason I had not appreciated that the airfield at St Louis, apart from being the facility from which MacDonnell Douglas flew, was also the main airport, so when I appeared and decided to give them a little display it was not long before I had a major violation filed on me. A sweet smile, a profession of ignorance, and an apology smoothed over my misdemeanour and I was cleared to do a proper display on the next day before leaving for Cherry Point. Having landed, I was met by Sandy McDonnell, John Fozard, Hawker Siddeley Aviation's Chief Designer for the Harrier, John Dale, Roll Royce's Chief Designer of the Pegasus, and Air Cdre Eric Burchmore, the MoD Harrier project Officer and Jack Crossthwaite, the Harrier Project man at MacDonnell Douglas.

The second part of the hot weather trial was meant to be a test during hot and humid conditions, but before we did that we had to give a demonstration to the US Senate and Congress. This was to take place at Quantico where the USMC had set up stands either side of the runway and many helos to ferry the high priced help in and out. We had a discussion as to what we could do; all we had was a clean aircraft or one with two 100 gallon tanks which was not going to impress anyone; but we did have all the weapons pylons—but no weapons. I decided that the only thing we could do was borrow some bombs off the USMC, load them on our aircraft for the demo and drop them off the aircraft once airborne before returning to do a V/STOL display. Fortunately there was a bombing range a very short distance from Quantico. It was, of course, highly illegal, for we had no clearance to carry US weapons let alone a clearance to drop them, nevertheless that is what we did. I can well remember arriving over the range, selecting all the pylons and pressing the bomb release in the hope that they all released and nothing went wrong. The display went well; that is I thought it did. I discovered many years later that many of the attendees had had their suits and uniforms covered in spots of molten tarmac. It seems that the USMC had just resurfaced the runway and the combination of the new asphalt and the Harrier was just too much for the tarmac and many of those standing a little bit too close to the action got sprayed with a very fine tar.

Having finished at Quantico we returned to Cherry Point to continue the Hot Weather Trial. We lived in a motel just off the base and, it being North Carolina, they had some pretty strange rules with regarding to drinking and bars. Our ground crew found it all a bit irksome and, by sharing rooms, they made a spare room into a bar. This became a very popular spot with a number of the locals and the management of the motel finally took umbrage at the arrangement, and demanded that we closed the bar or left the motel. We somewhat reluctantly acceded to their request.

Unfortunately the weather never achieved high enough temperatures and humidity to complete the trial so we decided to call it a day after a couple of abortive sorties, and dismantled the aircraft to take it back to the UK. Bill Scheuren and I climbed on a BOAC jet from Washington and went straight back home. All in all, apart from the somewhat abortive part of the trial at Cherry Point, it had been a successful trip. We achieved most of what we had set out to do, flown the aircraft all over the USA, and, apart from the incident of the burst air duct, the aircraft had been very reliable. Hot weather had not proved to be a problem aside from the effect that it had on the hover performance, but we had known that to be the case from the start; and over the years the improved Pegasus engines overcame the problem to an extent.

Back at Boscombe it was back to a mix of Phantom trials, mainly of the Recce pod, and Harrier trials including high incidence handling and some weapons trials, a weekend trip to Malta in a Hunter T7 for a bit of light relief and finally, the not so welcome news that I had been selected for the 1971 Staff College Course at Bracknell. Before I left I was tasked to undertake an operational assessment of the Jaguar A at Istres in the South of France. I went down there with Robin Hargreaves, who was the Jaguar project pilot and, having attended the French Test Pilots course at EPNER, was totally fluent in French. Robin was the arch typical Englishman—until he crossed the Channel when he donned a beret, had a Gauloises drooping from his mouth and became the arch typical Frenchman. This was just as well as I had some difficulty in understanding what was going on. It was the very early days of the Jaguar and it had some fairly severe limitations, not least of which were with the engines. On one engine you could only engage reheat for take-off but not once airborne. The other engine had a ridiculously high JPT limit. As I recall the JPT limit on the port engine was around 620° C and the other over 800° C. Robin borrowed a Dassault Mystère IV from the French Air Force and we did a bit a dissimilar combat—but not too energetic; even so I managed to exceed the incidence limit, which got the French a bit excited. I did two trips and I was impressed by the fuel economy at low level but not by much else. The fuel system was a disaster compared to most aircraft I had flown and appeared to be far too easy to mismanage. BAe and Dassault were trying to sing the praises of the machine by saying that it would go a long way at low level and would give the pilot a superbly comfortable ride; to me that was a euphemism for no thrust and no wing so that it would not turn worth a damn. Having subsequently completed a tour on Jaguars, my views have not changed although, funnily enough, it was an aircraft that I would have been comfortable going to war in.

My tour as a test pilot came to an end, one year at ETPS at Farnborough and four years at Boscombe. I was lucky compared to many as my tour coincided with the introduction of three new fighter aircraft, the Harrier, the Phantom and the Jaguar. It had been an interesting and challenging time with many interesting trials taking place especially with the Harrier. In those days, if you were unlucky with your timing you could do three years at Boscombe and not see a single new aircraft. We saw three and a myriad of challenges, including the air race which turned out to be a particularly significant event involving a certain amount of luck, and an event that I will not forget.

There followed a year at Staff College at Bracknell best described as six months work crammed into a year—but nonetheless welcome; there was plenty of time for golf, cricket and other sundry pastimes. Just before I arrived, I discovered that the new commandant was to be a certain AVM Michael Beetham. I had last met him as the station commander at Khormaksar when he had tried to have me and my Boss, Tam Syme, court-martialled, so I was more than a little concerned that I would be starting on the wrong foot. In the event I need not have worried as he greeted me like a long lost friend and, indeed, he has always done so ever since.

Some little time previously Tom Lecky-T and I had been told that we had been awarded the Harmon Trophy for Aviators for our achievements in the air race with the Harrier. In 1926 Clifford B. Harmon, a wealthy sportsman and aviator, established three international trophies to be awarded annually to the world's outstanding aviator, aviatrix, and aeronaut. A fourth trophy was later created to honour achievements in space flight. The Harmon Trophy—the aviator's award—is given for the most outstanding international achievements in the preceding year, with the art of flying receiving first consideration and the list of winners is like a Who's Who of aviation. Now came the news that it was to be presented to us by the President or Vice President of the USA. At first, the Staff College said that I could not go as it involved a week away. In the end they relented but insisted that I had to do all the work in any case. It just so happened that it coincided with a major exercise that we had been given a week to complete. I had to do it in a day and I remember spending a particularly busy Sunday. So off I went with my wife and Tom and his wife to Washington accompanied by ACM Sir Andrew Humphrey and his wife, Agnes. Because Sir Andrew was a C-in-C at the time we were given a VIP Comet for the trip and travelled in real luxury with just the six passengers. We were accommodated in Washington by the Air Attaché, Air Cdre Crowley Milling. On the morning of the presentation we went off on a so-called VIP tour of the White House returning with an hour or so to spare to change into No. 6 Uniform for the presentation ceremony. I was in the bedroom when I heard a sudden agonised scream from next door. Tom had gone to put on his uniform only to discover that he had no trousers. Tom is quite small; but so, fortunately, was Crowley Milling although not quite so short as Tom. In the end Tom had to borrow a pair of Crowley Milling's trousers pulled up to his armpits, and his own jacket.

The presentation was in the end made by the Vice President, Spiro Agnew. The Space award went to Messrs Armstrong, Aldrin and Collins for their Moon landing with Apollo 11 and the Aviatrix award to Turi Wideroe who was a Norwegian who became the first female airline pilot, helped, if I remember correctly, by the fact that her father owned the airline. The lunch afterwards was at the Army and Navy Club in Washington and I remember being ushered through to the top table whilst my wife was brusquely stopped with the words 'Not you!' Fortunately, Buzz Aldrin's father was behind her and immediately took her under his wing. I ended up sitting next to Neil Armstrong; he had a completely relaxed and very dry sense of humour and made a very enjoyable lunch-time companion. It was a memorable occasion made even better when Neil Armstrong presented me with a NASA book of photographs from space and duly signed it. Buzz Aldrin also signed it but Mike Collins escaped before I could catch him.

The staff college course wound its way to the end and naturally I was only interested in where I would be going next. The postings were finally announced and it was no surprise to me that I was sentenced to a tour in the Ministry of Defence as the man responsible for the Harrier desk in the operations branch. It was just a small office with Tim Barrett, wee Jock Kennedy (no relation to the Air Marshal of the same name) and headed by Wg Cdr Tony Hopkins. I had hardly been there two months when I was suddenly wheeled in to the group captain's office to be told that I was posted to go and take over the Harrier OCU at Wittering and that I was immediately to start refresher flying. I can just imagine how prisoners on death row feel when told that they have been reprieved—for that was how it felt to me. It did lead to a few domestic problems as we had only just bought a house in Camberley, so we decided to sell it and buy a house just outside Wittering which was a minor inconvenience compared to the attraction of the change in posting.

7

Tertius Primus Erit

March 1972 came around and I found myself on the Jet Refresher Course at Manby flying JP4s under the tutelage of Sqn Ldr Bob Hillman. The plan was to do a couple of months at Manby, followed by three months at Brawdy in South Wales flying the Hunter before finally going to Wittering to do the Harrier course. However, I had only been at Manby a few weeks before I got a signal telling me that my posting had been changed; it told me that I was no longer going to take over the Harrier OCU but I was going to become the CO of 54 Sqn. I had to point out that if that was the case I was being sent to the wrong OCU as 54 Sqn was equipped with Phantoms. Quick as a flash the appointments people came back to me and said that what they had meant to say was 4 Sqn not 54 Sqn. Since this was a Harrier squadron in Germany I was quite delighted, especially as teaching people had never been one of my favourite occupations. It did, however, bring further problems with regard to housing and I had to cancel the sale of my house in Camberley and the purchase of the house near Stamford and we decided to let the Camberley house to the MoD for the time we were due to be in Germany.

In less than a month at Manby I had managed to get over 30 hours flying and it was beginning to feel as though I had got my hand back in without too much trouble. I was fortunate in that I had only been off flying for 15 months and had not really had time to lose my touch. Occasionally some people had real difficulties when they had been on extended ground tours and getting back into the 'habit' of flying was not always easy.

Furthermore the system said that I was to forget about going to Brawdy and proceed directly to Wittering and join the Harrier course,

Early days at Cranwell, January 1955, 71 Entry being drilled by Flt Sgt Mitchell.

Our billet, having been trashed by 70 Entry.

The training duo of the 1950s, the Provost T1 and the Vampire T11.

The 'Gorillas' Skiffle Group, *from left to right:* Mick Ryam, Ted Nance, Jock Heron, GW and Alan Garside (subsequently killed in a Lightning accident).

2 Sqn at Cranwell, Advanced Flying Training on the Vampire, cadets and instructors.

Our course at Chivenor early 1958, *from left to right:* Bill Stoker, Jock Heron, Dave Cowley, Ted Nance and GW.

54 Sqn outside tour hangar at Odiham, May 1958.

David Harcourt-Smith, Clito, David Ross-MacDonald and GW in Clito's Wine Shop in Kyrenia, Cyprus, June 1958.

54 Sqn aircrew and groundcrew in El Adem, March 1960.

Right: The route followed on the first Gulf Ranger from 54 Sqn Mar/Apr 1960 (n.b. most ferry trips from Aden used this route, the north route going out and south coming back).

Below: The Hunter Dive Bombing team—Pete Phillips, Chris Bruce, Dave Scott, Dicky Dickenson (CO), GW and Terry Carlton.

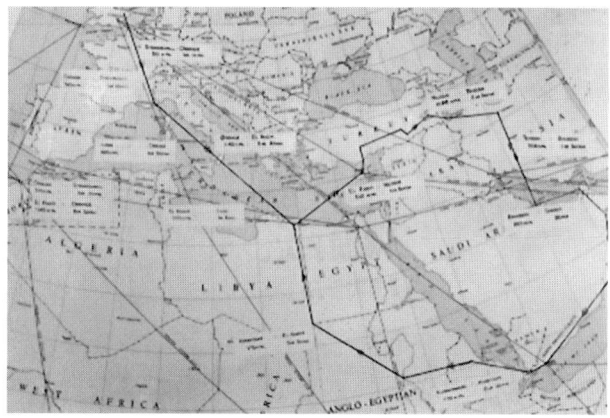

Wedding Bells at St Clement Danes—Sarah, (Judy's niece), David Williams (brother), Judy, GW and my father just behind me, 3 March 1962.

Mr and Mrs Castro at Chivenor, New Years' Eve 1963.

A Hunter 9 in its unique dive bombing configuration, bombs inboard, tanks outboard dropping a 25 lb practice bomb.

Above: No. 42 DFLS Course at Binbrook, February 1963.

Below: Whoops! A two wheeled landing at Binbrook, April 1963.

8 Sqn Bahrein Oct 63. *From left to right:* Nick Adamson, Chris Cureton, Tim Notley, Dave Baron, Jock McVie, the Boss Tam Syme, Gordon Talbot, Mac McCarthy, GW, Sid Bottom and Pete Sturt. Kneeling: Paul Constable, Roy Humphreyson and Owen Truelove.

Above: Christmas morning 1963 on the patio of the Station Commander's house at Muharraq, Bahrein.

Below: My trusty steed on 8 Sqn, XE 609.

Above: An 8 Sqn Hunter with a full load of rockets over Al Qara, Aden as depicted by Mal Grosse, a pilot on 8 Sqn.

Below: 2 × 8 Sqn Hunters in the configuration for the 'Beihan Patrol' as depicted by Mal Grosse.

Above left: A not so trusty steed provided by the Camel Corps of the Federal Republican Army! Khormaksar, Aden.

Above right: 1964 outside my room in the mess with my Mini—ideal transport round Aden.

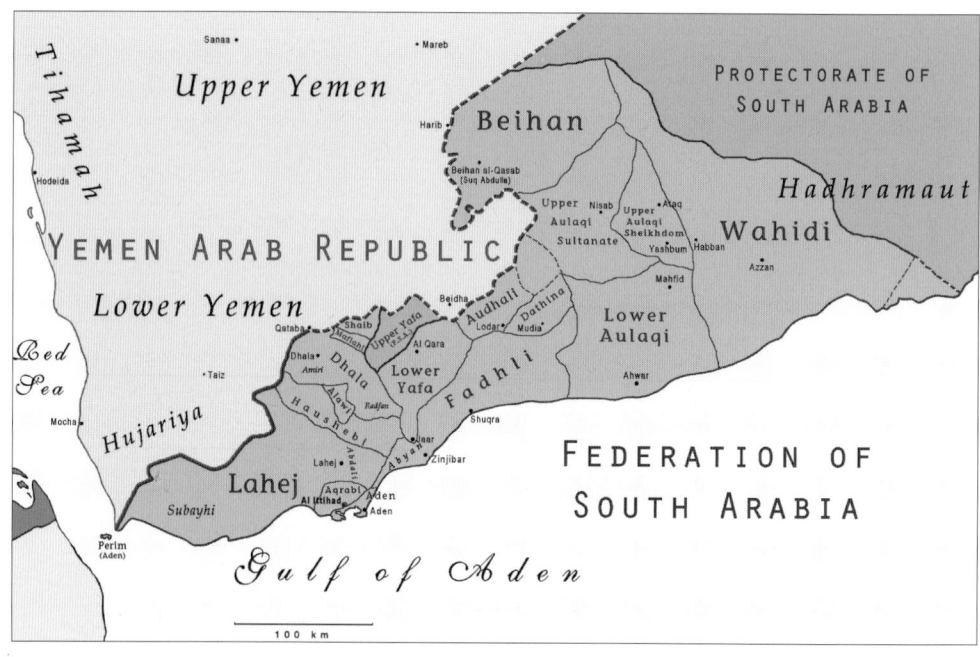

Map of South Arabia. Harib is to the top of the map in the centre.

Above: Map of the Arabian Gulf showing main airfields: (Aden, Riyan, Salalah, Masirah, Sharjah, Bahrein).

Below: The GLO, Capt. Phil Spooner, briefing Roy Humphreyson and GW for an operational sortie.

Above: The pre-strike photo of Harib Fort—nobody mentioned the 70 mm anti-aircraft guns in the brief!

Below: The post-strike photo of Harib Fort.

In the Jungle Bar at Khormaksar. *From left to right standing:* Mike Flynn, Mal Grosse, Mac Mackenzie-Crooks, Dai Rasdall, Chris Cureton, Roy Humphreyson, Lumpy Dix and Chris Hulse. *Seated:* Nick Kerr, Kiwi Hounsell, Tam Syme, GW, Ian Porteous, Mac McCarthy and Martin Johnson.

Judy with our son Mark on Tarshine Beach, Aden.

GW in one of the ETPS Hunters in 1966.

XT 795 a 'Mk 2½' at Boscombe Down—the original Mk 2a prototype with a straight wing, big ventral, big fin and cockpit layout similar to a Mk 3/6—probably one of the best Lightnings of them all—used mainly for CT.

Harrier air-to-air refuelling trials.

TLT and GW hovering either side of the bridge of the *QE2* as depicted by Mal Grosse.

Tom Lecky-T and GW hovering either side of the bridge of the *QE2* on its maiden voyage, entering New York.

Press interview on the pad in Manhattan with the Empire State Building in the background.

TV interview in the GPO Tower in London with JW, having completed the New York—London run

August 1969 at Edwards AFB, Californoa with 'Wally the Whale' (prototype F4K) and Dennis Sharpe, Dick Searle and GW.

March 1970—Approaching HMS *Eagle* for the Deck Trial.

July 1970—At McDonnell Douglas, St Louis with XV 741 (the Canadian marking on the intake was the result of a 'zap' when the aircraft was at Cold Lake) with Jack Crosthwait (MacDac), GW, Air Cdre Eric Burchmore (Harrier Project Officer MOD(PE), John Dale (Chief Designer Pegasus RR), and John Fozard (HSA Chief Designer Harrier).

August 1970—Demo to Congress at Quantico, GW with Bill Scheuren and Taff Johns—whatever it was it looks serious!

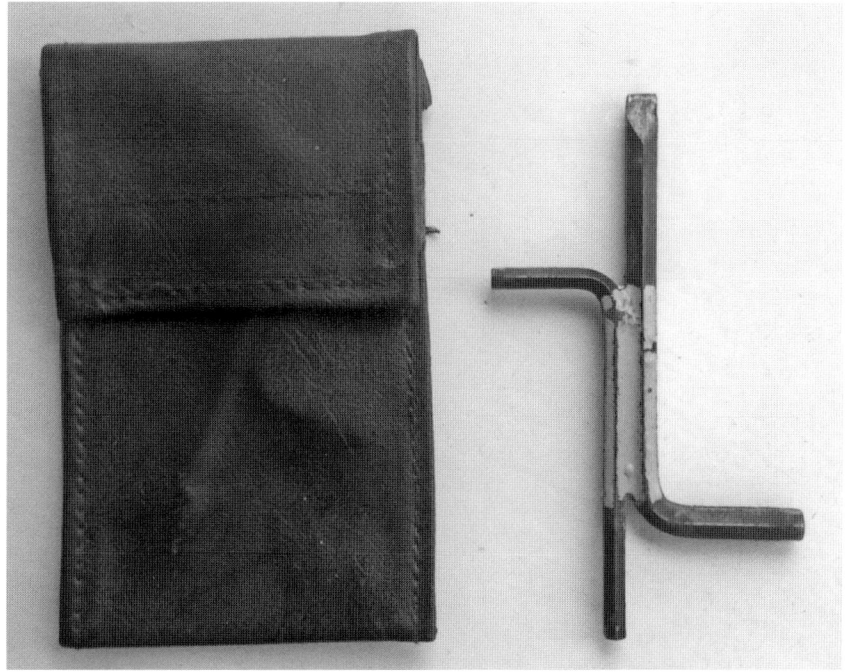

The ubiquitous Harrier toolkit!

1971—JW and GW and the Harmon Trophy.

1973—GW (as OC 3 Sqn) with Terry Nash looking on hosting a visit from the C-in-C AM Sir Nigel Maynard at Wildenrath.

April 1973, George Black, John McGarvey, Pieter van Vollenhoven and GW at RNLAF Deelen.

1973, George Black, AVM Neil Cameron (Dep Cdr RAF Germany), GW at Wildenrath.

August 1973—on an autobahn in Germany *From left to right:* Jack Rust (3 Sqn Exec), GW, Air Cdre Robertson (SASO) and John McGarvey.

1975—3 (F) Sqn.

Harrier GR1, XV741, started off in life in 1968 as part of the test fleet at Boscombe Down, then TLT used it for the Transatlantic Air Race in 1969. GW used it in 1970 for the Hot Weather Trial in Yuma and Cherry Point and touring round the USA - Los Angeles, Long Beach, El Toro, Amarillo, St Louis (McDonnells), and Quantico for a demo to Congress. It subsequently went back to HSA to be refitted and came out to Germany and became 'A' on 3(F)Sqn and GW's personal aircraft.

XV 741 in its 3 Sqn guise—my trusty steed.

1978 – A Brüggen Jaguar with a full warload—rumours that it needed the curvature of the earth to get airborne were totally unfounded.

Above left: Early 1978—AVM Tim Lloyd conducting the AOC's Inspection at Brüggen.

Above right: A visit from the Chief—CAS ACM Sir Michael Beetham outside Station HQ at Brüggen.

Being greeted in the Scruffs' Bar having just come off 'Q' by Nigel Walpole (OC Ops) and Richard Howard (OC 31 Sqn), Mike Gibson (OC 20 Sqn), Al Hudson (subsequently my PSO in MOD) and Joe Sim (OC 14 Sqn).

1979—With W/O Vic Cooper (CMC) and his wife Gudi (who also happened to be our housekeeper) at a dinner dance in the Sergeants' Mess.

1979—the 'Female Guard' of Brüggen's Der Adler Karnival Club strutting their stuff.

Exercise 'Strangled Sonata'—Padre Hubble (Wildenrath) at the keyboard prior to the event.

And after!

Above left: GW and JW Being presented to Princess Anne at the Royal Festival Hall on the occasion of the presentation of the Wilkinson Sword for Peace.

Above right: December 1979—the handover to Peter Taylor with Air Cdre Eric Macey SASO HQRAFG (and my new boss).

August 1982—at the end of the Buccaneer Course with (*left*) Chris Finn and (*right*) David Mullender.

July 1983—strapping in to the SE5a—white scarf and all at RAE Farnborough.

And safely back on the ground

1984—at A&AEE with Brian Childes (Chief Superintendent)

The Bassett—a comfortable way to travel

December 1983—the McKenna Dinner at Boscombe. *Top table from right to left:* GW, AM Sir Mike Beavis, Robin Hargreaves Headmaster and CO of ETPS (hidden behind the flowers), ACM Sir John Rogers—Controller Aircraft and David Bywater—Superintendent of Flying.

The Boscombe Sea Fury TT20

Dec 1985—The last flight in Hunter XE601, greeted by Ron Burrows Superintendent of Flying.

1988—An A&AEE Commandants' Reunion. *Back row left to right:* Reggie Spiers, John Brownlow, David Dick, Roger Topp. *Seated:* Alan Merriman, Geoff Cairns, David Bywater and GW.

Above left: September 1989—what goes around, comes around. On the steps of RAF College Cranwell as the Reviewing Officer.

Above right: 1990—making like the Commandant General of the Regiment with an SA 80.

1991—with my two brothers, David and Charles, in the RAF Club on the occasion of my son's wedding in St Clement Danes, just as I was about to retire.

which had already started. This course included among others, Jeremy Hall, who was going to take over as station commander, and Terry Nash who was going to be a Flt Cdr on 3 Sqn in Germany. Terry had been on the staff college course with me and had delighted in crowing about the fact that he had got a flying posting out of Bracknell whilst we lesser mortals had got staff jobs. It was difficult not to feel a little smug about the abrupt change of circumstances. I did have a slight advantage over the rest of the course as I was the only person who had flown the aircraft previously, so it held no mysteries for me and by the beginning of May I was back flying the Harrier.

On 26 June I was asked to deliver a Harrier to Wildenrath in Germany, which I was delighted to do as it would give me a chance to have a look at the place—I had never been there before—and find out how things were going. I remember vividly arriving in the circuit and turning downwind to land when I got a message that I was to report to the station commander, Gp Capt. George Black, in OC 4 Sqn's office. I immediately assumed that I had performed some dreadful misdemeanour (as you do when summoned by the station commander!) although for the life of me I could not think what it was. I did not think that I had transgressed but assumed that I must have inadvertently done so. It was with some trepidation that I climbed out of the cockpit and walked into OC 4 Sqn's office. George Black greeted me with a smile much to my relief, as he was not well known for his tolerant attitude and opened with the words: 'Welcome to Wildenrath. You think that you are going to be OC 4 Sqn, don't you?' My immediate thought was that I was going to be sacked before I had even arrived. 'Well, you're not. You are going to take over 3 Sqn.' His comment was a relief to me as at least I still had a job. 3 Sqn was the last Harrier squadron to form and was commanded by Phil Champniss. Unbeknown to me, as a result of a number of accidents, OC 20 Sqn had been removed and Phil Champniss had been moved across to take over as they were approaching their operational declaration and it was deemed that Phil's experience and wisdom was required to sort out the problems. 3 Sqn had not yet got its full quota of aircraft and pilots, so there was some time to go before they were declared operational. Meanwhile Jack Rust, one of the flight commanders, was going to stand in as squadron commander until I arrived.

I have heard it said that Phil was to some extent hoist by his own petard as he had personally preselected the pilots on 3 squadron and that therefore I was the fortunate beneficiary of his manipulation of the system. I am not sure that I believe it as my experience of these things is that such manipulation is difficult to achieve and often tends to backfire on you. I well remember that it was actually done by the CO of one of the Hunter squadrons some years back and it did not lead to success. Individually they were all very talented aviators; but they did not gel well mainly because they were all chiefs without any Indians. However there was no doubt that the change worked in my favour because I was to be blessed with a first class bunch of aviators and, just as important if not more so, another outstanding engineer officer—an absolute requisite for success.

I went to Wittering to finish the Harrier course and left there on 10 August 1972 before the main course finished, and a week later I took over 3 Sqn at Wildenrath. The course finished some weeks later although there had been a disastrous accident right at the end when Jeremy Hall, the station commander designate of Wittering was killed when he lost control of the aircraft whilst flying in cloud up in Scotland.

The station commander at Wildenrath was one George Black who had the reputation of being a trouble shooter and another hard man. If you had a problem George would sort it out, although there would probably be a few casualties along the way. That is why the previous OC 20 Sqn had departed somewhat in advance of his predicted tourex date. The local recommendation was that you looked round very carefully before you sat down at the desk in your office—just in case the chair was missing, and it was to be some months before I felt confident enough to sit without checking.

I arrived at Wildenrath one evening in August just in time to join some outrageously rowdy party in the mess. If I remember correctly it was a farewell party for Snowy McKee, the then CO of 4 Sqn who was leaving that week. I was introduced to the station commander's wife, Ella, who was at the time lying on the floor for some unknown reason—it was probably a comfortable place to be. The station might have been under the microscope mainly on account of the number of aircraft accidents, but it surely knew how to party.

The following day I had to go to the headquarters at Rheindahlen for an arrival interview with the senior air staff officer (SASO). He was a slightly odd character with some very fixed views. 3 Sqn was providing a five aircraft display who called themselves the 'Green Arrows' for the Farnborough Air Show. The SASO spent most of the time questioning me about the pilots who had been selected for this, telling me that one pilot in particular should not have been selected. Since I had no idea what he was talking about—I had not had time to peruse the pilots' records as he obviously had—I was somewhat at a disadvantage. And, despite my previous comments, there were one or two with a slightly chequered past. Nevertheless it seemed to me that to change things at this late stage after weeks of practice and with just a week to run before the event was not very sensible and I said so. We agreed to disagree; and it was a thoroughly unsatisfactory discussion. I cannot say that I was enamoured of the welcome. The squadron acquitted itself well and without incident at Farnborough, including the pilot who SASO had doubted the wisdom of selecting.

After the somewhat more relaxed attitude to rules and regulations of the test pilot world, I was now back in the more formal world of the RAF where there were rules and regulations for everything. Not having a full complement of pilots or aircraft, we could not fill all the posts as required by the air staff instructions. I remember standing by the ops desk one day when the ops officer told me that an air-test was required on a particular aircraft. This was a problem as we did not have a designated 'air test pilot' as required by the HQ RAF Germany rules. I was puzzling over this conundrum when I noticed that the pilots gathered around the ops desk were looking at me, waiting for me to say something. It suddenly dawned on me that if I was not qualified to do the air-test then no one was. So off I went, but it demonstrated how one's judgement could be affected by circumstance.

As we were the last Harrier squadron to form and the other two squadrons, 4 and 20, were heading towards their official operational 'declaration' to NATO, the tendency was that we were always last in the queue when it came to equipment and priorities. For the time being our operational posture centred around an on-base dispersal, imaginatively entitled 'Charlie', across the other side of the airfield. We were also used as the inevitable hosts for VIP visits to keep the pressure off the other squadrons. Within a very short time period we had a visit from the C in C of RAF Germany, a certain Sir Harold Martin, better known as Mickey Martin of Dambusters fame, closely followed by the new Deputy Commander, Neil Cameron.

Three days after returning from Farnborough, the squadron was on the move again, this time to GAF Fassberg, an airfield just 20 miles from the East German border and within striking range of Hamburg. Our first major task was providing a detachment of aircraft to go to Fassberg for a week to provide close air support for the Berlin Access Exercise called Live Oak. The detachment was to be led by me but with some 4 Sqn aircraft and pilots to provide reconnaissance expertise and make up the numbers. Fassberg was an old and well found pre-war *Luftwaffe* airbase, and it had also been an RAF base after the war, adjacent to the Inner German Border (IGB); it was now a GAF helicopter training school. There were rules about flying in the so-called 'Buffer Zone' which was a corridor ten miles wide from the border between East and West Germany. Basically flying in the Buffer Zone was forbidden although you could not avoid it going in and out of Fassberg. The exercise was a Tri-Partite one, namely British, French and American and the aim was to practice the procedures and air support required should the Soviets try to close off access to Berlin and the Allies decide to force their way through—which struck me as a tall order. It was combined with a large tripartite army exercise for which very large numbers of tanks were gathered in the Central German plain not far from Gütersloh. In fact it was the largest gathering of armoured vehicles that I have ever seen in one place; impressive, but also one of the best targets I had ever seen. On the air side, one squadron would be provided by each of the three nations and I was nominated as the UK detachment commander and senior allied officer. The French provided a squadron of F100s which deployed to Fassberg with us and the US provided a squadron of F4s although their rules did not allow them to deploy to Fassberg because of the proximity of the IGB. The GAF provided all the support at Fassberg.

This was the first time that Harriers had been involved in this exercise and I had made the not unnatural assumption that someone would tell me what was required and expected. However, advice was non-existent and there were no procedures laid down. I fell back on the alert procedures we had used in Aden in the 60s, namely a cockpit readiness, a 5 minute alert state and 30 minutes which could be held from the crew-room. Interestingly enough, those procedures were maintained for the life of the exercise which went on until the Berlin Wall came down. Unusually, for a Brit, I found the French a delight to have around. They certainly had a 'press on' attitude—a little bit too 'press on' for my taste at times and they made the best of their somewhat clapped out F100s. Their squadron commander, whose surname was, if I remember correctly, Colin, spoke English, albeit with a mix of a French and Cockney accent as he was married to a Cockney girl. He had an interesting mix of pilots including one of Vietnamese descent who drove a Porsche 911 with the words 'Fighter Pilot' painted all over it. One of his junior pilots had not exactly covered himself in glory as he had managed to get a bit lost and arrive via East Germany. Fortunately the East Germans did not notice or chose to ignore it; but the public dressing down of the offender by his mentor was wondrous to observe. Regrettably we saw little of the Americans as they operated out of their own base near the Mosel Valley. I have to admit that their location had much to recommend it; but Fassberg had its attractions as well.

Fassberg is actually on the Lüneburger Heide which is a renowned hunting area—not that we had time for such pastimes. It is also the area which produces a drink—I use the term loosely—called Ratzeputz. It is a mixture of schnapps, ginger and other spices which tastes so disgusting that it naturally had to become the 3 Sqn drink of choice. Schooner races with Ratzeputz became the order of the day and an order to be avoided if it was humanly possible. Fassberg is also close to Hamburg and the delights of the Reeperbahn, another German attraction which has to be seen once at least if only to prove how German tastes are occasionally somewhat dubious. And the final attraction, if it can be called such, of the area is the concentration camp of Bergen-Belsen. Although the camp buildings had been mostly destroyed, they had erected a museum on the site and marked all the mass graves. It was said that when you went there, you never heard any birds singing; and my experience tended to bear that out. It was totally mind-bending just to even think about what had been done at Belsen and it never ceased to amaze me that large numbers of Germans also flocked to the place, dressed in their Sunday best, with their children in tow and often with a picnic to hand. Ratzeputz, the Reeperbahn and Belsen—the choices were not particularly enticing; but the flying on the exercise was outstanding and the GAF were particularly good and attentive hosts. Fassberg was to become a firm annual favourite for 3 Sqn for both the aircrew and the ground crew.

We stayed for just over a week at Fassberg. On arrival I had been met by the group captain ops from HQ RAF Germany and given a quite unnecessary lecture on the importance of flight safety and not having any accidents. Initially I had not recognised him and then I had realised that it was Laurie Jones who, as OC 8 Sqn in the 60s, had had more fatal accidents than just about any unit in the RAF. The GAF provided us with transport wherever we wanted to go including coaches to Hamburg and Belsen; but we had to pay for the Ratzeputz. Personally, I believed that we should have been paid for drinking it. It was an excellent deployment and one which everyone enjoyed. The flying was good and the exercise well organised once we got the hang of what it was we were meant to be doing. The French, surprisingly, were great fun and the Americans noticeable by their absence; we returned to Wildenrath well satisfied. Shortly after our return we were joined by Ian Keppie who, having been my CO at Boscombe Down was going to take over as station commander at Wittering after the demise of Jeremy Hall. Ian chose to do his operational conversion in Germany rather than use the OCU at Wittering, and he spent a pretty hectic, busy and successful couple of months with us just flying as a normal squadron pilot.

One of the disadvantages of being the last squadron to form was that the other squadrons had 'stolen' all the decent kit and we always had to scrounge around for equipment. As new aircraft were delivered to the station, they were allocated to squadrons and a particular old favourite of mine turned up—XV741. This was the aircraft that had started out at Boscombe as my operational reliability trials aircraft—a trial that went by the board when aircraft had to be reallocated to different tasks because of accidents. It was the aircraft that Tom Lecky-T used for the transatlantic air race and it was the aircraft I had used for the hot weather trial at Yuma and flown all over the USA. After its time at Boscombe it had gone back to Hawkers to be refurbished and then sent out to Germany. Naturally I asked for it to be allocated to 3 Sqn and, when it was, it became 'A' and my personal steed for the remainder of my tour.

Another equipment debate that took place at the time was the allocation of engines to squadrons. We had three Marks of engine on the wing, Pegasus 101,102 and 103. The 101 was the original engine, the 102 the next stage of development and the 103 was the most powerful and hence, theoretically, the most desirable of the three. I had always felt that the 102 engine was the best and most well balanced of the bunch although it did not have quite the thrust of the 103. Because the number of different engines could cause some confusion among the pilots, I volunteered to take all the 102 engines, foregoing my allocation of 103s so that we could achieve some measure of standardisation. There were no facts to back my feelings and the only thing I can add in my defence is that we never had an engine failure on 3 Sqn with a 102 engine—unlike the 103s on the rest of the Wing. I have since discussed this with a Pegasus engine expert and he denied that there was any justification to support my theory, but I remain unconvinced.

Slowly but surely we were getting up to full strength of pilots and aircraft, with the addition of Mike Young, Rocky Goodall and Tony McKeon and, shortly after Christmas, Terry Nash and Al Cleaver as flight commanders and finally Bob Iveson. We lost one pilot, Geoff Hulley, who went to join 1 Sqn at Wittering—and subsequently found fame—I use the term loosely—after bailing out somewhat spectacularly from the hover at a demonstration in Cyprus. At least he proved that the ejection seat was fit for purpose! Nevertheless, we were approaching a full complement. We had demonstrated the flexibility of the aircraft by operating off a strip of autobahn in the south. Interestingly the autobahn had been designed and built as a stand-by airfield. The centre section could be easily taken out and there were lay-bys that were not really lay-bys at all but hard-standings for parked aircraft.

Having survived the excesses of Fassberg, Christmas and other festivities, the middle of February saw us deploy to Decimomannu for an APC (Armament Practice Camp). Deci, in Sardinia, was run by the Italian Air Force, with a large German contingent and the only aim of the exercise was to practise our weaponeering, namely retard bombing, rocketing (SNEB) and strafe with our 30 mm cannon. The range, at Capo Frasca, was run by the Italians who had a penchant for closing it at the slightest excuse. The telephone in the ops room would go and the Italian range safety officer would come up with the all too familiar words, 'Gentlemen, the range she is a closèd!' The usual reason was the wind being too strong which meant that the air sea rescue element was unable to do its job. I even went up to the range to try and understand what they were on about. I have to say that I was extremely well looked after; they had a very nice little mess and, having been shown all the facilities, I was invited to join them for lunch. As we were walking back to the mess we passed a fully equipped diver sitting on the jetty. The RSO, as he passed him, kicked him into the water, with the immortal words 'Hey, Mario, fish for lunch!' And sure enough Mario produced fresh fish for lunch which was grilled over a barbecue with a very nice wine to accompany it. They certainly knew about the creature comforts of life; but we did not manage to improve the availability of the range.

We used to fly around 24 sorties a day just going to the range which was about 50 nms north of the airfield. Serviceability was always an issue especially with the scarcity of spares available in Deci. John McGarvey, my engineer officer, was one of the finest and could nearly always find a way to fix a problem, not necessarily by conventional means. He and Owen Truelove, the engineer officer on 8 Sqn, had very similar attitudes; that was to ensure that they achieved the maximum serviceability with the minimum of resources. John used to be found patrolling up and down the line dressed in shorts, desert boots and no shirt every time a wave of aircraft started up just to make sure all was well. There would always be a spare aircraft just in case one went unserviceable on start. On one occasion he was patrolling as usual when the aircraft started up. As he was passing one of the aircraft he saw the outriggers starting to retract. He knew immediately what was happening—the pilot had unwittingly started up with the undercarriage selected up. Without hesitating he grabbed a main undercarriage lock and dived beneath the aircraft jamming the lock in the undercarriage before the main wheel had a chance to move. The starting cycle of the Harrier is comparatively leisurely; but even if the pilot had realised that was happening he could have done nothing to stop the undercarriage from collapsing in the circumstances. If he had stop-cocked the engine the residual hydraulic pressure in the system would have retracted the wheel. The only thing that could have prevented an accident was John's instant reaction, but we never discovered how or why the undercarriage had been selected to the up position with, coincidentally, the weight on wheels switch, which should have prevented the undercarriage from moving, way out of adjustment. John and the ground crew managed to keep most of the aircraft serviceable for most of the time, some claimed, as a result of the 'Doughnut Wave' concept—each pilot who returned with a serviceable jet was awarded a sticky doughnut.

While the main activity was obviously concentrated on flying, other activities included such things as playing cards, drinking with the Germans and eating. For some peculiar reason we used to have a competition which involved getting the biggest restaurant bill you could manage and the person who got nearest to the final total got a free meal. Surprisingly it was not the likes of Bob Iveson, a renowned trencherman, who ate the most. John Grogan, a slip of a lad, could usually excel at the table. Watching him eat a T-bone steak for his fifth course was a sight to behold. A restaurant called La Pineta, commonly referred to as Orange Chairs, because of the nature of the furniture, was usually the recipient of our largesse, and they even did not mind when Vaughan Dow stood on the table and carried out his well-known impersonation of the 'Stripper' which was as suggestive as you could imagine without him taking off a single item of clothing. In fact he had all the locals cheering him on like mad.

It was Alec Wedderburn, who was the local RAF unit commander, who persuaded us to venture miles into the hills to another restaurant which, he assured us, would give us an experience of the local cuisine. I felt it prudent to hand over the driving of my Land Rover to Jack Cobb, our tame regiment officer and squadron adjutant. As we went further and further into the hills, the road became narrower and windier and Jack's driving became more and more erratic until he finally bounced off the retaining rails and I thought our time had come. Jack seemed to regard the whole procedure as quite normal. It was with some relief that we finally arrived at our destination which did not show many signs of being a restaurant, but they served some magnificent food accompanied by pretty basic but fiery wine. My main memory of the whole occasion was of a cockerel which insisted on joining us at the table finally perching on McKeon's head which made eating a bit tricky.

No visit to Sardinia would be complete without a trip to Forte's Village ostensibly to carry out dinghy drill in the pool but in reality to have a decent lunch and the other memorable occasion was a Sunday visit to Oristano to witness the Carnival. Sunday was the culmination of a three day festival; the locals closed off all the streets covering the surfaces with sand and proceeded to have what was basically a medieval tournament on horseback with the riders wearing magnificent costumes. They rode through the streets at a full gallop culminating in trying to catch a silver star with a sword in front of the Duomo in the historic main square. And finally they performed acrobatics on horseback whilst galloping through the streets. There was some magnificent horseflesh on display and some really amazing displays of skill; it was an event not to be missed.

Cards was another activity which was used to pass the time at weekends. This included Bridge foursomes, not that the *aficionados* of the game would have recognised it as such, and another game which went by the name of 'Pot'. Pot was an extremely dangerous card game which could reach extremely high stakes in a very short time. The inevitable happened and people were getting very much out of their depth; one Sunday afternoon, Rocky Goodall was about to lose all his savings, a loss which would have been critical as he was about to get married. I did the only thing possible in the circumstances—declared the game null and void and banned it for ever more!

I suppose the only other activity which bears a mention was the tendency to partake of the odd beer every now and again. Because the bar in the Italian officers' club was not totally to our taste, the RAF squadrons had built their own bar in one of the upstairs rooms in the barrack block named the Pig and Tapeworm (ask me not why) where some serious late night imbibing could take place without interference. Having said that, there was a memorable night when we were having a 'quiet' get together with the Norvenich GAF F104 squadron which was very suddenly and rudely interrupted by the Italian duty officer who came up the stairs, waving a revolver, threatening all and sundry, saying 'You makea too mucha noise. You closa da bar and go to bed'. To which the German squadron commander's reaction was to pick the Italian up by the scruff of the neck, ignoring the revolver, and throw him down the stairs with the immortal words, 'Vy don't you shuddup. At least ve came second!' Who said that the Germans don't have a sense of humour!

We had a pretty good rapport with the German F104 Squadron in general and I with my opposite number—or so I thought, so when he came to me and asked if he could put some freight on our support aircraft to go back to Germany (as Norvenich was very close to Wildenrath), I readily agreed without asking any questions. Unbeknown to me these so called spares were in fact a couple of crates of duty free cigarettes and alcohol. Somehow the RAF police sergeant had got wind of this and all sorts of hell broke out with threats of courts martial and a major international incident. I managed to persuade the local authorities to drop all the charges; but our friendship with the Germans came to a rapid end. *Plus ça change!*

Such was the entertainment at Decimomannu, but despite the best efforts of the IAF, it was enjoyable and achieved the purpose of a weapons practice camp. We tried to beat the record by carrying out over 400 sorties which, in less than four weeks, would have been quite an achievement especially considering the number of times the Italians closed the range. However we did not quite make it, and to add insult to injury, our return to Wildenrath was delayed by four or five days because the RAF air transport had been required to go elsewhere. This caused much dismay and consternation amongst the families back at Wildenrath and my wife and Grace Smith, the flight sergeant's wife, had to go round passing on the bad news, receiving a certain amount of flak in the process. Eventually, on 26 March, to the relief of everyone, we finally returned home.

It was on one such return from a Deci detachment that I got myself into hot water with the wives on the squadron. They had decided that the crew room and coffee bar was a disgrace. It stank of stale cigarette smoke and sweaty flying suits and behind the coffee bar was a rest home for cockroaches. In fact it was just like most aircrew coffee bars, totally unhygienic! So, while we were away they had given the place a thorough spring clean. I walked in and, without thinking, said that the place smelt like a tart's bedroom and asked what had been going on. It took some days before I was spoken to again by the wives! In fact even today some of them do not hesitate to remind me of the incident.

Life returned to normal—if indeed life at Wildenrath could ever be described as such. Slowly but surely we had built up to full strength with 13 aircraft and, with the arrival of New Zealander Arthur Gatland (a.k.a. Adolf Galland or just Kiwi) and Roger Gault, 16 pilots. We were the first Germany Harrier squadron to achieve its monthly flying task, a fact which owed much to the senior engineering officer and all the ground crew. We used to have a regular aircrew/ground crew get together in the crew room to discuss life with a few beers. After a lengthy dialogue concerning the interface of technological and aviation affairs, most aircrew were seen to retire with a peculiar deformity of the ear and a bruise on the chest! However the squadron was generally reckoned to have the most cheerful ground crew, the most serviceable aircraft, and the most professional aircrew who continually flew more than the rest of the wing. No doubt there would be some who would disagree with that statement, but that was our (unbiased!) view.

In April I had to fly to the RNLAF base of Deelen to fly Pieter Van Vollenhoven, the husband of Princess Margriet of the Netherlands, in the Harrier T2. He had served in the RNLAF and I believe he was also a qualified pilot. He was a pleasant fellow and seemed to be quite keen on a flight in a Harrier and also appeared to enjoy it. A little later on I checked the rear cockpit after the flight and found a used sick bag tucked down by the side of the seat—something he had failed to mention.

Because the weather was invariably poor, and in order to keep up with the flying task, we would often send aircraft away for the weekend, usually to the UK. Valley was a favourite location, not because it was a particularly nice place to go but because they were more willing than most to accept a visitation. We would leave Wildenrath on a Friday afternoon, fly a couple of sorties on Saturday and then return leisurely on Sunday.

May 1973 was made memorable for me on account of the Queen's Birthday Flypast at Rheindahlen. The plan was for a sixteen-aircraft flypast of the parade ground at the headquarters of RAF Germany at Rheindahlen. It would be led by four Phantoms, followed by four Buccaneers, then four Lightnings and, finally at the back end, four Harriers. Each section had an airborne spare just in case anyone went unserviceable. The first couple of rehearsals went pretty well but the final full dress rehearsal was a different story. The weather was appalling and as we were going around the racetrack route, the whole formation went into cloud. Almost immediately the leader in the F4s declared 'everyman for himself' and that the 'flypast was cancelled'. Being down at the back end I could see what was coming and, with my airborne spare, I ducked beneath the cloud. I headed back towards Wildenrath and, as I did so,

I saw Rheindahlen through the mist and rain. I looked at my watch, saw that the timing would be about right, and decided that at least the Harriers would put on a show, so I called in the airborne spare, forgetting that there was a flying order which expressly forbade formations of more than four aircraft (for some unknown reason), and we flew from north to south instead of west to east across the main parade ground about 15 seconds early on the schedule.

I thought no more about it and returned to Wildenrath. I had to keep the five aircraft airborne for 50 minutes to ensure that we met our monthly flying target again, so I passed the time by giving the airfield the benefit our formation flying expertise and as I turned downwind to land, I got the message that the squadron commander was to report to the station commander as soon as he landed. I realised I had in some way sinned but really could not think what it was that had caused such a violent reaction. As we walked in from the line, Terry Nash, who had been No. 3 in the formation, thought the station commander might want to congratulate us on achieving the flying target; I said that I did not think so. Ten minutes later I stood in front of the station commander and found out what the problem was. It turned out that the leader of the Phantoms, Derek Bryant, having said that he was cancelling the flypast, had neglected to say that he was going to carry on just with his four aircraft, so, 15 seconds after I had flown over the parade from north to south, four Phantoms came across west to east, threading the so-called needle. Whilst the effect was quite spectacular, it was not quite the effect that was required or expected. I had sinned and George Black left me in no doubt that I had sinned; in fact I had to class it as one of the finest bollockings that I have ever received. George has told me since that when we flew past, his chest swelled with pride that his boys had made it despite the weather. Just for 15 seconds that was, until the Phantoms came from the other direction. The then group captain ops at Rheindahlen, Laurie Jones, went apoplectic with rage and thus on the following Monday, after a Phantom from Brüggen had crashed, it was no surprise when I found myself as the President of the Board of Inquiry. But I cannot say that I appreciated the telephone calls from Derek Bryant, the leader of the F4s and CO of 14 Sqn, who kept cackling down the line at me that he could 'hear the chains rattling'.

Although it distracted from my primary duty as a squadron commander, I found that the onerous duties of a President of a Board of Inquiry interesting and quite demanding. The Phantom in question had crashed on the approach in bad weather. The pilot and the navigator had bailed out but, unfortunately, the navigator was killed when he was struck by the canopy from the front cockpit. We at least had the benefit of being able to talk to the pilot of the aircraft. He was adamant that the primary flight instruments had failed and that the stand-by flight instruments had also been affected. Barring a very unlikely coincidence, this was theoretically impossible. That was until we started looking back at all the records and found that it had inexplicably occurred a number of times previously—fortunately not at such critical times of flight in poor weather. The pilot involved was just about the most experienced pilot on the Brüggen wing, added to which he was also the Command Instrument Rating Examiner, so there was little doubt of his ability to fly an instrument approach. However it was almost impossible to ascertain what had occurred and in consequence we decided to set up a trial using the Phantom simulator. We got 12 crews and, without warning them what we were going to do, failed the flight instruments at the same stage that we suspected had happened in the crashed aircraft. Amazingly, the flight profiles of 10 of the 12 aircraft followed exactly the same path; so we were as certain as we could be that the flight instruments had failed in the way described by the pilot. We were never able to find out the exact cause of the double failure; the death of the navigator was caused by the fact that the timing of the two ejections was such that the canopy from the front hit the navigator just as he was exiting the aircraft. Again, despite the very high number of Phantom ejections that had taken place since the aircraft had gone into US and, subsequently, UK service, there was no record of this happening previously. However, on looking rather more carefully at the records it was found that there were several instances where it had been suspected that such an event had occurred.

Forgetting the very tragic outcome, I found it an intellectually interesting and demanding exercise. We had the help of the AIB who, I have to say, were not quite as expert and professional as I would have expected. When their report made its way back to me, their analysis had the aircraft impacting the ground with the starboard wing down when, in fact, it was port wing down. I had to point out their error and they took their report back, apologised, and then sent me an amended one. So despite all the claims that a double failure could not possibly occur, the evidence all pointed to the fact that it could—and had—actually happened. While I did not welcome the diversion from my primary duties as a squadron commander, I did enjoy the intellectual challenge—and at least it got me off the hook from the dreaded Queen's Birthday Flypast.

At this stage it is probably worth saying something about the RAF Germany Harrier concept of operations. Flying a ground attack aircraft in Germany was probably one of the most demanding yet exhilarating jobs going at the time. The Close Air Support (CAS) role was basically to provide support for the armed ground forces of NATO in Germany so that Forward Air Control (FAC), armed recce and pre-planned attacks were the squadron's bread and butter. Virtually all of the training is centred on these tasks although the squadron also had to keep up to scratch in weaponry, reconnaissance and combat; and added to that there was the challenge of both an on-base concept and an off-base concept. Operations from on-base involved operating from the hardened dispersal—Charlie in our case—across the other side of the runway. In effect we operated just like any other tactical fighter squadron from a hardened base. However the true Harrier concept of operations envisaged deploying forward to aircraft sites nearer the front line. The wartime sites would make use of a straight strip of road, a shopping complex or a factory complex—places that could provide natural cover and facilities. Obviously in peacetime we could not use those pre-surveyed sites and we relied upon a number of grass strips in the Sennelager area. All was well if the weather was fine; but if it was not, then you were in for an exciting (and mucky) time. Speaking personally, I never believed in the Harrier concept of operations and I had written a short paper when I was at staff college in which I concluded that the best way to use the Harrier was deployed around a hardened base so that the logistics problem could be reduced to a minimum. I believed that keeping a forward strip supplied with fuel, weapons and food would become a nightmare in a war scenario, and site moves when an original site was compromised—as it almost certainly would be—would become an even bigger nightmare especially if the roads were clogged with refugees as indeed happened in France in 1940. However, ours was not to reason why but just to get on and do it. I have to say that over the period of my time as OC 3 (F) Sqn it led to some of the most enjoyable and challenging flying of my whole career and, strangely enough, in view of the challenging environment, no accidents.

We were by now approaching our formal declaration to NATO. Bruce Leigh, our long suffering adjutant, was posted out to Naples; we got a new junior engineering officer, Les Walsh, another new pilot, Brook Blackford and, most importantly, a new GLO in Major Dick Ablett of the Royal Corps of 'Truck' (RCT). The RCT was an unusual background for a GLO but it turned out to be extremely useful. Much of our life was spent moving around with large convoys of trucks; and suddenly I was presented with a professional who knew what he was talking about. Not only that, he turned out to be a very capable 'scrounger' with excellent contacts, so despite suffering with a lack of equipment, being the last squadron, we found ourselves better equipped than most.

On 1 June 1973 the squadron was at last declared to SACEUR as combat ready. This declaration only applied to on-base operations. Another significant period was to elapse before we were declared operational both on-base and off-base. Life continued at a pretty hectic rate. The station commander would have his own readiness Mineval exercises from time to time to ensure that the wing was ready and capable. HQRAF Germany would then up the ante with a similar exercise called a Maxeval and then the hooter would go for real and a team from SACEUR's Taceval team would appear over the horizon and the assessment was then for real. The whole scenario led to an ever-increasing crescendo of activity. The only problem was that the NATO Taceval team had yet to come to grips with the Harrier concept of operations in the field and insisted on asking many inappropriate questions. One such instance was the requirement to have a cross-servicing capability which was, of course, easy to achieve on base but a different question off-base. Thus when one of the 4 Sqn NCOs was asked what he could do for a GAF F104 if it arrived at the strip, the answer of 'I'd provide the pilot with a 6 ft wooden box and bury him over there' was not quite what the assessor was expecting. Exactly how a 104 was going to land on a 600 ft strip was not explained; the requirement was to be able to cross service other NATO aircraft and it did not seem to matter that it was a totally impossible proposition.

We had taken to training in phases as a practical solution allowing us to concentrate on various facets; we had a combat phase, an attack phase and a recce phase so that over a period of time we would cover all the capabilities. We also gave the running of these various phases to the experienced pilots on the squadron rather than leaving it all in the hands of the flight commanders as it freed up the flight commanders so that they could carry out the overall supervision of flying without getting drowned in some of the detail. It also gave responsibility and experience to the middle ranking guys who were tasked with the organisation of the flying. All in all it worked well. Quite apart from my doubts about the Harrier concept of operations, I was also concerned about the rather blinkered (in my view) notion that the only way to defeat the threat was to fly fast at low level. While I did think that it was the most likely path to success and therefore should remain a priority in our training, I also thought that it was worth retaining a medium level capability just in case on Day One it was found that the low level tactic did not work. I was therefore not averse to introducing some flexibility into our training, undertaking high-low-high strikes against targets in UK defended by Hunters and/or Lightning.

The other pleasant diversion was to be able every now and again to be able to take a couple of aircraft away on a 'Southern Ranger', and at the end of July 1973 I took a couple of aircraft to Akrotiri in Cyprus, staging through Luqa *en route*. We were looked after well by the resident Lightning squadron in Cyprus and some kind fellow inadvisedly lent me a car so that we could go and gate-crash a supper party hosted by Owen Truelove who was now based in Cyprus. I thought that he was very trusting and generous—and unwise! We certainly had a very good evening and on Monday we flew back to Wildenrath via Luqa.

Having been formally declared as an operational squadron, we participated in the 'On Base' Taceval at the beginning of September. As so often happened on these occasions the formal Taceval was not as searching as the more frequent station commander's Mineval or the Command Maxeval; so while I would not be tempted to say it was a breeze, we did manage to acquit ourselves reasonably well. No sooner was that over that we were off to Fassberg again for a repeat of the Berlin Access Exercise. As usual the French turned up with their F100s which were by now getting very long in the tooth, but they entered fully in to the exercise. The USAF were still forbidden by their rules from operating out of Fassberg so they flew from Spangdahlem. As ever the GAF were magnificent hosts and by osmosis we had arranged for the Germans to supply the beer, the French the champagne and the Brits provided the brandy as we could get it cheaper than anyone else, all of which combined to make for a very good formal allied officers' guest night in the mess at Fassberg.

I have several memories of Fassberg, some repeatable and others which I could well forget. One of those memories was giving a couple of the French pilots trips in the Harrier T2. I flew the first sortie and remained in the cockpit whilst the ground crew strapped the second Frenchman in to the back. I was just about to start up when suddenly John McGarvey came rushing up and said that there was a problem. It seemed that the airbrake, which normally should have been in a mid-position with the undercarriage down, had failed to sequence properly and had been fully extended when I landed and had scraped along the runway, damaging the bottom half, but in so doing it had gone back to the mid-position. After a quick discussion with John, he decided that he could fix it without delaying the sortie. What he did was take a hack saw to the damaged part of the airbrake with the comment that if the sequencing did fail again, it would not hit the runway. I have to say that the noise coming from beneath the aircraft as I sat there during the turnround was horrendous. Even the French were somewhat stunned by this somewhat basic approach to engineering and everyone came out to watch this performance. In fact the airbrake worked normally and the aircraft flew like that for quite a few weeks as spare airbrakes were in short supply. So much so that we had almost forgotten about it until one day we had to take the aircraft to Wittering, the erstwhile home of the Harrier. There was a realisation that if someone saw the aircraft like that, they might just be tempted to ground it. Some artistic work with some duck tape followed and nobody noticed it.

The guest night was memorable although I must admit that I did have more than a couple of nervous moments as the senior allied officer. The French squadron commander insisted on teaching me how to open a champagne bottle with a sword and as the evening progressed, I became reasonably adept at it; and he also introduced us to a game which I had never experienced before and never wish to experience again. The final incident which occurred after the dinner was one which I thought could easily bring my career to a premature close. I was standing talking to the German base commander, a GAF colonel, when suddenly with a roll of drums a curtain went back on a balcony and Tim Smith, one of my pilots, appeared doing a very creditable impersonation of Adolf Hitler. There was a stunned silence followed by a click of the heels of the person standing next to me—and then absolute pandemonium. The French thought it was marvellous and the even the Germans seemed to appreciate the joke. Indeed the next thing I knew was the German base commander was giving Tim lessons on how to do it better. It turned out that he had been a very highly decorated pilot in the Second World War who had met Hitler on several occasions. His remarks centred around the word *unglaublich*. Tim could give a more than passable imitation of the Hitler rant and rave, being a reasonably fluent German speaker. But what was most incredible according to the German colonel was that Tim's facial bone structure was exactly the same as Hitler's; quite what that said about Tim I am not too sure, but it was a pretty riotous and memorable evening.

The German base commander was an interesting character. He did not wear any wings or medals but he had been a pilot during the Second World War ending up as a test pilot at Peenemunde. He gave me a very graphic description of the last days of the war when he was tasked with getting together a bunch of biplanes with the equivalent of a bazooka (a *panzerfaust*) strapped to each wing connected to the pilot by a system of wires. The idea was to go tank-busting but only at night as they were so vulnerable. His description of going down the dive at night, aiming these devices and pulling the wire trigger device, followed by total blindness from the flames of the missiles was very graphic. He said that they finally gave up when on his last sortie they lost 50 per cent of their aircraft for very little achievement.

The exercise followed the usual format of giving close air support to the 'friendly forces'. My main memory of the flying was that I had never seen so many armoured vehicles gathered together in one place, and what it also brought home was their vulnerability as, when they were moving, you could see them from miles away. The engine exhausts combined with the dust thrown up by their tracks acted like beacons; I was not convinced that they were aware of how vulnerable they were.

One last memory of that week was a trip with the French in their two-seat F100. We took off as a four-ship in the most appalling weather. We had hardly been going five minutes at low level when the weather forced us to abort and climb up to medium level through some fairly thick and nasty clouds. Inevitably the formation became split up and after ten minutes we managed to gather everyone together again. In the midst of all this, it became evident to me that the leader was totally lost, or to be generous 'temporarily uncertain of position'. Fortunately, it being in an area with which I was very familiar, I was able to help out and get them to overhead Gütersloh after which we headed back home through the weather. Quite where they would have ended up without my local knowledge, I do not know, but I could not say that I was very impressed with the F100 or the performance of the FAF on that day. Before being too critical, it is fair to say that we all have our 'off days' and they got 10 out of 10 for press on spirit!

A week at Fassberg was about all that our constitutions could stand. The weather had not been particularly good for that week which was probably a blessing in disguise as the social commitments had been pretty demanding, including the usual trip to Hamburg. Nevertheless it had been an enjoyable week made even more memorable by the camaraderie of the German base personnel and the French squadron plus the occasional USAF visitor.

While the on-base Taceval assessment had taken place at the beginning of September, the off-base assessment did not occur until the beginning of October. 3 Sqn had not participated in off-base deployments at that stage and our first deployment to 'Kestrel', the code name for our site, took place in the week after the rest of the wing had suffered their off-base Taceval assessment. All I remember was that the weather was appalling and we suffered from a determination to get in to the field no matter what. Having persuaded the force commander, George Black, that the weather was acceptable, we departed Wildenrath in the pouring rain for our first deployment. The rest of the wing had decided that the weather was not suitable for flying and that better entertainment would be gained by listening on the net to 3 Sqn's attempts to find the field site on a typical murky German autumn day, and quite entertaining it must have been. I found the landing site with the first pair of aircraft and landed. The subsequent aircraft had some difficulties with the weather and if it had not been for Roger Gault circling above the site in a small gap in the clouds talking the subsequent aircraft down, we might have had a few problems. However everyone got safely down but not without our antics causing some amusement to the rest of the wing.

Kestrel was a site in the Sennelager training area not far from Gütersloh called Moosdorf. To say that it was one of the more challenging and exciting sites was probably an understatement. It was a fairly short strip and immediately on take-off you had to turn to aim for a gap in the trees; it was also pretty boggy, in fact that was to be a recurring theme of many of our deployments. While our war sites would have made use of local roads, barns, factories, etc., peacetime regulations meant that we had to use grass strips usually in or near woods and, unless it was in mid-summer in a good year, that usually meant mud up to the axles. Terry Nash briefed all the guys with particular reference to being careful to avoid digging the nose wheel into the mud. Ironically when he was the first to taxi out he managed to get the nose wheel so far in the mud that we had to dig him out—much to the amusement of the rest of the squadron.

The remainder of the year passed fairly uneventfully; the weather deteriorated, the flying rate decreased although the visitors did not. The Harrier force, being somewhat of a novelty, was never short of visitors including senior military officers, press, local dignitaries and others. The list was almost endless, but in the main it was a pleasure to show them around and try and 'sell' them the Harrier concept; and most of them were only too pleased to listen and learn.

We marked the end of the year with a 'squadron ladies guest night' and cabaret. We dined out three of the original squadron members, Alan Whittaker, the junior engineering officer; Chris Bain and Tim Smith. We had gained a few as well; John West who was a first tourist and Neil Gilliard who had replaced Bruce Leigh as our adjutant. The cabaret was a great success and became the foundation stone of a future event—of which more later. The Christmas festivities included a very successful all ranks Christmas draw and the usual aircrew versus ground crew football match. I elected to be the goalkeeper as I thought it would keep me out of trouble; how wrong was that! I gathered a ball just as the centre forward was trying to kick it. I was wearing gloves at the time and did not realise anything was wrong except that one of them seemed to be very wet. I took the glove off to find that the wetness was blood and the bone of the finger was sticking out; I was taken off to the hospital at Wegberg to get it fixed. I do not think they made too good a job of it as the finger has never worked since. I cannot remember quite why but the hospital insisted on keeping me in overnight, which would not have been much of a problem normally, but it coincided with the Christmas draw party—which upset me a bit. Unbeknown to me, George Black and others hatched a plan of activating the train, which existed for hauling ammunition between the ammunition dump and the 'Clutch' stations, and leading an expedition to the hospital to kidnap me. Fortunately, probably for everyone, the plan was never executed.

John West was one of the last pilots to join 3 Sqn and his arrival was very nearly a major disaster. John was one of the early 'University Graduate Entrants', and he made no secret of the fact that he thought this ought to earn him accelerated and early promotion, despite his lack of experience. Predictably this upset some of the older and more experienced hands and they resolved to teach him a lesson at his arrival party. The plot was to get him incapable, put his leg in plaster, tell him that he had broken it at the party and leave him like that for a week. The theory was good but the execution was poor; it did not seem to matter what he was given to drink, it had no effect. That was until he suddenly keeled over a table full of glasses, then stood up again amongst all the broken glass and then keeled over again. I had to leave at that stage as I was going to a formal dinner party with the station commander. I told the boys to put John to bed and, as a precaution, get the SMO to have a quick look at him. I was unaware of the fact that the SMO took one look at John and rushed him off to hospital where he remained for three days. Fortunately for me and the rest of the squadron, it was George Black, the station commander, who managed to sort out the consequences of this little episode.

By 1974 we were up to full strength on all counts. Jack Rust was my Exec, OC A Flt Terry Nash, and B Flt Al Cleaver. A Flt consisted of Mike

Shaw, Vaughan Dow, Bob Iveson, Mike Young, Arthur Gatland and Brook Blackford. B Flt had Tony McKeon, John Grogan, Jim Downey, Rocky Goodall, Roger Gault and John West. Ritchie Profit, who was in fact the wing standardisation officer, also joined us for all operational exercises (and when he had nothing better to do). The engineers were John McGarvey (SEngo), Les Walsh (JEngo), Bob Matthews (Sqn WO) and Bill Smith (Sqn Flt Sgt), two RAF Regiment officers, Len Laithwaite and Jack Cobb, two GLOs Ian McFarlane and Dick Ablett and a squadron adjutant Neil Gilliard. I do not think that I could ever have asked for a bigger bunch of troublemakers and ne'er-do-wells who could always be relied upon to go the extra mile to deliver the goods—and get you in to trouble. The ground crew, led by John McGarvey, were of a similar ilk. No matter how unreasonable my requests, they would always do their damnedest to produce the aeroplanes and more often than not succeeded. They were a happy, fun-loving, hard-working bunch and it was a pleasure and a privilege to be part of it. However, now we were going to have to put our money where our mouth was as we were due to be formally declared as operational both on and off-base.

As in most military organisations, life had its occasional amusing moments and Wildenrath was no exception. One morning an Army officer came to visit and he was stopped at the gate and, as was normal practice, asked for some form of identification. For some reason the Army officer, a major, objected to having to show his ID card and remonstrated with the corporal policeman on the gate who was a well-built individual. 'Is this the way the RAF entertains its guests?' he said somewhat petulantly. 'No sir, we can do better than that,' replied the corporal and proceeded to do a song and dance act in front of the car to the tune of 'Gimme the Moonlight'. The major went apoplectic and put the corporal on a charge. However the corporal policeman achieved instant fame on the base and was for ever known by all as 'Corporal Moonlight'.

And then there was the incident of the station commander's hi-fi kit. We had been to a very good party in the mess and on the way home George Black invited some of us back to his house to continue the party. George had a brand new and very expensive Bang & Olufsen hi-fi kit of which he was inordinately proud. So he put on some music and we continued dancing in the lounge. I was dancing with Angela Champniss and Ella Black when we tripped and fell all over the hi-fi. There was a horrendous screech followed by a silence. George went apoplectic (just like the major!) and went off to bed in a huff. We all decided that it was a bit late and time to go home, which we did. A week or so later, I was stopped at the gate by Corporal Moonlight and asked if it was true. I had no idea what he was talking about and he explained that there was an advert in the latest copy of *Zulu*, the station magazine, saying that I wanted to swap my car, a brand new BMW 520i, for a Bang & Olufsen hi-fi. I have no idea to this day who put the advert in *Zulu* and I had not realised that the fact that I had ruined the station commander's pride and joy was common knowledge. He did forgive me subsequently.

January and February 1974 were fairly slow months mainly due to the usual appalling weather at this time of the year. This was just as well as I had expressed some dissatisfaction to the station commander at the quality of the officers' mess entertainment on a Saturday night. In a rash moment, as a result of our successful Christmas cabaret, I said that 3 Sqn would provide a cabaret for the whole mess on 25 February. The deal was that the other squadrons would then follow suit so that we got a variety of home-based relatively low-cost entertainment. My offer was taken up with alacrity although the rest of the squadron were not over pleased with my generosity with their time and talent. In fact what ensued was one of the finest evenings I can ever remember. There were nine acts, culminating in a 'This is Your Life' treatment of the station commander, George Black. And I don't think we upset anyone, except perhaps Padre McNeil, who had to be treated for shock after John West's sneezy violinist with a third hand act. However, the idea of shaming other people into providing Saturday night mess entertainment slightly backfired as the general view was that no one could equal that so that they would not even bother to try.

It was time for a new station commander and George Black was replaced by Gp Capt. Paddy Hine. George had had a hard two years one way and another, but there was no doubt in our minds that George had formed the basis of what was to be a very successful wing and that Paddy Hine benefited from George's hard work and then proceeded to put the icing on the cake. Meanwhile on the home front Vaughan Dow decided that his talents were heading towards civil aviation and he left us for 'greener pastures'. He was replaced by Gemmel Ross who immediately managed to break his arm falling of his bike and had to wait a couple of months for it to mend.

Come March and we deployed in strength to two off-base sites, Geseke (code named Tiger) and Eringerfeld (Panther). By this time we had made good use of our GLO, Dick Ablett. He had scouted around Germany and found a couple of expander trucks to serve as our ops rooms. They actually belonged to the HQ at Rheindahlen but they never used them. They were pretty sophisticated pieces of kit, being extremely well equipped and NBC proof. Dick somehow persuaded them to lend the trucks to us and they said yes with one proviso; that they provided the drivers. Since we were always short of drivers, this was music to our ears and we accepted with alacrity. Jack Cobb found a very nice little 'commander's mini caravan' for me to have while on deployment. It would have been relative luxury compared with a tent but, unfortunately, Paddy Hine got wind of what we were up to and exercised *droit du seigneur* and took it back. Nevertheless, despite being the tail-end-Charlie with regards to deployment equipment, we ended up in pretty good shape as a result of our scrounging ability. The Royal Engineers were a vital part of the whole set up as they were responsible for laying out the sites and laying any planking required plus the vertical landing pad. Equally as important were the Royal Signals and we had our own dedicated signallers who provided all communications for the sites, and lastly, the RAF Regiment who were responsible for guarding the sites. Then there were all the peripheral but vital facilities such as field kitchens, air traffic, firemen, etc. The end result was that there were 200 to 300 people on each site.

The format of the flying from off-base took the form of very short sorties, usually no more than 30 minutes, and cockpit tasking. You would climb in to the cockpit first thing in the morning and complete four or five sorties on the trot without getting out. The ops room would provide the tasking which was master-minded by the GLO who would provide the pilot with a short brief, a target description and maps to match. Taxy out and a short take off from the strip; complete the task and return to the site for a vertical landing on the pad. A quick debrief followed by a retask and off again. Weather was always an issue flying from the sites and we were unable to fly unless the visibility was 5 kms and the cloud-base 1000 ft. We would often send up a weather check aircraft and we had a code to tell us how suitable the weather was for flying. If the weather checker reported it as 5 clicks (kms) then it was OK; if he said it was a marginal 5 clicks, it was probably between 3 and 5 clicks; and if he said it was a poor 5 clicks, it was below 3. The squadron ops would then make the fly/no fly decision based on the information given. Basically it was never said to be below 5 clicks mainly because the decision was never straightforward and once someone had said it was below 5 clicks, it was difficult to reverse the decision.

To say that 3 Sqn, aircrew and ground crew, took to off-base deployments like ducks to water was probably an understatement. We flew a record number of sorties out of the two sites and then, added to that, were the extra factors of guarding the site against intruders during the night, keeping the logistics (fuel, etc.) replenished. The fuel was stored in pillow tanks, which were replenished every night, and that was a significant logistic problem in itself when you had six aircraft flying 40 or so sorties during the day. If the problem was exacerbated by the demands of weapons that would be needed in the war scenario, then it was not difficult to imagine how this could easily transform into a logistical nightmare. Add in refugees, fifth columnists and so on and the recipe for chaos was always there, and the more I participated in these off-base exercises, the more I was convinced that it probably would not work—or at least it would not work quite as envisaged. But that did not lessen the challenge and the fun of off-base flying, it could almost be described as legalised hooliganism and I am pretty sure that some of the high-priced help did not appreciate the risks that were taken. But, as a peace time exercise, it worked; and it worked well.

We stayed out on deployment for two weeks. The first week was used for familiarisation and work-up and the second week for evaluation—the off base equivalent of the on-base Mineval and Maxeval. As ever in Germany, there was no flying at the weekends, so usually the wing would get together at some German *gasthaus* or other. The other trick was to try and find an Army or RAF barracks with a shower facility as by the end of a week one was beginning to get a bit ripe. Coping with mud, even snow and certainly rain in March in the woods in Germany was not always the picnic that some imagined. Nevertheless the troops coped well and of particular note was the performance of the RAF field kitchens. They produced good high quality hot food at almost any time which was just as well because Bob Iveson always had to have a 'chip butty' at ten o'clock in the evening before retiring to his tent.

After the off-base sites it was back to the comforts and delights of Wildenrath, and just to keep us on our toes, we were to be the recipients of a Royal Visit by the Duke of Edinburgh on 17 May 1974. For some reason that was not clear to me, it was decided that we would not do any flying at all and the programme was all on the ground. My only involvement was to attend a couth tea party with my wife that was to take place just before the Duke departed. However it turned out that he had complained to the station commander that he had been there all day and not seen an aircraft fly, so as the station commander came past me at the tea party, he asked me if I had an aircraft available and, if so, would I do a display. I rang the squadron and John McGarvey answered the phone. Needless to say when I asked him for an aircraft he answered in the affirmative and by the time I arrived it was on the pan waiting. I ended up doing a full display for the Royal Visit, completely unrehearsed. I don't think that it was one of the best I had ever done as it was a long time since I had done any display flying. But the Duke got his wish.

That May we had a grand programme of flying attack profiles against targets defended by Phantoms, Lightnings and Hunters. The F4s were from our next door neighbours at Brüggen. The Lightnings were from Binbrook when we were flying against targets in the UK and the Hunters from Wittering. Leading 4 and/or 8 ships certainly stretched and tested the leadership capabilities of the younger pilots—and some of the older ones. It is quite an art to be able to maintain control of a formation when you are being attacked by other aircraft from all directions. Quite apart from being spatially aware of what is going on and the tactics involved, you need to be able to progress the formation towards the target and then finally you need to be aware of the fuel needs. Often as not we would use the Holbeach Range in the Wash for live targets and it was surprising how far you could go on relatively small amounts of fuel. If you got 'lights' (the low level fuel warning lights) in the climb out of the target area in the Wash, you could be certain of having enough fuel (just!) to get back to Wildenrath—a fact which surprised some people. We did have an air-miss filed on us by a helicopter from Lowestoft. We had failed to notice that there was a helicopter base there for North Sea oil platform support and it just so happened that, as we crossed in across the coastline, we were bounced by half a dozen Hunters from Wittering. The ensuing mêlée was quite exciting but we all failed to notice a helicopter in the midst of it. According to the helicopter pilot, he was in the hover over Lowestoft and could not move up or down because there were aircraft under him, round him and over the top of him. Somehow I managed to talk us out of any retribution for the sin.

It seemed that after the display for the Duke of Edinburgh I had been *de facto* elected a display pilot for the wing, so during the following month I went to the Canadian Base at Soellingen to do a display for the tactical weapons meet. That was immediately followed by the next field deployment, called Exercise Fir Wander; it was notable for the most awful weather. Jagergrund was not too bad but the Buchenhof site was by far the worst as it was pure mud. The only good thing was that at less than a foot down you came to clay so that at least you could not sink in any further, however taxying was difficult as you slid all over the place. When you tried to park the aircraft in one of the hides, as soon as you touched the brakes, the wheels locked and you just kept going until the ground crew could leap underneath with chocks. An added danger was an adjacent German flying club who were determined to be hospitable and, I regret to say, we succumbed to their blandishments on the Sunday night. They really did throw a memorable party.

The Monday was a public holiday in Germany and as such no flying was permitted, so we had arranged to take six aircraft to Leeuwarden, a joint RNLAF/USAF base in Holland, so that we could at least fly. The aircraft were absolutely filthy with mud all over the fuselage—and the pilots were not a lot better and a bit bleary eyed. As I taxied in, I was met by the RNLAF base commander and a USAF colonel dressed in their best uniforms. Unshaven, unclean and somewhat dishevelled after the previous evening's hospitality at the German flying club, I have often wondered what they thought of the sight that confronted them. Tony McKeon took it upon himself to give a VSTOL display which, I have to say, did not show the aircraft at its best; however we had a good day and flew back to Buchenhof in the evening.

This deployment was notable for the fact that it was the first one to include weapons deployment as well. There was a centralised logistics site from which all the logistics were organised; it was an impressive achievement but I was still not persuaded of its efficacy. We also exercised a site move, the idea being that if a site was compromised in any way we just moved to an alternate in as little time as possible. The site move was from Buchenhof to Jagergrund and in a record time. It was also somewhat of a relief to find that Jagergrund was comparatively dry despite all the rain since this was a site that we were going to use for Taceval in the final deployment of the year, the portents were good, for Buchenhof had been a nightmare.

Buchenhof had not been without the odd amusing incident. Usually it is the aircrew that have a penchant for getting one into trouble, but on 3 Sqn, the ground crew were equally up to the challenge. On a previous deployment, I had already had a rather difficult time explaining how and why the 3 Sqn crest had appeared on the roof of the church at RAF Gütersloh. In fact the culprits, who shall be nameless, had not realised that it was a church as it was just a rather nondescript Nissen hut, but on this deployment they excelled themselves. It so happened that a bunch of our ground crew met up with some girls in a local hostelry. Nothing unusual in that, you might think, except that these girls were from the local 'Gymnasium', the German version of an up-market ladies boarding school. To cut a long story short, these girls invited them back to their dormitory. However the headmistress got wind of it and interrupted proceedings and called the police. All of the ground crew managed to escape—except one who had fallen asleep in the toilets. He was arrested by the German police but we managed to persuade them in the end that it would be easier if they released him to our custody and allowed us to deal with the matter, and that was what happened. The young man appeared in front of me on a charge; but I think that he was more concerned about what his wife was going to say than what I was going to do to him—which was not much.

By July we were back at Wildenrath, but not for long. First of all we lost two of our founder members, Jack Rust, the Exec, and Mike Shaw. Jack had put a lot of hard work into the squadron and Mike Shaw had many talents, not all connected to flying; they would both be missed. Terry Nash took over as Exec and Stu Penny took over A Flt from Terry. On the farewell station guest night I was 'advised' by my pilots not to pull my chair back and sit down after the padre had said grace. I should have known that some devious scheme was afoot—and it was. As soon as grace had been said, the top table pulled back their chairs to sit down with the most unbelievable clatter, for every single item of cutlery went onto the floor—except for mine! The boys had spent the afternoon tying the cutlery to the chairs with black cotton. No one had noticed and hence the clean sweep of the top table. The evening deteriorated from then on in!

One of the more enjoyable arrangements of NATO forces was the Squadron Exchange, and in our case we were teamed up with 421 Sqn of the RCAF at Baden Soellingen who were equipped with F104s. Just before we left, the on-base part of Taceval occurred, the most important aspect being having to meet the weapons qualifications for bombs, guns and rockets. That we achieved without too many problems, so off we went to Soellingen with eight aircraft. Soellingen (or Slingen as the Canadians were wont to call it) is in the southern part of Germany and it was good to be able to fly in an unfamiliar area. It was also interesting to exchange views and tactics with another NATO squadron. I flew in their 104 and I cannot say that I was that impressed, and they flew in our two seat Harrier. We flew combat sorties against the 104s, but when it came to hospitality, the Canadians took some beating—especially on a Friday night. I do not think that I have ever seen a bar floor with so much broken glass and beer on it. By 10 o'clock in the evening you were wading through ankle deep broken glass and beer and this seemed to be the norm for a Friday night at Soellingen; it was a pretty memorable week that cost us more than a few brain cells. We flew out on the Saturday morning and I remember being somewhat annoyed with the new flight commander, Stu Penny, as he broke another one of our records in that we never left an aircraft behind after a deployment. His excuse was that as he taxied out the fire warning light came on and he felt forced to close the engine down. Looking at it now, I suppose it was a reasonable decision; but I did not feel that way at the time!

Back to Wildenrath for August and just for a bit of variety, a recce training phase. By default—as it seemed that I had been elected as the display pilot for the wing—I went to the Dutch airbase at Twenthe for their open day. But really the accent was on the final field deployment in September during which we would be assessed for off-base operations for the first time. As usual we had managed to get the use of the big expander trucks from the HQ and we had managed to overcome all the shortages of equipment that we had suffered from. We had two sites allocated to us, Jagergrund (Tiger) and Moosdorf. The primary site was Jagergrund where I was based with OC B Flt and Terry Nash ran the secondary site. For the first time we had a full weapons outload on the sites just to prove it could be done. Many of the activities of Taceval, site ground defence, day and night, logistics, command and control were so important that I was unable to do much flying. And as was often the case the formal Taceval was not as demanding as some of the previous evaluation exercises had been. It was amusing to record the fact that we captured an attacking team who were totally lost and had thought that they were infiltrating a 20 Sqn site. Nevertheless it was a demanding three days of evaluation with plenty of flying although, as I recollect, the head of the evaluation team spent more time flying in the Harrier T2 than on the ground, but it paid to keep him occupied and the net result was a 'One' for Mission Effectiveness, the highest evaluation possible. It was a good result for our first outing and one of which we were very proud. When I arrived back on the site after the debrief at about 9 o'clock in the evening, I found that the cooks had prepared a celebratory dinner for me of fresh trout and new potatoes served on a silver platter. It was in fact an ordinary plate covered in tin foil; but, as they say, it's the thought that counts! Having not eaten for most of the day, it was absolutely delicious and much appreciated; but I was requested not to ask from whence the trout had come!

We just had a couple of days to refresh ourselves back at Wildenrath before we were off again to Fassberg for the annual tri-partite Berlin access exercise and for a change we had some pretty decent weather as I personally flew 17 sorties in six days. In fact we flew a record number of sorties for a Fassberg detachment, so much so that it even curtailed some of the evening activity. It did not curtail the final formal dinner night where as usual, the French provided the champagne, the Germans the beer and we provided the brandy. I had been wondering what I could present to the German base commander as a memento of our visit when I had a brain wave. The Germans had what one could only describe as a 'honkatorium' in the men's toilet so that, if you had the misfortune to have over-imbibed, you could lean over, hold on and relieve yourself. There were meant to be handles either side of the bowl so that you could hang on for grim death (or whatever). Unfortunately one of the handles was missing so that you tended to fly left wing low and were in danger of missing the bowl. I got our engineers to make up an identical handle to replace the missing one and added a 3 Sqn crest to it. I presented it to the base commander at the formal dinner and he was well pleased—or at least he made pretence of being well pleased. So my final deployment to Fassberg came to an end and we flew back to Wildenrath.

When I got back to base I found that I had been posted; which was no surprise as I was coming to the end of my 2½ years of tenure. I was evidently going off to attend the Air Warfare College at Manby. A certain Wg Cdr Dick Johns had been designated to take over from me, but before I left, there was another little surprise awaiting me. It turned out that we had been chosen to undertake an extensive night ground attack trial with the Harrier. Since I was going to move on in the near future, I chose one of my flight commanders, Terry Nash, to lead it and we selected three other pilots for the night team. These were Bob Iveson, Tony McKeon and John Grogan. It meant that we had to shift the whole working day to a 1000 hrs start so that the last wave of sorties was always done at night.

The aim of the trial was to look at the practicality of achieving close air support at night. The Harrier was the first single seat aircraft to be equipped with a full inertial navigation and weapons system and it was not unreasonable to expect that you could achieve rather more with it than just with a map and stop watch. The trials unit was to work up starting with night low level cross countries, night formation, culminating with a FAC controlled run with weapons delivery under a Lepus flare, the flare being released by the leader and the weapons by the following aircraft. We started the trials flying in October with four chosen trials pilots. I would occasionally fly a sortie just to get some understanding of what they were up to.

One Monday morning in December, I was sitting minding my own business at the station commander's weekly conference, as usual wondering how long it would be before we could get away. Suddenly I heard an ominous double bang come from the airfield which sounded just like an ejection seat going off. And so it was; and unfortunately it was one of my aircraft. Flt Lt Jim Downey had suffered a catastrophic engine failure just as he took off which caused the aircraft, not surprisingly, to drop back on the runway from about 50 ft. An outrigger sheared off and he ended up running off the runway and across the grass. It would not have been disastrous had he not caught a concrete drain which wiped off the main undercarriage and, as he slid to a halt in front of the fire section, the fuel from the drop tanks caught fire and he was enveloped in flames. Being a sensible lad he decided that it was time to leave despite the fact he was stationary on the ground and he pulled the ejection handle; and that was the double bang that we had heard as we sat in station headquarters. He was so close to the fire section that they were literally underneath him ready to catch him as he landed. It was proof, if we needed it, that the Martin Baker seat had a true zero/zero (zero speed/zero height) capability as Jim landed totally uninjured. I got the message that he was unharmed and despatched my wife to tell Jim's wife, Jenny, that all was well and went back to my office. The next thing is that Jim Downey himself knocked on my door and burst in apologising profusely for breaking my 'record'. 'What record?' I asked. And then he explained that we had had no accidents whatsoever during my tenure of office in nearly 2½ years and he had spoilt it. It had not occurred to me at that time but what he said was true. We had had no accidents whatsoever when the other Harrier squadrons had been less fortunate. I assured him that he had no reason to apologise and that the accident was not of his making. More importantly he had come through the whole incident unharmed. Unfortunately Jim was killed a year or so later when he was an instructor on the OCU in a mid-air collision with another Harrier.

I have often wondered about our accident record and why. That was the only incident during my time and even that aircraft was not a write-off. The fire very quickly subsided as Jim had had the courtesy to plant the aircraft right by the fire section and they very quickly doused the flames. We had never taken a low risk strategy, flying in poor weather, and sometimes pressing on to extreme limits. We certainly had a superb bunch of ground crew led by one of the best aircraft engineers I have had the fortune to know. John McGarvey did not know how to say impossible, no matter how unreasonable my demands might seem, so there is no doubt in my mind that they had a major responsibility for our success. Luck is always an essential ingredient and there is no doubt that we had that from time to time—and some might claim that we had more than our fair share of luck. I have always thought that my decision to persevere with the 102 engine had a part to play. We never had an engine failure with the 102 (Jim's aircraft had a 103 engine as we had by then run out of 102s) but we had had 102s for most of my time. I have since discussed this with Andrew Dow, an engine expert from Bristol Siddeley, and he stated that there was no evidence to support my conjecture, but I remain to be convinced. Finally there were the pilots themselves; they also were an exceptional bunch of professional aviators who could be relied upon to go the extra mile and a little bit beyond—not always in quite the direction you expected!

By now I was getting ready to move on. We had a short detachment down to Deci in December getting back to Wildenrath in good time for Christmas. I was due to leave in mid-January and Judy went home a few weeks early to our house in Camberley. I had arranged to take all our worldly goods back to UK in the PSI Transit van and also committed myself to pick up all of Dick Johns' household stuff on the way back. It was while I was at Dick's house that the telephone went and, much to my surprise, he said, 'it's for you'. It was the station commander, Paddy Hine, telling me that my posting was changed. I was being sent to the Royal College of Defence Studies (RCDS) in Belgrave Square, London as the junior RAF Directing Staff. At the time I did not have any idea as to what this was; indeed, in my ignorance, I had never heard of RCDS (in fact it was the new name for the Imperial Defence College), so it was all a bit of a mystery to me; but it sounded interesting and a lot better than some anonymous post in the Ministry of Defence.

I was formally dined out—in some style I might add—and given a number of mementos which still hang on my wall today, not least the ejection seat pins out of Harrier GR1 XV741. It had served me well ever since Boscombe Down and I had travelled far and wide with it and it never let me down. And on 15 January 1975 I handed over the squadron to Dick Johns. And so my tour of duty as OC 3(F) Sqn came to a close. It had been a challenging, enjoyable and satisfying tour and one that I shall certainly never forget.

8

Concordia Artus Roborat
(Strength through unity)

We moved back to England firstly into our old house in Camberley which we sold almost immediately and looked for a new base from which to operate. We looked at a number of options but came to the conclusion that Buckinghamshire was a sensible solution on two grounds. Firstly it was not as expensive as other commuter areas at that time and secondly it was convenient for RAF Strike Command at High Wycombe which, I reckoned, would almost certainly feature in some future posting. We finally settled on buying an old cottage called Devil's Dyke in the village of Ballinger near Great Missenden. It needed quite a lot of work doing to it but, in my new job, I had the time.

In February 1975 I arrived at the Royal College of Defence Studies (RCDS) at Seaford House in Belgrave Square. The proclaimed charter of the RCDS was 'to give selected senior officers and officials of the UK the opportunity to study, with representatives of the Commonwealth and other nations, the problems of defence related to international relations and public policy with emphasis on the strategic aspects.' The staff consisted of a commandant (4*), four senior directing staff (2*)—one from each service and a diplomat from the Foreign Office—and five junior directing staff (JDS) at Wg Cdr level (or equivalent)—one from each service, a civil servant and a coordinator. In addition there were a number of administrative backup staff, a college secretary, a librarian and a number of secretaries and messengers. Not least we had our own excellent and well-run restaurant in the basement. There were 76 students on each course of whom approximately 50 per cent were British and the remainder from the Commonwealth and overseas.

It is worth mentioning how fortunate we were to work in one of the most gracious houses in one of the most attractive London squares. It was built as Sefton House in 1844 for the third Earl Sefton and when the fourth earl died it was bought by Lord Howard de Walden in 1902; and as he was also the 4th Baron Seaford, renamed Seaford House. Town houses in those days were designed primarily for receptions, balls and dinners, not for guests to stay overnight. Thus there were seldom more bedrooms than were necessary for the family and its servants, and Seaford House was typical of its genre. Of particular note was the broad grand staircase of noble proportions made of a rare pale green onyx. All in all it was somewhat different to the usual gloomy MoD office and we were privileged to be there.

I took over the post of RAF JDS from a Wg Cdr Dink Lemon who, in turn, took over the coordinating post. My boss was AVM Ross Harding. He had responsibility for a number of phases of study including economics, finance, the Middle East and a number of other aspects. There were a number of tours during the year's course, a regional tour in UK, a NATO tour on the continent including Berlin, and a world tour in which the course was split into six or seven individual groups and went for a month to various parts of the world. My responsibilities included arranging relevant lecturers for the various phases of study, arranging regional tours and the world tours; and being the airman on the staff, all air travel (which was a nightmare!) fell to me. I became very familiar with the British Airways office in Victoria!

In addition, as the College 'travel agent' it fell to me to organise all the various jabs required for all. This was done by the central medical establishment in London, but they did actually come to Seaford House rather than having a bunch of senior officers travel across London—they would have got lost in any case. The man who actually carried out the injections was a retired air commodore doctor who worked as a locum at CME. He was an interesting character; he had been a prisoner of the Japanese at the end of the war and had been close to Hiroshima ground zero when the first atom bomb went off. His description of the event over lunch was not to be recommended whilst eating. He told me that it had been a blue sky day and they had seen the B29 aircraft approaching because of the contrails. Of course no one had any idea of what was going to happen but because it was only one aircraft half of the prisoners stayed above ground watching. The other half decided to dive into a trench. Those in the trench—of which he was one - survived; the ones who stayed watching were almost completely 'vaporised'. He described how all that remained of one person who had been near him was reduced to an outline of the body on a wall. Equally graphic was his description of the tests the US medics did to him after they had been released It might have put me off my lunch but it certainly did not put him off his food—or the wine!

The commandant was Air Chief Marshal Sir John Barraclough who, I have to say, was one of the most talented officers it has ever been my privilege to work for. He used to stand up after each lecture and summarise the lecture and the subsequent discussion in the most succinct manner and, often, rather better than the lecturer himself. He was physically a rather imposing individual, tall and saturnine; but his bark was worse than his bite.

The life was not quite as frenetic as life on a squadron and it was most definitely a more 'gentlemanly' existence. The first lecture usually started at 1000 so that you rarely had to be in the office before 0900. Even as junior directing staff we had to attend all the lectures and seminars, but afternoons were frequently clear of any commitments and that was when we did most of the administration relating to the course, such as arranging lecturers, arranging tours and visits and so on. Stress was not a word that had any relevance to our daily life; having said that, we did have a Commonwealth naval officer on the course who suffered a nervous breakdown and I could never understand why or how!

The highlight of my first year was the 'European tour' with the commandant and 12 students. It covered France, Germany, Italy, Yugoslavia and I was the inevitable 'tour guide'. I had never realised that some senior officers could be so hopeless when it came to international travel. During the tour one of our UK brigadiers was recalled to the UK on urgent business. He was quite unwilling and unable to go to the airport unescorted; so I had to leave the rest of the tour and take him to the airport and guide him to his aircraft. I then had a nightmare which every 'tour guide' dreads. We were in Munich and when we arrived at the airport to fly to Rome, it was to find that Alitalia were on strike and there was no way of reaching anywhere in Italy from Munich. I looked at every option—coach, car, train—but none of those solutions would get us to Rome in time for our next event which was a formal dinner with the ambassador and many guests that evening. The only solution was to fly back to Paris and then to Rome. It was going to be a very narrow squeak but, all being well, we should make it in time. The commandant was somewhat less than pleased but had no option but to accept my suggestion.

In fact the travel arrangements became an even bigger nightmare. We lost another tour member in Paris as he became unwell and I had to dive into the depths of Charles de Gaulle Airport to retrieve his bags. I saw parts of the airport that I had never seen before and will never see again. And then, just to make my day, the commandant, who had gone off to have lunch with his daughter who worked in Paris, was unable to get back in to the airport. All I could see through the glass partitions was this irate senior officer scowling at me from the outside. Fortunately I could not hear what he was saying, but by dint of fast talking to some French official, I managed to get him back in.

We reached Rome just in time and, I have no idea who arranged it, but the Carabinièri turned up in force and escorted our coach through the rush hour traffic in Rome. That was quite an eye opener in itself; as I would not have believed that a coach could have made the journey in such a short time. Even so this disaster was seen to be totally my fault and any goodwill I might have had had totally disappeared. Even worse was to follow. When we arrived at the dinner, there were about a dozen different tables and I was seated on the top table with the ambassador and next to the most attractive lady in the room who happened also to be an Italian contessa. I could feel accusatory eyes boring in to my back thinking that I had arranged this for my own benefit. In fact I had nothing to do with the seating plan and I regarded it as my payback for a thoroughly miserable day. But our visit to Italy did not get much better because while we were in Naples, the commandant managed to lose his wallet which led to many phone calls trying to block his credit cards. Meanwhile I was being pestered by one particular member of the course who saw it as his duty to take every opportunity to try and endear himself to the commandant and was continually getting in the way. I thought that no one else had noticed what was going on until a brigadier came up to me and said, 'Don't worry Graham, we have chalked his name on the bottom of his shoes so that when he disappears up the commandant's arsehole, you'll know who it is!' It didn't really help but I felt better.

We had a particularly interesting and satisfying visit to Yugoslavia. It started with a couple of days 'rest' in Dubrovnik which was very welcome (for me at least). This was in the days of Tito and the Yugoslav Army looked after us particularly well. We were taken out on a field exercise with their specialist mountain troops who demonstrated their capabilities and were very impressive. Equally impressive was the *al fresco* lunch they provided. It was a banquet served in the field with some style; and there was no doubt at that stage who they regarded as the 'enemy'. It was not the West but it was the Soviet Union. The British Embassy official who looked after us for this visit, whose name, sadly, I cannot remember, had been with the partisans during the war and was highly respected by the Yugoslavs. Our visit to Yugoslavia ended with another couple of days in a hotel by Lake Bled; it really is a beautiful area and one to which I have always meant to return but have never yet managed.

The next crisis for me was to arrange the air travel for the visit to NATO and Berlin. The tour lasted about a week and in the past the RAF had always provided a Britannia aircraft to take us around the various destinations, but they had just gone out of service and nothing else was available. However, I knew of one Britannia that was still in service and it was owned by A & AEE Boscombe Down. They used it for supporting overseas trials; but there were not so many of those occurring at this time. I called the superintendent of flying at Boscombe and suggested that they might like to allocate it to us for this tour and, because they were having some difficulty justifying its continued existence, they jumped at the opportunity. We therefore had our air transport for the tour, and in fact the Boscombe Britannia was used by RCDS for a number of years until it too finally fell by the wayside.

Life went on in its own sweet way at Seaford House; lectures, seminars, and a relaxed form of life even for the staff. I cannot say that it was really my cup of tea but it was preferable to and more enjoyable than slaving away in Whitehall and we had overseas tours, UK industrial tours, visits to the City, a NATO tour and so on. AVM Ross Harding was replaced by Norman Hoad and Barraclough by Admiral Sir Ian Easton who was a somewhat more relaxed commandant—to judge by some of the parties that took place in his apartment behind the College.

Norman Hoad was a lovely man to work for. He was at this stage of his life more interested in painting than his RAF career. He was, of course, a well-known and highly regarded aviation artist, but he had decided to concentrate on horses rather than aircraft and he specialised in horse portraits which was a rather more lucrative subject with the interest coming from the Middle East. As soon as the formal lectures or seminars were over, he would allocate the work on a 50/50 basis between the two of us so that we could complete our commitments as soon as was humanly possible. He would then leg it to spend the rest of the day painting and leave me to my own devices.

After a year or so, the job became a little boring mainly because of the fact that the course was for a year and you were then attending lectures for the second and, later on, the third time. It was interesting to note that some of the lecturers, especially those of an academic nature, were almost word perfect in their delivery every time. Goodness knows how many times they delivered the lecture in a year but it was almost certainly a lucrative way of making a living. Within the four walls of Seaford House lecturers were free to say exactly what they thought without any fear of it being leaked out to the wider world, and some of those views, especially of politicians (of all colours) and trade union leaders were quite surprising.

The highlight of the year was always the world tour and because I was in my second year I was allowed to choose, so I chose to go to the Far East. The tour started in Hong Kong, and included South Korea, Japan, Thailand, and Singapore. This tour was led by Ian Easton—somehow I always managed to end up with the commandant and it most certainly was not by design. South Korea was impressive in terms of their work ethic. We went to visit a shipyard building container ships and the workers were like ants all over the place with the ships coming together like a giant Meccano set. We visited a similar shipyard in Japan and the contrast could not have been greater. You viewed the activity from a platform and there was barely a person in sight; the assembly of the ships was completely automated. One of our tour members had served in the Korean War as an RAF pilot and, quite how the Koreans knew I have no idea, but they fêted him everywhere we went. A visit to the UN Cemetery at Pusan was impressive because it was so beautifully kept—and it was also a sobering reminder of the cost of such a conflict in terms of human lives.

A visit to the Bridge over the River Kwai in Thailand was equally impressive. The fact that it is not entirely original nor is it actually over the River Kwai does not matter—the Thais solved the problem of the name by renaming the river over which the bridge stands. Equally, if not more impressive and sobering, were the cemeteries—immaculately kept and with an air of tranquillity and beauty which made it difficult to envisage the cruelty and savagery involved in the building of the Burma Railway. It was a visit that I have not and will not forget.

Just before we left to go home, I was summoned to join the rest of the members of the tour to be presented with a pair of gold cufflinks as a 'thank you' for the way in which I had organised and arranged the whole Far East tour; what a difference from the European tour of the previous year. The only point of debate used to come when I had to allocate seats on the aircraft. Travel was always first class, mainly because of the foreign students. There were 14 people on the Far East tour and usually only 12 first class seats. Inevitably I had to shunt myself down to cattle class; but I always had to ask one of the tour members to join me, and it was always a matter of some dissension. It was even worse when travelling from Hong Kong to Seoul by Cathay Pacific when the crew took pity on me and asked me to join them in the cockpit. That was seen as preferential treatment not worthy of the junior directing staff.

All good things come to an end, and in the spring of 1977 I was told, as I had feared, that I was to be posted to the Ministry of Defence to take over the operational requirements desk for the Harrier replacement aircraft from Jerry Cohu. I had not really expected anything else and the job, as Whitehall jobs go, was a challenging and interesting one; so I had no complaints. Then, just a couple of weeks later, I received one of those mysterious telephone calls from the air secretary's department asking me whether, if I was to get a command appointment, my wife would accompany me. To which I replied that I was not even allowed to go to the NAAFI without her and there was no way that she would allow me to disappear off to some distant shore without her. The following week I was called in to Norman Hoad's office to be told that my posting had been changed and that I was going to become the station commander at Brüggen in Germany. That involved six months of refresher flying including a Jaguar course at Lossiemouth—all infinitely preferable to MoD although Jerry Cohu and his wife did not seem to want to share my good fortune.

9

Seek and Strike

As ever the first step in getting to Brüggen was to go through the refresher flying machine. For some reason it always seemed to take an inordinate amount of time, anywhere from six months to a year once you had gone through all the various stages. Normally that would include basic refresher flying on the Jet Provost, followed by a session on the Hunter at Brawdy, an aviation medicine course and finally the relevant OCU Course—in my case the Jaguar at Lossiemouth. However, I did not have all that time and I did a short ten day course on the Provost at Leeming in which time I did 14 hours and then straight to Lossiemouth for the Jaguar OCU, all of which suited me fine.

I arrived at Lossiemouth at the beginning of September 1977 and I was delighted to find that I had been allocated to 1 Sqn at Lossie which was commanded by John Grogan who had been one of my pilots on 3 Sqn at Wildenrath. There were 12 of us on No. 20 Jaguar Course including Wg Cdrs Bruce Latton, Jim Watts-Phillips and George Robertson who was going to take over one of the Coltishall squadrons, seven first tourists and a French Air Force Exchange officer, Jean Allier who was also going to Coltishall. Lossiemouth is, in my view, a wonderful place to be if you wanted to fly, drink whisky, play golf and walk on the beach. I have never been addicted to whisky so I avoided that particular trap and had a wonderful two months flying. In fact John Grogan made sure that I had very little spare time and I flew 65 hours on the Jaguar in less than two months which was good going by any measure in those days. I had originally flown the prototype Jaguar at Istres in 1970 when I carried out the original operational assessment. The GR1 was a little more refined—but not a lot. I seem to remember that, among other things, I had criticised the fuel system severely and that had not been improved. The engines were a vast improvement but the NAVWASS (the inertial navigation and attack system) was very unreliable and it was not unusual to get a great big 'cross' coming up on the head up display (HUD) as you rotated on take-off indicating that the system had gone tits up, after which it was back to the good old map and stopwatch. Even when it was working—and I use the term loosely—it was not usually that accurate. But it was a thoroughly enjoyable two months, thanks in the main to John Grogan, which came to an end at the beginning of November.

The remainder of the month was spent preparing for the move to Germany, renting our house in Ballinger to the local orthopaedic surgeon whose house a few doors down the road had succumbed to dry rot throughout and had to go through a major refit. Judy went to stay with friends a few doors in the other direction and I went to Germany, arriving at the beginning of December. Judy's stay with our friends was notable for one event. The girls were sitting there one evening having a quiet drink when the husband arrived back from work. He opened the conversation by saying that he had been to see his solicitor. His wife said 'Oh yes, what was that for?' 'To talk about our divorce', he said. You could have heard a pin drop and Judy said immediately that she would retire to the kitchen. She was told in no uncertain terms to remain where she was and so found herself in the position of umpire in the subsequent discussions. It turned out that the husband, who had a couple of insurance companies in the city, was going bankrupt in the grand manner and indeed did so a few weeks later. He had managed to transfer the house to his wife before anyone could get their hands on it and he was left with nothing. The next time I saw him, about two or three years later, he was living in pretty desperate conditions in Houston, Texas, working as a porter for an antiques dealer. He did subsequently recover to some extent going back to the insurance business in the US.

Brüggen was one of the largest, if not the largest station in the Royal Air Force. It had 4 Jaguar squadrons, Nos 14, 17, 20 and 31; a wing of around 60 aircraft all with a nuclear capability. It had the Headquarters Flight of 25 Sqn with Bloodhound surface to air missiles, 37 Sqn RAF Regiment with Rapier missiles and No. 431 Maintenance Unit. In all it amounted to some 2500 service personnel, plus another 500 locally employed civilians and with families for which, being overseas, the station commander had responsibility, it amounted to some 7000 people—the size of a small township and many of the problems that go with such a community. Quite a responsibility! I arrived at Brüggen at the beginning of December and had a week's handover with my predecessor, John Walker. We had known each other for many years, having been cadets at Cranwell together and also been on the same squadron at Chivenor in the 1960s. John was a pretty focused individual and had worked up the station to a very high level of operational readiness and effectiveness; he would be a hard act to follow. He was moving on to be the group captain offensive operations at HQ RAF Germany at Rheindahlen.

The major concern was Taceval which was due to take place sometime in the New Year. The Tactical Evaluation (Taceval) was the major vehicle by which all operational units were judged by the Commander Allied Air Forces, Central Europe (ComAAFCE) on behalf of the Supreme Allied Commander Europe (SACEUR). There were four main categories of the evaluation. The first was alert posture and reaction (AP&R) for which the Taceval team would descend on the station unannounced and require the station to adopt a war posture, recalling all personnel and generating a maximum number of aircraft fully armed. To most RAF units this was never a problem. The second category, and perhaps the most important, was mission effectiveness (ME) during which the evaluators would judge the operational capability of the unit to perform its war role. In the case of the Brüggen Wing this was nuclear strike and conventional attack. The third part was support functions which was self-explanatory and would cover just about any activity on the station that you could think of. The fourth was ability to survive which looked at the unit's ability to operate in nuclear, biological and chemical conditions and to recover from attack from the air or from the ground. Many were critical of Taceval as being unrealistic and time-consuming, but it did force you to look carefully at many aspects of operations that would otherwise have been ignored as too difficult to manage. As such it was a valuable training tool which, whether you liked it or not, led to improving your overall operational capability.

During my first week the station underwent a Maxeval. There were three levels of exercise. A Mineval which was an exercise run by the station commander for the station's own benefit and rehearsal, a Maxeval which was conducted by the HQRAFG staff and was usually more representative of the final Taceval conducted by COMAAFCE. It was the result of this latter evaluation which really mattered. For that first Maxeval, I mainly stood and watched to see how it was done. My biggest worry was the nuclear procedures which were esoteric to say the least and with which I had no experience whatsoever. A simple mistake there could lead to a devastating assessment and negate months of work and hard training. I watched carefully but could not claim that I was much the wiser at the end of it all. Unfortunately the evaluation team were unable to award a rating for Mission Effectiveness due to the very bad weather conditions which restricted flying to a minimum, so we achieved a '1' for AP & R, N/A for ME, and '2s' (satisfactory) for support functions and ability to survive, and it was with some relief that we stood down for the Christmas break.

January came, and having seen the children safely back at school in England my wife arrived. She vividly remembers the day; she arrived at our quarter on a Monday morning to be told that she would be hosting a SSAFA committee meeting in the afternoon. She had not been aware that she was chairman of the local committee and certainly not aware that she had to host the committee in our house. In fact she had never in her life attended a SSAFA meeting before, let alone been its chairman. Fortunately we had a wonderful housekeeper, Frances Boon, who was the wife of the officers' mess manager, WO Danny Boon, and her helper, June, who referred to herself as the 'scrubber' but was anything but; they were always on hand to help and advise. Station commanders' wives in those days were unpaid general factotums, hostesses, charity workers, counsellors and mentors and their time was never their own especially on a big station overseas.

January and especially February were notable for bad weather, ice and snow. I had started flying the Jaguar again and I decided that I would fly with each squadron in turn so that I could become familiar with the units and the pilots and their operations. This was a system I maintained throughout my two years at Brüggen. We had another Mineval in January to keep up the level of training and, not least, to try and ensure that I was as familiar as possible with procedures in the combat operations centre (COC). Fortunately I had a very capable deputy, Wg Cdr Nigel Walpole, and an equally capable squadron leader ops in Max Craghill who would do their best to keep me out of trouble.

HQ AAFCE's Taceval team descended on to the station on a Sunday lunchtime and their activities continued for three days, without any admin breaks, to assess the station's ability for continuous operations. Proper evaluation of flying operations was yet again hampered by bad weather and many sorties had to be simulated by taxying through and parking on a special dispersal for the planned duration of each sortie. The mission evaluators however remained behind after the formal Taceval and were able to complete their assessment. The Canadian team chief read his preliminary report to an assembly of officers and we were delighted to hear that we had been awarded the highest possible gradings in all fields—the first time that this had ever been achieved. The following message from the Parliamentary under-secretary for defence (RAF), James Wellbeloved, reflected the general reaction:

> I have just heard about the outstanding success of RAF Brüggen in the recent NATO Tactical Evaluation. The results you attained represent a remarkable achievement and I am delighted that it is an RAF Station that has been the first to achieve such a distinction.

It was, of course, a result that it was impossible to beat and just as hard to equal—a rod for our own back and especially mine, but that did not stop us having a party to end all parties which certainly still sticks in my memory; not least because OC operations wing, Nigel Walpole, managed to break his ribs that evening in a valiant attempt to try and open the door of the toilet in the mess. Having consumed a fair amount of ale there was a need to go to the toilet but the door had unfortunately jammed. Nigel, not to be thwarted, said leave it to me and charged the door. Apart from breaking the lock, he went straight through the door and impaled himself in a basin, breaking a couple of ribs. He was out of action for some weeks and was in fact the only casualty we suffered in the whole of Taceval. But I have to say that our success was founded on the work done by my predecessor, John Walker.

Brüggen, being close to the Headquarters, was a constant recipient of visitors. The only advantage was, that being so close to Rheindahlen, it meant the visitors usually stayed overnight with the C-in-C or the deputy commander rather than with the station commander, so at least we avoided the constant overnight hosting of visitors that was the bane of many station commanders. No sooner had Taceval receded than we hosted Winston Churchill MP for a full day. I briefed him on the role of the station and then took him across to 31 Sqn where he had a trip in Jaguar, an informal lunch in the crew room—and a lively discussion about pay and conditions. It was during the 70s that the services were very poorly paid and, for the lucky ones in Germany, the local overseas allowance (LOA) kept us afloat.

With the arrival of March the weather perked up a bit. 20 Sqn decamped to Decimomannu in Sardinia for their armament practice camp (APC), 14 Sqn was preparing to take part in the Strike Command tactical fighter meet and 17 Sqn had a series of three bird-strikes. Being low level attack squadrons, bird-strikes were constant hazards which were difficult to avoid. Most of the time the damage was not too bad but every now and again it could be disastrous. Pete New of 31 Sqn collected a bird on take-off at Lahr, a RCAF base in the south, and ended up ejecting. I flew down to Lahr with Terry Nash, now OC 31 Sqn, to survey the wreckage—not that there was much we could do. Fortunately New was uninjured, but the Jaguar was a total write-off but, at least, it had not done any other damage. To complete my month we had the annual formal inspection by Air Vice-Marshal Tim Lloyd, the deputy commander, RAF Germany. It was also Tim Lloyd's time to leave and, as a former station commander of Brüggen, we dined him out in style. He, in his turn, wrote all station commanders a personal letter advising us, among other things, on how to deal with the C-in-C., AM Sir John Stacey The last sentence of the letter asked us to destroy the letter after reading, an instruction with which I complied.

With the coming of spring, the pace of flying activity perked up significantly. 14 Sqn hosted a detachment of 11 Sqn Lightnings to carry out low level air combat training, 17 Sqn had an exchange with 132 Sqn Villafranca (IAF), 20 Sqn had a busy and varied month training for the forthcoming tactical air meet and 31 Sqn, not to be outdone, hosted a detachment of 5 Sqn Lightnings. Last but not least, the squadrons competed in the Salmond Trophy, the best performance being that of 14 Sqn who came second. The whole wing was involved in a plethora of exercises with the FAF and the RDAF. One of the more memorable moments was provided by Margreet Walpole, the wife of my wing commander ops. We had a visit from a group of Dutchmen from Roermond who had made a formal complaint about noise, the town being almost on the periphery of the airfield. Since she was Dutch, Margreet was co-opted to act as interpreter. However, because she had mainly spoken English for many years, she had trouble with the correct Dutch word order and the Dutchmen were so fascinated by this and charmed by Margreet that they appeared to forget precisely why they had come to see us. Suffice to say the heat was taken out of the complaint and the Dutchmen went away quite happy. Another significant visitor was the new deputy commander, AVM Mike Armitage and his wife Gretl. I had met him before when he was a student at RCDS and he was not someone to whom I warmed; so I was somewhat apprehensive of his appearance on the scene.

I still managed to fly quite frequently. I rotated around the squadrons and would fly three or four sorties with one squadron before moving on to the next. In that way I achieved some form of continuity and familiarity with each outfit so that I could fit in with their operational training without being an embarrassment; and it seemed to work. Fortunately the spate of visitors had eased off and, having had such a successful Taceval, I felt the station deserved some relaxation from the endless rounds of Minevals in order to improve the quality of life. That this was a mistake only became clear to me later; once you relaxed the training regime, it became difficult to get the system into gear again. At this stage we also lost our squadron leader ops, Max Craghill, who had played a significant and important part in our success.

Spring moved on into summer and 20 Sqn participated in the central region tactical air meet at Wildenrath. This was a biennial event open to attack, recce and dual capable squadrons. 13 squadrons took part and, after a tactics phase, the second week was devoted to a weapons competition between 2 ATAF and 4 ATAF. 2 ATAF won and 20 Sqn achieved the highest score of the participating 2 ATAF Sqns.

It was in June that I called our first Mineval since our Taceval in February. With a large number of new personnel on the station, this was a huge learning exercise and served to bring home to us how rusty you can get after a short time without any practice. It was going to an upward climb to get back to our old high standards.

July was a pretty good flying month marred by a tragic and unnecessary flying accident at Deci. The pilot had taken it into his head to 'beat up' one of the many beaches in Sardinia trying, I understand, to impress a couple of young ladies he had met on the previous day and flew straight into the sea. He had only just joined the squadron and his wife had only just arrived at Brüggen. Judy and I had the unpleasant duty of calling on her to tell her the sad news; not one of the best of tasks especially as the lady in question thought that we had arrived on her doorstep to welcome her to the station. I did fly down to Deci in a Jaguar to find out first-hand what had happened; but it did not really improve on what I already knew.

My wife had been suffering for some time with a bad back which, on some days, would be so painful as to make even walking very difficult, and it chose this stage of the proceedings to give up entirely. She had been at a wives' farewell lunch for Lorna Nash, whose husband commanded 31 Sqn. She had been in such pain that she could barely get back to the house, which was only a very short walk from the mess. The mess manager rang me to say that Judy was in some difficulty and she was admitted to Wegburg Hospital in very short order. It was fortunate that, at the time, one of the RAF's best orthopaedic surgeons, Air Cdre Bob Povey, was stationed at Wegburg and he decided that there was no alternative but to operate and perform a laminectomy. At that time such operations were not without risk and Judy was warned that there was only a 50 per cent chance of success. She spent three weeks in hospital where she was looked after superbly and, I am glad to say, recovered completely. Indeed, as I write this some 40 years later, it has remained successful, so we shall always be very grateful to Bob Povey. One of the consequences of her sojourn in hospital was that she missed the summer ball in the officers' mess at Brüggen to which she had been looking forward if only for the magnificent seafood bar they always put on, but the mess staff ensured that she did not miss out by sending her a very large tray full of seafood for her to feast on in her room.

The mess at Brüggen was a good place for entertainment. Being overseas, we had a captive audience and the mess was always very well supported for any function from Burns night (a speciality of our senior medical officer, Jim Greig), Jazz luncheons with Monty Sunshine's Band, and various other forms of entertainment. Friday nights in the bar were almost a parade, and with such a large station we had a fair amount of talent. One of the pilots on the wing was a very talented pianist and I well remember walking through the mess at the end of the summer ball to find him playing the piano in the ladies' room accompanying Monty Sunshine on the clarinet. He could also do a very fine impersonation of Victor Borge. In fact, I was never quite sure what he was doing in the RAF! Danny Boon, as the mess manager, saw that we lacked for nothing. All of which helped to sustain a happy and vibrant station.

The summer finally produced some really decent weather. 14 Sqn exchanged with the French Jaguars at St Dizier and 17 Sqn lucked out, being selected to trial the new NBC protective clothing with a team from the Institute of Aviation Medicine. Personally speaking, I am very glad that we never had wear all this kit for real as I was less than convinced of its practicality. It was very uncomfortable to wear and, probably, even more difficult to fly in. However, it has to be said that it was as good as anyone else had and at least would have given us a fighting chance of surviving in a nuclear or chemical environment. And then, just to ensure that the other units did not feel left out I called a Station Mineval; but it was again painfully obvious that we had a very long way to go to achieve our previous peak.

On 19 August, as a result of a series of bomb attacks by terrorists on British bases in Germany, we activated the combat operations centre

(COC) and spent the night there supervising Brüggen's response which was basically increasing security precautions without placing the whole base on alert. We had a nominated emergency force of 30 men on permanent standby. This was a regular station duty for all airmen which lasted for a week and could provide an immediate response to any emergency—be it burst water mains or terrorist attacks. As far as I can recollect, this was the only time that it was ever invoked.

The summer season usually brought on a series of visitors and this was no exception. In quick succession I hosted visits from COMAAFCE, Gen. J. W. Fauly USAF; the UK Milrep to NATO, ACM Sir Alisdair Steedman (who I took flying in a Jaguar); CAS, ACM Sir Michael Beetham; the Chaplain in Chief, the Ven. J. H. Wilson; the International Police Association and the advanced staff course. CAS, having recently been C-in-C RAFG dispensed with the usual briefings and after visiting several units on the base and having lunch in the mess spent the afternoon on the golf course.

The golf course at Brüggen was a particular feature of the base which deserves mention. It was a championship standard golf course tucked away at the far end of the station out of the way of any operational activities. Legend has it that it was constructed by the sappers at the time the base was built and there was said to be some question about the legality of it. I was told that there had been a large inquiry and, unfortunately, all the paperwork had been lost when the aircraft taking it back to UK crashed. Somehow I doubt the truth of this story although I have no doubt that the construction of the golf course was a little questionable. When I arrived, one of the first things I was asked by the headquarters to do was to sign off the heating bill for the club house. My predecessor had a distinct dislike of the game and regarded the golf course as a carbuncle on a handsome beast, so he had refused to have anything to do with it. As a golfer, I was seen to be an easier prey. I was told that the club house had a war role as a 'hospital' and, as such, that justified the use of public funds for heating. I refused to sign off the bill (which was for a substantial sum) and told the headquarters that, if it was legal, they might like to sign it off themselves. Which I believe is what happened in the end, as I certainly never signed anything. But it was a beautiful golf course with an excellent club house run by a German couple, the husband being the resident golf professional. I have to admit I spent many happy hours down there as did the C-in-C and many others from the headquarters.

Flying activity remained at a pretty high level. 14 Sqn spent most of September at Deci on APC followed by anti-shipping missions against

US Navy task groups defended by F14s. 17 Sqn were preparing for the Jaguar's first ever participation in Red Flag (of which more in Cp 10) and 31 Sqn went off to Fassberg for the tripartite French/UK/US exercise to provide air support for ground forces conducting simulated operations for access to Berlin. This was an annual exercise which I had volunteered for when I was OC 3 Sqn. Terry Nash had been one of my flight commanders at the time and when the option to take on this commitment was offered he grabbed it. It was a hard-working, hard flying exercise matched by an equally rigorous international social programme, one that tested one's stamina to the limit; and for old times' sake, I flew up to Fassberg for a couple of days to participate. 20 Sqn was the only squadron not to be affected by deployments and thus ended up being responsible for most on base commitments, and to make sure that they did not feel too left out, I called for another Mineval. We were making progress but there were still too many areas of unsatisfactory performance.

The Red Flag training showed up a problem with batteries in the aircraft. It seemed that the high speed jinking manoeuvres used to avoid missile and radar acquisition was causing battery acid spillage with consequent corrosion. This was fairly rapidly cured by modifying the batteries. They deployed to Nellis AFB in Nevada, USA and early Red Flag sorties also revealed an engine surge problem. Despite these technical setbacks they had a very successful deployment and the Jaguar was considered to have acquitted itself well. Targets were hit on time and confirmed kills from ground and air threats decreased as threat awareness and tactics improved; all of which was the main purpose of the exercise. It highlighted the need for self-defence air-air missiles, more power, improved ECM and better avionics especially with regard to reliability. This was not exactly a surprise to most of us, but it was good to have a firm basis on which to base our needs.

One of the features of Brüggen was 'QRA'—quick reaction alert. We had a dispersal completely wired off and guarded in which we had four aircraft fully loaded with nuclear weapons, with four pilots on 15 minutes standby, 24 hours a day and 365 days a year. A squadron pilot usually spent a three day stretch in the QRA compound and the ground crew a week. Each aircraft would have a pre-designated target with all the pertinent maps and target information. It was a pretty unpopular (and boring) occupation as you had to sleep and eat in the compound; but it did give you some release from domestic duties. I decided I should savour 'Q' for my own satisfaction. So I went through all the necessary qualifications, target study, nuclear procedures, etc. However I did exercise *droit du seigneur* and only did 24 hours rather than three days. It was different from QRA in air defence, in which I had participated when I was on 54 Sqn, from which you did get scrambled from time to time. If you were scrambled from Q at Brüggen, it only meant one thing. Doomsday! It was a pretty soul-destroying duty of which the inference did not bear thinking about.

Moving into autumn and winter we had, as ever, long spells of poor flying weather. I had another Mineval and workup for Taceval but very poor weather marred the whole affair. Indeed the unintended highlight of the exercise was when I decided to launch half the wing on a simulated conventional mission following a somewhat optimistic weather forecast. In the event there was a rapid deterioration in the weather at Brüggen and, although several aircraft managed to return, 18 Jaguars, whose pilots included three of the 4 Sqn Cdrs, found themselves at Jever. Despite, or was it because of, traditional German hospitality it was three days before the aircraft were able to return; and even then that was in very marginal conditions. I was forced to end the Mineval a day earlier than planned.

For the second time we were invaded by a bunch of the British headmasters' and careers advisors. Normally I would not have considered it as being of any special significance except on this occasion I found myself talking to the headmaster of Bloxham School in the bar before dinner. And I suddenly realised that I knew him; in fact he had the master in charge of the RAF CCF section at school when I had decided to join the RAF. I obviously had not made too much of an impression on him as he did not remember me. As a result of the conversation and the fact that I needed to find a school for my daughter to take her A Levels, we ended up visiting the school. My wife and I were very impressed by that visit but unfortunately it turned out that the fees were somewhat out of our league.

December 1978 was a quiet month with poor weather allowing the squadrons to catch up on servicing. I called yet another Mineval concentrating on nuclear strike procedures and a subsequent wing launch. Fortunately, this time, we managed to recover all the aircraft to Brüggen. 37 Sqn still had two Rapier fire units deployed in Belize and Ed Durham, the CO of 25 Sqn, was posted to Strike Command at High Wycombe.

January was only notable by the snowfalls and freezing temperatures, going down to -9° C, black ice and freezing rain. It was as much as we could do to maintain flying currency. All in all, it was a month best forgotten apart from a Maxeval called by RAFG. Despite the freezing conditions, requiring all diesel engine vehicles to be warmed up in hangars, we managed to load 29 aircraft with CBUs and ammo in 4 hrs 48 mins compared with the required 12 hours. The notified Maxeval phase took place ten days later. Yet again it was badly affected by weather although the taxi through procedure enabled the evaluators to award ratings in all areas, however they proved to be somewhat disappointing—2s for mission effectiveness, support functions and ability to survive. 31 Sqn got a 3 for strike mission effectiveness because they broke nuclear regulations by carrying out a wheel change on an aircraft without first unloading its nuke. It was, in the main, procedural and incorrect actions which detracted from an otherwise good performance.

The main visitor for the month was a Miss Pauline Bramhill. You might well ask who she was, but I have to say that she stayed for three days and attracted unprecedented interest from everyone and managed to make herself seen in almost every corner of the base. She was, in fact, Miss RAFA, and ostensibly came to collect a cheque of £2000 donated by the station charities committee. The following month entailed a visit from AMSO, ACM Sir Rex Roe and DUS(Air), Mr J. H. Nelson who unfortunately had the very bad manners to drop dead the following morning when a guest of the C-in-C. I had not appreciated that we had that effect on people.

The weather did not improve much in February with winter not releasing its grip. Full flying was only possible on seven days with a further ten days when no flying at all was possible. I only flew four sorties in January and February; without a doubt it was one of the worst winters I can remember, and having been frozen over the last few months we then had the wettest March since Brüggen records began in 1954. Despite that, there were some reasonably good periods of flying weather and all the squadrons were able to catch up with most of their flying. Even I managed to fly more than 20 hours that month. Unfortunately 17 Sqn suffered a disaster when a Mallard struck the canopy of their T2, shattering it and the pieces going down the engine intakes causing both engines to stop and the pilots to eject successfully.

It is worth at his stage saying something about the social life at Brüggen. An overseas station like Brüggen has the advantage—if you can call it that—of having a captive audience. By that I mean that all personnel and their families live on or near the base and that the social life inevitably centred around the various messes. In the UK everyone tended to merge with the local population and mess life is not such an important factor and not so well supported. At Brüggen, if there was a mess function, it would be extremely well supported and it all added to the team spirit and feeling of symbiosis. To me it was an important part of life in RAF Germany and one that could not be ignored. Strangely enough, even though we were close to Holland and the easy accessibility to drugs, they were never a problem; mainly, I think, because of most RAF servicemen's aversion to drug abuse. Drink was certainly a bigger danger as it was cheap, plentiful and readily available and it certainly led to a few problems. One of my key personnel became an alcoholic and I had to bring him into my office on a Monday morning, with the SMO waiting outside, and give him the option of reporting sick or facing a court martial. It took over an hour before I was able to persuade him to accept the former, and after a period in hospital he did return to work totally teetotal and finished his tour in good shape. Sad to report that I heard he lapsed a few years later.

There was plenty of fun and enjoyment to be had during one's spare time. Being on the Continent meant that one could climb into the car at the drop of a hat and drive to Italy, France or wherever; and generally speaking most took full advantage of that ability. Friday night happy hours were always celebrated with gusto and ended up in some disarray. There was the night when certain young officers ate all the flowers which the wives had spent hours arranging for some function. When I interviewed them on Monday morning and asked why, they replied that they had been hungry. It was difficult to get very angry although I have to say that my wife was not best pleased. On another occasion a young visiting Harrier pilot from Gütersloh had been entertained in the bar for some hours until he too said he was hungry. His hosts said they knew of an establishment where he could get fed and drove him round the perimeter of the airfield (about ten miles) and planted him at my front door, which was actually only a hundred yards or so from the mess. At the time, about 11 p.m. on a Friday night, my wife was producing egg and bacon sandwiches for me and a few of the wing commanders after we too had indulged at happy hour. When the doorbell went and I was confronted with a very confused young Harrier pilot, who had been deserted by his hosts, leaving him on my doorstep. We took pity on him and gave him an egg and bacon sandwich as well.

One night we decided to have a senior executives' dinner in the mess as the wives had deserted us on some feeble pretext (as they do). We had just got to the dessert stage when who should roll into the mess but John McGarvie. John had not only been my senior engineering officer on 3 Sqn but had also been Nigel Walpole's engineering officer on 2 Sqn with

Hunters. John had by this time left the RAF and was, I believe, working for Ruston Gas Turbines. Anyway what followed was a fairly riotous reunion and by the time it came to go home, John was in no state to drive to catch the ferry. It was agreed that he would stay the night and so saying he said he would follow us to married quarters. *En route*, only a very short distance, he disappeared, and that was the last time I ever saw John McGarvie. I have often wondered what happened to him.

Jazz nights, balls, Christmas parties, all sorts of live music at a weekend—there was always something to cater for all tastes; and the mess was superbly run by Warrant Officer Danny Boon whose standards in everything were of the highest. We were privileged and very lucky to have such an excellent facility on our doorstep, add to that the sporting facilities of the base and there was always something to do.

Spring came and the Salmond Trophy was beginning to rear its head again, so a lot of the flying was concentrated on practising for the event. 17 Sqn led a multi-national flypast to say farewell to Com2ATAF and also provided four Jaguars to join four Buccaneers to welcome the new man, ACM Sir Peter Terry. However the highlight was a visit by the Hon. Fred Mulley, our secretary of state for defence, and Herr Doktor Hans Apel, the FRG secretary of state for defence accompanied by the C-in-C and numerous and varied hangers on. I decided that we would take up a full war posture for the duration of the visit to demonstrate how we would go about business for real. All personnel were armed and clad in full protective clothing for the period of the visit. I included an 'R Hour' launch from the COC to demonstrate the close supervision of nuclear operations and the subsequent take-off of 33 Jaguars, local defence actions against both air and ground attack, an operational turn round in an NBC environment and a visit to the QRA compound. With the detailed planning and rehearsals and the actual visit, this event required as much effort as any exercise and must rank pretty high among all the visits that Brüggen hosted over the years. It was not unremarked as Fred Mulley said in his message afterwards:

> I had come to expect high standards from RAF Brüggen and I was not disappointed. The sheer professionalism of all that Dr Apel and I saw at Brüggen was quite outstanding and reflected the very greatest credit on yourself, your officers, Warrant Officers and airmen. Please accept my congratulations and thanks.

At least he did not fall asleep!

Other visitors included the C-in-C, Sir John Stacey on his farewell, followed by the editor of *Der Fliegel* Magazine, Herr Franz Kanahl who had a trip in a 14 Sqn T2 and finally we were treated to the annual formal inspection by the Dep Cdr, AVM Mike Armitage, all of which seemed a bit of an anti-climax after the visit of the two defence ministers. Nevertheless we went through the usual rituals of cleaning, repairing and painting and I went round the station with the deputy commander and Judy looked after his wife, Gretl.

Somewhat amazingly we had snow for the first five days of May and then, to compensate, temperatures of 26 to 30° C during the last three days of the month. It was a pretty busy month what with two Minevals and the Salmond Trophy. The squadrons entered teams and, as I recollect, each individual sortie consisted of a couple of pinpoint targets, a line search and a couple of bombs on the range at Nordhorn. Everything was marked according to timing and accuracy and I decided to challenge Kip Kemball, the station commander of Laarbruch, to a personal competition. Although he could have used a Jaguar from 2 Sqn thus ensuring a level playing field, I am sorry to say that he cheated by using a Buccaneer thus employing the aid of a navigator; and by such underhand means he managed to beat me even though I scored 85 per cent in the event, quite a reasonable effort, I thought. 20 Sqn came second and would have won but for a bomb hang-up which cost them 40 points; 14 Sqn was third, 17 Sqn fifth (but one pilot scored 100 per cent) and 31 Sqn seventh after an unfortunate oversight which caused a disqualification. The Salmond Trophy was called in the middle of one of the Minevals so I was forced to cancel it, and just to complete our joy, the new C-in-C, Air Marshal Sir Peter Terry spent a day in our company. More importantly, my deputy and Wg Cdr Ops, Nigel Walpole left for pastures new. With his experience, he had been a great source of wise advice and I knew that I would miss his help and support. He was replaced by George Lee, who was someone I had not come across before.

I decided to attend the Innominate Club dinner at the RAF Club in London. This was a club formed just after the war to foster the relationship between the GD Branch of the RAF and the RAF Medics. It just so happened that my senior doctor (SMO), Jim Grieg, was a member as well and he wanted to attend the same dinner. So we took a Jaguar T2 to Abingdon, cadged a lift to London and spent a very pleasant evening with a 100 or so fellow members of the club before returning to Abingdon the following morning and flying back to Brüggen. It sure as hell beat the so-called comforts of the cross channel ferry and was a bit quicker and certainly more convenient. I also picked up the SASO, Air Cdre Paddy Hine, from Finningley and brought him back to Brüggen in a T2 and flew a sortie in a 14 Sqn training mission to give him some idea of what we managed to get up to.

One of the biggest drawbacks on the Jaguar was that we could carry laser guided bombs but we had no way of providing the laser beam to guide them, generally referred to as 'designating'; therefore we had to rely upon a third party to provide such a facility and this was usually the Buccaneers from Laarbruch. In order to give more options we looked at inter-operating with USAF F4s equipped with the Pave Spike designating pod. In fact there were few difficulties encountered but there was a conflict in tactics. The USAF were great believers in medium altitude operations with the benefits of an extensive electronic counter- measure capability. The UK, not being quite so well equipped electronically, relied on low level operations to avoid the many Soviet threats. The two philosophies were not compatible and we felt that we would be very vulnerable using the USAF profiles; but there was no technical barrier to such cooperation.

In the middle of June, Danny Lavender, the station commander of Wildenrath—which was equipped with F4s in the Air Defence role—rang me up to issue a challenge; and so was born Exercise Strangled Sonata. Basically he was going to put a piano on Nordhorn range and the challenge was that in 30 minutes the Jaguars would be unable to hit it with a practice bomb. The losers of the bet would pay for the subsequent Friday happy hour. Actually, to call it a happy hour was a bit of a bit of a misnomer as it usually went on for far longer than that. The piano was, in fact, a pretty small target and I was by no means sure that we would be able to do it although I was going to give us every chance of achieving it. I decided that I would lead a formation of 25 Jaguars which I reckoned could complete four runs each on the range (we carried four practice bombs each) in the allocated 30 minutes. On the morning of 21 June 1979 I was in my office just clearing up a few things before going off to brief the sortie when who should appear on my doorstep but the inspector of flight safety (Air Cdre Ken Hayr) to make one of his 'surprise no-notice inspections'. I was mortified and had no idea how he would view Exercise Strangled Sonata. However there was no option but to continue as though it was nothing unusual; and I did the only thing possible and invited him to fly in one of the two-seat Jaguars with Wg Cdr Joe Sim, OC 14 Sqn. The weather was pretty dank with mist and poor visibility; however we went ahead and flew the sortie, each aircraft making four passes. The range safety officer entered into the spirit of the occasion by playing piano music over the radio after unsuccessful attacks and the piano remained stubbornly upright until one of the last passes by Sqn Ldr Mike Gray who was, appropriately, the wing weapons standardisation officer achieved the all-important direct hit. In fact it turned out that we had had more than one hit, our bombs going straight through without collapsing the piano. Nevertheless our honour was saved and the subsequent happy hour at Wildenrath's expense quite memorable. Unfortunately we could not think of a similar challenge for the F4s although they did manage to get their revenge some 12 months later when they accidentally shot down a Jaguar! Ken Hayr never said a word about Exercise Strangled Sonata and his only real comment was to compliment admin wing on the way that they supported all personnel widely dispersed around the station. As a special prize on the following day we were subjected to a visit by the new secretary of state for defence, Francis Pym, at less than two hours' notice. I gave him the usual Brüggen briefing (which by now I could almost do in my sleep!) and we showed him an operational turn round on 17 Sqn; and the whole thing went off without a hitch.

We moved into the usual summer routine of squadron exchanges and deployments to Deci and, as the continental holiday season gained momentum, our exercise commitment reduced. The main activity for July was a three day Mineval with continuous manning which only proved the inadequacy of current manning levels to maintain 24 hour operations. It also highlighted yet again that it was quite difficult to keep up with the continual turnover of personnel as the inexperienced replaced the experienced. Regrettably, Graham Wardell of 14 Sqn crashed during the Mineval when he hit a television mast doing in excess of 400 kts. It certainly did not improve television reception in that area and Wardell was extremely lucky to survive having little or no time to decide to eject. However, the ejection seat functioned perfectly and he was uninjured. Wardell went on to become the RAF's first exchange officer flying F117s, the secret stealth fighter, with the USAF before the programme was public knowledge.

20 Sqn went off to Deci and I flew down to join them for a couple of days, flew a couple of trips on Capo Frasca range for old times' sake and flew back to Brüggen. We had the usual bunch of visitors; Controller of the RAF Benevolent Fund, Air Marshal Sir Denis Crowley-Milling; VCDS, General Sir Patrick-Howard-Dobson; the Commandant of the RAF Regiment, AVM Henry Reed-Purvis. I had had the privilege of joining 37 Sqn when they deployed to Benbecula for their annual

missile practice camp. It was interesting to watch although only 17 of the 28 missiles fired were assessed as successful. Obsolescent missiles, inadequate range facilities and operator inexperience all contributed to the poor results. But the most important visit of the month was by the Direktor of Kreis Viersen, Dr Rupprecht, in order to improve our relations with the local community. His nearest UK equivalent would be CE of a county council. I took him flying in a Jaguar and we gained a good deal of favourable publicity in the local press. In fact our relations with the German population were reasonable, many of us did mix with the local population and we were fairly well regarded. One of the vehicles of goodwill was Bruggen's Der Adler Karnival Club. Karnival is a great tradition in Germany and most towns in North Rhein Westphalia have their own Karnival Club. Not to be outdone, Brüggen had its own Karnival Club which could compete with most of the German versions. A *sitzung* (session) would be organised for a Saturday evening and the two clubs involved would compete with various acts, bands, male and female dancing troupes. Judy and I used to attend whenever possible and it has to be said that the standard set by Brüggen was as good if not better than most of the locals, and our efforts were very well appreciated and led to some very good relations with the locals. The penalty for attending these sessions was usually a headache from the noise and, to some extent, the beer. But it was worth it in my view.

It was also the season of summer balls and, as usual, Judy and I were invited to the summer ball at Rheindahlen. As a station commander, we were invited to join the C-in-C at his table with all the other HQRAFG hierarchy. I can well remember warning Judy not to make too much of a pig of herself on seafood (one of her weaknesses) as it could be a bit dodgy at times. It was an enjoyable evening and the following evening we were due to have dinner with a local German family, the husband being the local president of the 'returned German prisoners of war association', Paul Amende. They had all been taken prisoner in the West or by the Russians, and a few of them had not been allowed to return from Russia until many years after the end of the war. One of them always said that he spoke 'perfect Oxford English' mainly because he had been in a PoW camp just outside Oxford; unfortunately that was the only English sentence he could speak. However, they were a very friendly and hospitable bunch and we usually went out every two months or so with them to have a meal and play skittles in a local hostelry. Paul had been very insistent that we should come to dinner at his house but it had been very difficult to find a free Saturday. Finally, the Saturday after the

Rheindahlen summer ball was the agreed date, and as the day wore on I began to feel unwell. In normal circumstances I would have gone to bed, but I knew that Paul had gone to great trouble to arrange this evening and I did not want to disappoint him, so I persevered and went to his dinner. But the evening had barely started before I knew that I was not going to last the pace. There was a special barrel of beer and when they brought on the main dish, some sort of pork swimming in fat, I was certain that I was not going to make it. I called for my car and was driven home, only to find the SMO on my doorstep awaiting my arrival. It turned out that the food at the Rheindahlen ball had been contaminated although it was only the top table that had been affected. According to the SMO, I had an extreme case of Salmonella poisoning and, when I asked him what he could do about it, he said 'nothing!' For seven days I was extremely ill, not even being able to hold down water and then on the following Friday when it was time for the Brüggen summer ball, I suddenly felt better—and extremely hungry. I thoroughly enjoyed the evening.

Without a doubt the major worry was the impending Taceval and our continuing struggle to achieve the standard of the previous year. In order to maintain the station's operational capability, a reduction of flying hours had been imposed RAF-wide because of the effect of an engineers' industrial action back in the UK. 14 Sqn spent most of the month in Sardinia while 17 Sqn's APC was cancelled because of the critical spares situation. Frank Mitchell took over from Mike Gibson as OC 20 Sqn and the squadron continued its workup for Maple Flag which was due to start on 15 October. I called a three-day Mineval with 24 hour continuous manning again throughout designed to mirror future Tacevals. Considerable progress was made during the three days but some of the reaction to incidents, poor communications security, inadequate knowledge of mass launch procedures and unsatisfactory NBC procedures were all further pointers to the considerable drop in experience levels since the last Taceval. A welcome feature of the exercise was the full time participation of 52 Field Sqn RE, normally based in UK but whose war role was at Brüggen providing our airfield damage repair service. They added to the realism of the exercise by physically blocking roads with aggregate (instead of using flags and tape to indicate damage, and by setting off suitably loud explosions at appropriate moments. They also blew up sections of taxiway so that they could exercise their repair capability. In one incident they nearly gave me heart failure when a Jaguar, ignoring the carefully laid down instructions, taxied past a section of taxiway just as the Engineers were lighting the blue touch paper. It certainly got his attention—and mine—but fortunately the aircraft escaped unmolested..

The major exercise of September 1979 was a Maxeval; the alert posture and reaction phase took place at 0500 on 28 September. If ever there was an ideal time 0500 was it, as most people had had a reasonable night's sleep and were available in their billets and quarters so that the full call out plan could be put into motion without delay. The result was one of the fastest loadings ever of the Jaguar force with conventional armament. The senior evaluator was heard to comment that it was so fast that he had not had time to use many of his 'situation injects' when he had to call a recess until the 20 November. We had yet another Mineval at the beginning of October which, although planned to last three days, I had to suspend during the second day after an alarming series of errors by armament personnel responsible for nuclear generation. After a 'come to Jesus meeting' with those responsible, we resumed and the general performance was otherwise good.

The effects of the engineers' strike had disappeared and we got back to our normal flying rate of 20 hours per pilot per month at the beginning of October. I spent a couple of days at Lossiemouth with 31 Sqn tossing laser guided bombs at Garvie Island from low level with the designating being done by Buccaneers from Laarbruch. It needed careful coordination but it worked quite well; it was certainly better from a tactical point of view than the medium level designating with the USAF F4s. Garvie Island, a rock sticking out of the sea just off the northernmost coast of Scotland, has to be the most seriously abused pieces of real estate in the UK having had more bombs thrown at it than anywhere else.

20 Sqn went off to Maple Flag in Canada although they only took six aircraft and ten pilots. Maple Flag was similar to Red Flag and provided a unique opportunity to train in a permissive environment. And the long awaited appearance of the Taceval Team made itself felt. But the AP & R Phase got off to an unfortunate start when the evaluating team produced the wrong codes and were unable to persuade the COC staff to initiate the alert procedures. But once the *impasse* had been resolved 70 per cent of the aircraft (30 aircraft as the 6 at Maple Flag were exempt) were generated fully armed in 3 hours and 1 minute. By now everyone was getting thoroughly fed up with Minevals, Maxevals and the threat of Taceval. It somehow affected everything that you did and the thought of it was beginning to keep me awake at nights. I was right when I thought that the 'Ones' we had achieved the previous year were a rod for our own back.

As a bit of light relief, we had a couple of visits. The first was from Geoffrey Pattie and his wife accompanied by the C-in-C. Pattie was the under-secretary of state (RAF), and whilst the ladies were confined to the mess for lunch, Pattie met a cross section of personnel and showed a good understanding (for a politician) of the problems and rewards of service life in Germany. The other visit brought back memories from my time as JDS at RCDS as 80 or so staff and students, headed by the then commandant of RCDS, General Sir David Fraser, descended upon us. I decided to give them Brüggen in a full war posture (we hardly knew any better by then!) and that seemed to impress them.

In December and the long awaited Taceval team arrived. At the end of three days we achieved 'ones' for AP & R, mission effectiveness in both the strike and attack roles, support functions and a 'two' for ability to survive. Slow and inaccurate dissemination of contamination levels led to a marginal result in the NBC survival phase in the ability to survive category. The award of a marginal rating in any subsection precluded an excellent rating award for the whole section; thus the award of a 'two' indicated that all other subsections in the ability to survive category were of a high standard. While I was disappointed not to achieve the four 'ones' of the previous Taceval, I was relatively pleased at the outcome when I considered the trials and tribulations of our Minevals and the Maxeval, but it was a little frustrating to miss the four 'ones' by such a narrow margin.

And thus my reign at Brüggen came to a close. It had been a challenging time and it had also been a privilege to command one of the UK's premier and largest RAF Stations—another memorable and unforgettable tour of duty, but it had also been at times stressful and demanding. I had been posted to the Headquarters at RAF Germany as the group captain offensive operations taking over from, yet again, John Walker. Peter Taylor was taking over from me (again) and on 12 December 1979 we flew a pairs sortie in a couple of Jaguars and on landing, shook hands on the dispersal pan and that was the handover complete. One final footnote was that, in addition to our reasonably successful Taceval, we also won the Wilkinson Sword of Peace which was awarded annually to the unit making outstanding contributions to community relations. Nevertheless it was time to move from being prince of my own principality to doorman at the palace. One aspect that sticks in my memory is the professionalism and enthusiasm of the pilots, ground crew and of all the support functions without which I could not have succeeded. I doubt that many of the great British public appreciated the effort that went into maintaining their military capability. The *esprit du corps* was outstanding and I was privileged to be a part of it.

10

Keeper of the Peace

I served for the next two and a half years at the Headquarters in Rheindahlen as the group captain offensive operations from 1980 to 1982. After Brüggen, where we had a decent house and good house staff, I am afraid to say that our house at Rheindahlen was not in the same league; nor did we have any domestic help. My immediate boss was Air Cdre Eric Macey, an ex-V Bomber man who had never been out of East Anglia. It could have been a disastrous recipe as he readily admitted that he did not fully comprehend tactical offensive air operations having spent most of his time on Vulcans. However, he was always ready to listen and accept advice. More importantly he had a very fluid pen and once pointed in the right direction could provide a very persuasive argument; so I always appreciated the 'partnership' and, once persuaded of a cause, he would give me 100 per cent support. More importantly my immediate staff got on well together and it was a very happy team, David Mulinder, Taff Lewis, Graham Gibb, and Chris Strong. The deputy commander was John Sutton, a man with whom you could argue—but rarely persuade him to change his mind! Nevertheless it was a pretty happy headquarters with the overall direction being provided by Air Marshal Sir Peter Terry at the start followed by Air Marshal Sir Jock Kennedy towards the end of my time there.

As an ex-station commander it was inevitable that, as group captain ops, I would be the first point of contact should any of the bases require advice and/or guidance. Three of the four main bases were strike/attack, attack and recce bases—Brüggen, Laarbruch and Gütersloh. Brüggen had four Jaguar squadrons; Laarbruch, two Buccaneer Squadrons and a Jaguar Recce Squadron; and Gütersloh two large Harrier Squadrons. Wildenrath was the odd man out having two F4 squadrons in the air defence role. Sad to relate that is not far different to the current total RAF offensive front line strength of today.

One privilege granted to station commanders was the use of the C-in-C's house in Berlin by the side of the Wannsee which was fully staffed. Because I had not taken advantage of the facility when I was at Brüggen, I was offered the opportunity to spend a week there; so I piled my family into the car and we drove to Berlin through the corridor—which was an interesting experience in itself. Because of my knowledge of RAF Germany operations, I had a police escort through the corridor. The East German Police stopped you on the slightest excuse, photographed you; and then round the back of the customs post would try and sell you bits of their uniform, buttons, cap badges. I found it all a bit sad really, but the RAF police kept a very sharp eye on our progress to ensure that we kept out of trouble. Once we got to Berlin, we established ourselves in the C-in-C's house where we were looked after in style. The RAF police offered to take my wife and children across to East Berlin for a tour, an offer they took up with alacrity. Unfortunately I was not permitted to cross into 'Indian Territory', so I had to leave them to it. Suffice to say, they had a magnificent guided tour of the East and my children began to appreciate how fortunate we were. It was best summed up by my son who, after some time touring the East, said, 'Please may we go back to the decadent West now!' But it was a very pleasant and enjoyable week, made even more so by the attention and care of the C-in-C's house staff.

One of the advantages of living on the Continent was that it was easy to just throw a suitcase in the car and drive off to a number of attractive destinations. And, as a 'staff officer' the pressures of the job were not quite as bad as when one commanded a unit. We took full advantage of the situation and spent some enjoyable times in the south of France, in Munich at the Bier Fest, skiing in Austria (not a great success as far as Judy was concerned!) and trips to Italy. One Italian holiday was particularly memorable. I had been reading *The Sunday Times* one weekend and noticed an advertisement for an apartment in Sarzana. It sounded quite attractive and ideal for a family holiday so I answered the ad and booked the apartment for a fortnight. It turned out that the apartment was in a block of flats which used to be the Bishop's palace in the town centre of Sarzana. It was owned by a family called Pini who filled the whole building. The father, Stefano, used to own a restaurant in London and had retired back to his home town of Sarzana. Mother,

Angela, was a London Cockney who spoke fluent Italian with what even I could tell was an atrocious Cockney Italian accent. Their daughter was a very beautiful dark haired lady who taught English at the local university, and their son was a barrister in London who spoke perfect upper class Oxford English. Stefano had owned an Italian restaurant in London before the war and, it turned out, had modelled it on Judy's great uncle's (Marchesi's) Italian restaurant near King's Cross. He was an interesting man who would hold court every evening in the local bar in the town square where he would demolish a bottle of Remy Martin in one session. He had been interned in UK as an 'enemy alien' at the beginning of the war and put on a ship to be sent to a camp in Canada. Unfortunately it was torpedoed just after leaving Liverpool; he survived but never made it to Canada, and judging from his consumption of Remy he was not going to last too much longer anyway. But it was an excellent holiday, made even more so by the hospitality of the Pini family.

One of my other duties was to be the detachment commander for the RAFG Red Flag detachments at Nellis AFB just outside Las Vegas. The origin of Red Flag was the unacceptable performance of US Air Force fighter pilots in air-to-air combat during the Vietnam War in comparison to previous wars. An Air Force analysis had shown that a pilot's chances of survival in combat dramatically increased after he had completed ten combat missions. As a result, Red Flag was created in 1975 to offer USAF pilots and weapon systems officers the opportunity to fly ten realistically simulated combat missions in a safe training environment with measurable results. Many US aircrews had also fallen victim to SAMs during the Vietnam War and Red Flag exercises provided pilots and backseaters experience in this regime as well. The Red Flag mission was to maximize the combat readiness and survivability of participants by providing a realistic training environment and a post-flight training forum that encouraged a free exchange of ideas and tactics. Combat units from the US and its allies could engage in realistic combat training scenarios conducted within the Nellis Range Complex which is located north-west of Las Vegas and covers an area of 60 nautical miles by 100 nautical miles, (approximately half the area of Switzerland). This space allowed the exercises to be on a very large scale. In addition there were aggressor aircraft flown by USAF pilots using Soviet tactics, and many Soviet SAM ground threats both simulated and real—real in that they were real systems but they did not actually fire SAMs; but they did fire off what was referred to as a 'smokey joe' so that you were aware that you had been acquired and fired at; they also provided records of whether the aircraft had been acquired, whether it was within the firing parameters and so on for the subsequent debrief. Maple Flag was and still is a Canadian version of the same exercise.

Red Flag was a very impressive set up and ended up getting just about as near to combat as one could get without actually going to war. It was very frustrating for me in that I was the non-flying detachment commander so that I had to sit around all day listening to the briefings and debriefings—and keeping my fingers crossed that we did not have any kind of accident, always a possibility when you are flying that close to the margins. We had, on a previous exercise, had a disaster with a Buccaneer when the main spar fractured and the aircraft crashed. Frustrating it might have been, but it was infinitely preferable to being at Rheindahlen; and there were always the dubious attractions of Las Vegas to provide some entertainment. I lived on the base at Nellis in BOQs and very comfortable it was as well. Most of the rest of the RAF detachment had to live downtown Vegas in hotels which meant that they were never far away from the slot machines. When the first detachment arrived, I gave them an extensive briefing concerning the 'do's and don'ts' when in Vegas, with the usual warnings about the dangers of getting hooked on gambling, to beware of the laws concerning under-age drinking (some of our ground crew were quite young and under the legal age of being able to buy alcohol.) My credibility was almost immediately blown when two sergeants won $30,000 on the slot machines on the first night. They did say that it was an interesting experience in that as soon as the winning numbers came up, all sorts of bells and whistles blew; they were immediately surrounded by security men and marched to a private room and searched to ensure that they did not have any illegal devices on them. As soon as they had passed all the tests, which were carried out firmly but politely, they were given their money and sent on their way.

In those days in Vegas, you could eat pretty well for a dollar at one of the many buffets in the hotels. We were actually paid a daily rate of some $25 to live on and so I would generally eat at one of the buffets, then sit down and play Blackjack with the remaining $20 or so which meant that you could drink for nothing. All in all it made for a very pleasant evening's entertainment and at the end of the first six-week detachment I was about $300 in credit. I have been back to Vegas not so long ago and I have to say that I found the place a shadow of its former self. It was much more expensive to eat, there were no free drinks and the 'Strip' had a distinctly sleazy feel about it. When I was talking to one of the barmen in my hotel about it, he explained that the reason for the fall in standards was that it was no longer run by the 'Mob' who would have never permitted standards to slip.

I did two Red Flag detachments and I never failed to be impressed by the whole set up. There was no doubt that we benefited greatly from our participation and, although it must have been quite expensive, it was certainly worth it and enhanced our operational capability. The RAF's only participants in those days were Jaguars and Buccaneers. Unfortunately, the Jaguars did not bring a T2 with them and the only trip I did was in the back of a Buccaneer flown by Peter Norriss—not something that I wanted to repeat too frequently. I did actually get a couple of trips in a USAF F15 and a Canadian CF5. I think they felt sorry for me! The F15 was impressive, having that wonder aid to manoeuvrability called a wing and a large amount of excess power.

Back in Germany, there were other little distractions from the normal headquarters routine. My wife and I spent a very pleasant couple of days down in Decimomannu standing in for the deputy commander to carry out his annual formal inspection. It was a place I had always enjoyed despite some of its drawbacks. Sunshine (usually), good beaches and some half decent restaurants—what more could one want. And then I had to attend the Paris Air Show because McDonnell Douglas wanted me to fly the F18. I took Judy with me and we were well looked after by the company staying at some plush hotel in the middle of Paris. She declined to go to the Air Show and spent her time undertaking a bit of retail therapy. I flew the F18 out of Le Bourget and was less than impressed, mainly because it seemed to be incredibly short of fuel. It certainly did not seem to be anything special to me.

As I came towards the time to go back to England, we decided to sell our cottage in Ballinger and build a new house in Chearsley. I discovered that I could save a lot of money by buying a German kitchen in Germany and shipping it all back in the PSI van which one could hire at a cheap rate. It seemed to be quite a good wheeze until the Customs at Dover demanded to check the serial numbers on the oven which, of course, was buried right under all the other units at the most inaccessible part of the vehicle. It was raining, it was 1 o'clock in the morning and the Customs had little to do except irritate a senior RAF officer! He relented in the end when it seemed that the only way he was going to be able to check it was to give me a hand unloading, and much to my surprise and gratification the kitchen fitted perfectly.

Our domestic arrangements were becoming a little difficult at this time, mainly because my son had decided to go back to school to try and get at least one A Level—he was even idler than I was at school! So he was going to have to stay in Germany two or three months longer than us and I had to find someone to look after him. Fortunately Chris and Brenda Strong volunteered (Chris would question the word 'volunteer') and you could not have asked for any better surrogate parents. They looked after Mark as though he was their own son and Mark always remembers them with fondness. He did have a horrendous accident whilst staying with them, tripping down the stairs and falling through the sheet glass front door. He suffered a very nasty cut to his wrist and managed to wrap his arm in a towel and stagger in to a nearby school for help. Quite what they thought I do not know; he was covered all over in blood and looked like some escapee from Dracula. I was still in Germany and the first I heard of it was a telephone call to say that he was in hospital. Fortunately—and very luckily—no permanent damage was done; but the powers that be did take steps to replace all the front doors with toughened glass.

As my time ran out, there came the question of my next posting and when it came through I could scarcely believe it. I was posted to be the station commander and CO experimental flying at the Royal Aircraft Establishment at Farnborough. While it was in one way good to get another flying appointment, it could be regarded as a bit of a backwater when one had commanded one of the largest stations in the RAF. Certainly I was less than happy and when the C-in-C asked me what I thought I said so. His response was that I had better go and see the deputy air secretary in London and discuss it with him.

So off I went to London by courtesy of Uncle Ronnie's Sunshine Airways. Ronnie had been the squadron commander of the Pembroke transport support squadron at Wildenrath in 1974 and he had long since left. But I still thought of the Pembroke squadron in those terms. And I had a meeting with the deputy air secretary, AVM Les Phipps at the time. I had always heard of people who had objected to a posting and got something far more to their liking, so I thought I would try that line and the only answer I got from Les Phipps was that he would be happy to change my posting but it would be something that I would like even less. I went back to Germany with my tail between my legs, and when I got back the C-in-C called me in and asked whether I had got any satisfaction from my meeting. When I said, 'No' and told him what had happened he said that that was ridiculous and, as I sat there, he called the air secretary, Air Marshal Sir Charles Ness on the phone. 'I've got Graham sitting in front of me,' he said. 'Can I tell him exactly what the plot is?' Charles Ness replied in the affirmative and Jock Kennedy then told me what was going to happen. It seemed that I was going to be less than a year at Farnborough and then be posted to become the commandant of the Aeroplane and Armament Experimental Establishment as an air commodore, and that put things in a completely different light. I have never understood why they could not have said that to start with. I returned to the UK in a far happier frame of mind. Not only was I going to get promoted, all being well, but I was also going to get two more tours during which I could fly.

11

Cody's Tree

In March 1982 I had been to visit RAE Farnborough as soon as I knew I was going to take over as CO experimental flying from Chuck Charles. That visit in itself was quite interesting. The COEF had a very nice office in the control tower which had a panoramic view of the airfield, and I arrived one late spring morning to find out from Chuck what the job was all about. I went into the office and Chuck was busy signing off some papers, so I sat patiently waiting for him to finish, drinking a cup of coffee and surveying the airfield before me. A two seat Hunter, painted green, taxied out followed by a BAC 111. The Hunter was a 'one-off' T12 with an experimental fly by wire system fitted to the right hand seat. It roared down the runway and suddenly exploded into a ball of fire closely followed by two ejections. I was moved to exclaim what the hell was that? Chuck looked up from his desk and saw the BAC 111 waiting to take-off and said, as though I was a complete idiot, 'That's a BAC 111.' I quietly responded, 'Not the 111, Chuck, but look at the black smoke at the far end of the runway and the two parachutes'. I have never seen anyone move so fast. He was down the stairs in a flash and into his staff car, closely followed by me. We arrived on the scene just after the parachutes landed; the fire and rescue crews had beaten us to it. Apparently the engine had suffered a catastrophic turbine disc failure right at lift off. Rod Sears, the RAE pilot who was the captain and John Leng a company test pilot from Holme-on-Spalding Moor were both injured and a little burnt having landed in the fireball; but they were lucky to survive. I had not appreciated that life at the RAE was quite so exciting!

Back in England again after nearly five years in Germany, and I was asked what I would like to do for refresher flying. Since I had never flown helicopters and never flown the Buccaneer, I said I would like to do a proper helo conversion course and a Buccaneer familiarisation course. So the powers that be decided that I should go firstly to Shawbury for a Gazelle course, followed by a short refresher on the Hunter at Brawdy and then the Buccaneer Familiarisation course at Honington. It sounded pretty good to me and a damned sight better than pounding around MoD or some headquarters.

We settled in to our new house at Chearsley which was not without a few problems, the biggest one being that the builder left all the seals in the waste pipes that they put there to do a pressure leak test. The outcome of that was a flood in all the downstairs rooms when my daughter emptied her bathwater and it just came up through the downstairs toilet with all the usual unpleasant detritus, which, of course, ruined all the new carpets. The builder was good enough to put his hand up and say *Mea Culpa* and put the damage to rights.

At the beginning of June 1982, I arrived at 2 FTS RAF Shawbury and in one month did a complete helicopter conversion course on the Gazelle. The Gazelle really was a very pleasant machine (I hesitate to use the word aircraft). It always reminded me of a little sports car with very forgiving handling characteristics. It was, in fact, great fun to fly and I very much enjoyed the course. I did a little bit of everything, instrument flying, sloping field landings, confined areas, mountain flying and night flying. In just over two weeks I did over 20 hours flying.

July and I moved on to RAF Brawdy and the Hunter OCU. This was like putting on a familiar and well-used old boot. The pace was a bit slower than Shawbury and, as I recollect it, Brawdy had some issues with aircraft serviceability which slowed down progress. The Hunter was beginning to get a bit long in the tooth and, in any case, never had the reputation of being one of the most serviceable aircraft, but there was little sense of urgency around the place and it seemed to be run for the benefit of the staff rather than the accent being on the students. Nevertheless I did manage to get 17 hours flying in just over two weeks which was not too bad.

Finally in August 1982, I moved on to Honington and the Buccaneer OCU. Fortunate to relate, David Mulinder, who had been one of my wing commanders on the staff at Rheindahlen, was the CO of the OCU. He was quick to tell me of a certain group captain test pilot who had blotted his copy book by losing control of the aircraft and baling out on the approach. Test pilots (or ex test pilots) were not exactly flavour of the month! The theory was that I had to do the 10 hour acquaint course for senior officers, but David had other ideas assuming I could shape up. I must have done so because in two weeks I did 22 hours of flying, and I covered just about all aspects of the Buccaneer long course including all weapons (toss bombing, dive bombing, bunt retard) on ranges around UK, strike attack profiles, low level navigation. In all of this I was teamed with one of the staff navigators, Chris Finn, who was a pleasure to fly with. Being primarily a single seat man, navigators were a bit of an unknown entity to me, but I had to admit they had their uses and definitely made life a bit easier in the low level environment. The only disagreement we ever had was that I insisted, to his disgust, on carrying a marked up map in the front cockpit which he considered to be superfluous and an insult to his ability. My argument was that if anything happened to him, I wanted to be in the position of being able to carry on or at least find my own way home.

That month at Honington was my first experience of the Buccaneer and I have to say that I was impressed by the performance of the aircraft. It might have only been subsonic—just as all other strike/attack aircraft were once you slung weapons and fuel on externally—but it had a bomb bay to carry weapons internally which enabled it to accelerate quickly to high subsonic speeds making it very difficult to catch at low level. The only problem it had was some very dated avionics making it very much a 'steam driven' device. I have always been of the view that we the RAF missed a trick with the Buccaneer and that the 2* Buccaneer which was proposed as an alternative to the TSR2 and F111 projects would have been a very capable machine and far more cost effective. Unfortunately it suffered from the disadvantages of being primarily a subsonic aircraft designed for the Fleet Air Arm and therefore obviously, in the view of the Air Force Board, not worthy of consideration for the RAF. There were also RAF fears of unwittingly renewing the claims of Naval airpower, so the Buccaneer 2* (and the 2**) became a victim of MoD politics and in the end we had a Buccaneer without any updates at all. In my view, this was a great shame and an opportunity missed, but I very much appreciated the opportunity to fly the Buccaneer and to explore its many capabilities. Chris Finn had been a delight to fly with and David Mulinder left no stone unturned to ensure that I had a very successful and enjoyable experience.

It had been a very enjoyable three months of varied flying without any responsibilities, and now it was time to take over from Chuck Charles.

As far as I knew, no one was aware of the plan for me to move to Boscombe Down in less than a year. I looked briefly at the house offered to the COEF and decided that it really was very substandard and not worth moving into for a short time, so I got permission for my family to remain at our house in Chearsley and I moved into a suite of rooms in a separate bungalow which was part of the officers' mess. The mess itself was a unique building. Legend had it that when it was built, sometime in the 1920s, it had been a prefabricated building destined for India. The design tended to confirm that rumour as it was all single storey with a veranda all the way along the front. In fact it was a very comfortable place, not exactly overcrowded and with a reasonably good dining facility. Chearsley was only an hour or so away and the prospect of being a weekend commuter was not too depressing.

The handover period was just at the time of the Farnborough Air Show. It is perhaps necessary to explain the role of the commanding officer experimental flying. Firstly, you were the station commander of RAF Farnborough. This was not quite in the same league as being the station commander of Brüggen as, for starters, there were only about 100 RAF personnel, including the Institute of Aviation Medicine, which was a lodger Unit with an air commodore (medic) at its head; and as the title of COEF implied, you were responsible for all the experimental flying carried out by the Royal Aircraft Establishment. As COEF you were also a member of the RAE's management board which met every Monday morning. COEF's responsibilities included the airfields and operations at Bedford, Aberporth, West Freugh and Llanbedr. Bedford was probably the most significant as it included the operations of Aero Flight which really undertook the most demanding research flying. Llanbedr was important because of the Jindivik target drone operations. West Freugh did not have any resident operations but was an airfield used mainly for the range facilities in the bay, and Aberporth was just a small strip used for communications flying for Aberporth range personnel—also a part of the RAE. And then there was the Farnborough Air Show for which COEF was responsible for all the flying operations.

The theory was that I would shadow Chuck during the Farnborough Week so that I was fully prepared for the next Farnborough Air Show in two years' time. My main memories of that week were being a member of the Flying Control Committee which was responsible for the conduct of all display flying during the week. The main duty consisted of sitting on the roof of the tower watching all the displays with my fellow committee members, Brian Trubshaw and Robbie Robinson. Brian, of course, was well known for his exploits in Concorde and Robbie was Chief Test Pilot for Avro. We had a system of 'yellow cards' and 'red cards'. Any display deemed to be dangerous earned a yellow card and a second transgression would lead to the grounding of the offending pilot, not something that would please the manufacturer. We awarded a few yellow cards and one instant red card to the pilot of an F18 who we all thought had killed himself, but managed at the last moment to avoid hitting the ground. Sitting on top of the tower in the sunshine, especially if one had lunched well, could be quite soporific despite the noise and it was also a little tedious, only enlivened by moments such as described above. Trubbie, having lunched extremely well, frequently surrendered to the arms of Morpheus. Nevertheless it was a pleasant week and I was happy in the knowledge that I would not have the overall responsibility in two years' time.

After five years in Germany, Farnborough was a relative backwater but an enjoyable one. As COEF one was a member of the RAE's board of management which was headed by Tom Kerr; a lovely man and also an ex RAF pilot. The board met every Monday morning and my main recollection is of endless discussions concerning intellectual property rights and fighting off the establishment secretary who was always wanting to close the officers' mess as a savings measure. We spent very little time discussing the running of the Establishment.

I settled in to a relatively humdrum life. We had a fairly diverse aircraft fleet; we used a collection of Devons for transport support between all the various establishment's airfields (Bedford, Llanbedr, Aberporth, and West Freugh), a couple of two-seat Hunters, one of which belonged to the IAM, a couple of Buccaneers, a Dakota (which is now used by the Battle of Britain Memorial Flight, I believe), a Jaguar and that was about it. It was obvious that, if I was going to be able to maintain a reasonable amount of flying, it would have to be on the Devon and that I would have to get myself qualified to carry passengers and an instrument rating in the Devon—a 'Transport category' no less; which I did. And I found myself making like a transport pilot flying the schedule from Farnborough to Bedford and so on, but at least it kept me in the air. The Devons were most definitely coming to the end of their lives and I was tasked to look at possible replacements. We looked at the Titan and the Chieftain (second-hand of course), either of which would have done the job more than adequately. Although I think I preferred the Titan, but nothing came of it apart from showing us how dated our fleet was.

I did the occasional trial in a Buccaneer and acted as a guinea pig for the IAM in their Hunter. The doctors were always good at dreaming up some sort of trial which involved esoteric flight profiles, usually extremely uncomfortable and not very enjoyable and the IAM did not disappoint on that score. I was never quite sure what we were trying to achieve. All I do know is that it involved maximum amounts of 'G' and sick-making manoeuvres. Unfortunately, because the amount of trials flying was always very limited, it was difficult if not impractical for me to get fully involved. The most interesting work going on during my time was the use of FLIR at night and at low level using a Hunter and a Jaguar and it was not really the sort of work you could do every now and again. It required continuity and a depth of knowledge of the systems that I could not afford the time to acquire. More importantly it would have taken flying time away from the trials pilot and that was unacceptable. I did do a couple of trips—enough to frighten me and even suggest that I was probably getting too old and set in my ways. Added to which, knowing that I was only going to be at Farnborough for less than 12 months coloured my judgement. Apart from the FLIR work done at Farnborough, a lot of the more interesting flight testing was carried out at Bedford, such as BLEU (blind landing experimental unit) and VSTOL work.

In the early 1970s RAE Bedford was tasked by MoD with a work package to enable Sea Harriers to recover to a vertical landing on a ship at night in poor visibility. A two seat Harrier, XW175, was allocated as the trials aircraft and thus began its illustrious 38 year research career at RAE Bedford and then at QinetiQ Boscombe Down. During 1977/78 two sea trials were completed with HMS *Hermes*. The research programmes included recovery using MADGE guidance, VSTOL Head Up Display symbology, ski-jump launch, auto-stabiliser and autopilot development and FLIR demonstrations.

In the early 1980s, studies into advanced VSTOL aircraft concepts suggested that control at low speed and hover could be more complex than with the Harrier. The need for research into novel control methods led to XW175 being adapted for one pilot to have fly-by-wire control, when it became the Vectored thrust Aircraft Advanced Control (VAAC) Harrier, a unique UK VSTOL research vehicle. This decision was taken by the RAE Board and I have to admit that I voted against it; the reason being that my cynicism was at its peak and my view was that it was a very expensive exercise that would lead to little gain.

Over the period 1986–2004, several 2-inceptor control concepts were progressively developed, first with simulation and then, from 1990, with extensive flight trials in the aircraft, including the first ever deck landing with unified control (HMS *Illustrious*, Sept 1998). In 2002 this Bedford 'Unified' control concept, having been shown to demand minimal pilot workload while maximising safety, was selected for the STOVL variant of the Joint Strike Fighter (Lockheed Martin F-35B). Several ship trials with HMS *Illustrious* and HMS *Invincible* were completed up to 2008 to further support JSF and to demonstrate the capability to UK and US pilots. These trials included automatic recovery and automatic vertical landing to a ship at sea, some 30 years after the original HMS *Hermes* trials with XW175 in 1977. Thus it would seem that I was very wrong!

One never ceased to be amazed at the variety and capabilities of various entities at RAE. I discovered that I had responsibility for the RAF personnel in the parachute test section at Cardington (another part of the RAE), so I sallied forth to find out what they got up to. They used one of the airship hangars at Cardington for their balloons (for static drops) and I have to say that you can have no idea of the size of those hangars until you go inside. The head of the parachute test section was a small but nonetheless impressive individual who was a civilian, the remainder of the staff being mainly RAF PTI parachute jump instructors (PJIs). I asked him how he had ended up doing parachute research and he came out with a fascinating tale. It seemed that in the 1940s as a young man he had been working at RAE Farnborough. In those days, the only way to test spinning characteristics of aircraft was by dropping models from static balloons. He and a colleague used to go up in the balloon and drop the models from about 800 feet. They were equipped with parachutes but no one had ever said why or told them how to use them. One day they went up as usual in the balloon and someone had interfered with the cable; so that as they unwound it the cable flew free and the balloon drifted off into the far distance. The two lads in the balloon saw what had happened and suddenly realised why they had been provided with parachutes. They debated long and hard about what to do next and after half an hour or so concluded that there was only one way out of their predicament as they were rapidly heading off to the east. So they jumped; and that was how my host ended up as a parachute specialist!

Aero Flight at Bedford was run by Dennis Stangrom and he rang me one day to say that they were about to get rid of their Gnat which was the last airworthy one of its type and did I want to have a quick trip in it. Since I had never flown a Gnat I was more than happy to oblige; so off I went to Bedford. Dennis started to brief me on the peculiarities of the aircraft which had a particularly complex flight control system with an emergency procedure that was easy to get wrong—with disastrous consequences.

After attempting to explain the system, it was obvious that it was going to take too long to ensure that I understood all the nuances of the system and Dennis gave up. Since it was the last flight of the aircraft before it went to the knacker's yard, he just said 'if anything goes wrong, just eject!' an instruction that fortunately I did not have to follow; so I had a very pleasant hour in a Gnat which—apart from its complicated flight control system—was a very pleasant and fun aircraft to fly.

Spring was turning towards summer and it was time for the Paris Air Show. It was traditional that COEF invited the French colonel who ran the Paris Air Show to Farnborough and *vice versa*. So I was invited to Paris to have lunch in the president's chalet and spend the day. I took one of our Devons across to Le Bourget and was met by the French colonel whose name I regret to say I forget. However he did a splendid job of hosting and the lunch was, as only the French can do, sumptuous with plenty of fine wine and brandy with the coffee. It was only after the third brandy that the colonel reminded me that, as I had to fly home, it might be prudent to desist from having any more. What he did not know—and I did not tell him—was that I had taken the precaution of having a spare pilot in the aircraft, so when it came to flying back to Farnborough I was safely tucked in the back and fast asleep for most of the trip. I'm not sure what the colonel thought of the apparently irresponsible British.

It was shortly after the Paris trip that the telephone went one morning in my office and I was informed that the one and only original SE5a, a First World War fighter, would be ready shortly to be air tested and that it was my responsibility. The aircraft had been on the ground for a couple of years going through a full refurbishment and the CAA would be present to be able to give it a Permit to Fly. I did have a moth-eaten type-written copy of so called *Pilots Notes* which Chuck Charles had given me, but I had not flown a tail dragger for some time and I looked around for something to try my hand at before flying something that could be considered a national treasure. I rang Roger Beazley, the wing commander at Bedford, and it turned out that he had access to a Tiger Moth, so I made a quick trip to Bedford and, under his supervision, had 45 minutes in the Tiger. A few days later the SE5 was ready. My secretary, Heather Crisp, who had been at RAE for some time, felt that I had to be properly dressed for the occasion, and went and got a long length of silk scarf from stores. According to her it was the genuine article, and I tend to believe it. It was only at RAE that you would find such items in stores.

So, suitably attired with a long white silk scarf, I strapped myself in to the SE5. The cockpit had all the original instruments in it, but you could unlatch a panel behind which were some more modern variants just in case you needed them. It was a beautiful day with little wind and I have to say that I did feel somewhat nervous. Bend a Harrier or a Jaguar and you would probably be forgiven. Bend the one and only SE5 in the world and no one would forget. The first thing you notice is that the cockpit is very small—there is no doubt that our average size has increased somewhat since 1916 when the aircraft was designed. It was a pretty tight squeeze and not very comfortable. The aircraft had a 200 hp Wolseley Viper engine and it is, by modern standards, very low revving. Max rpm is less than 2000. But despite the low rpm, it is relatively powerful with plenty of torque. The aircraft flies not unlike a very powerful Tiger Moth with a fairly impressive performance and rate of climb. On that first trip, being of a somewhat nervous disposition and being under the eye of the CAA and half of the RAE, I climbed staying overhead the airfield; and just as well, because as I hit 5000 ft the engine started misfiring badly. I immediately pulled it back to idle and rapidly put the aircraft back on the ground. Unlike the Tiger Moth, the ailerons of the SE5 are not too effective at low speed which can give you a problem on landing particularly in gusty conditions. Perhaps because I did not have time to think about it, I did just about the perfect three point landing.

It turned out that all was required was a good clean of the plugs and we were back in business, and later that day I managed a full sortie of general handling and a couple of days later the CAA inspector came back to give his official blessing and 'Permit to Fly'. The SE5 has a .303 Vickers machine gun mounted on the fuselage and synchronised to fire through the propeller and a Lewis gun mounted on top of the wing which could be pulled down by the pilot so that he could change the magazine. Out of curiosity, I did try this in flight and all I can say is that it was extremely difficult to achieve. God knows how they managed to change magazines in the middle of a dog fight. Anyway it was an honour and a privilege to fly this aircraft. The RAE decided that they could no longer afford to keep such aircraft as a 'hobby' so they handed it over to the Shuttleworth Trust and on 15 July 1983, I delivered the aircraft to Old Warden.

My time at Farnborough was coming to an end and at the beginning of August I handed over to David Scouller before going off to take over the reins of the Aeroplane and Armament Experimental Establishment (A&AEE) from Reggie Spiers.

12

Probe Probare

September 1983 and I moved to Boscombe Down for what was to be my last flying appointment in the Royal Air Force. There were only two appointments for air commodores in which the incumbent had aircraft under his control which he could fly. One was the commandant of the CFS and the other was that to which I had just been appointed. I considered myself to be very fortunate indeed. The first problem was of a domestic nature. Martlet House, the commandant's married quarter, had suffered from a number of years neglect and was stuck very firmly in the 1940s—or maybe the1950s if I was to be generous. Reggie Spiers, my predecessor, had his own house not far from Boscombe and had not been too concerned as he only used the quarter on a part time basis for convenience. I was persuaded that it was time that the housing people were allowed to get at it to modernise the house and we acceded to their request. Consequently I was sentenced to another sojourn in the mess, although I have to say that the VIP suite was a very comfortable but lonely existence.

The organisation of Boscombe was always somewhat arcane, especially to the outsider. The commandant was head of the establishment and the chief superintendent was the technical authority for all testing. There were a number of divisions, trials management who were responsible for the coordination of all trials; performance division whose main concern was the handling and performance of aircraft; navigation & radio who carried out all the testing of aircraft systems; armament division who generally tested all weapons; engineering, who looked after all the aircraft servicing and tested the reliability and probity of the aircraft systems including environmental testing; photographic who recorded the outcome of trials and tested reconnaissance systems; and flying division which carried out all the flight testing and included the Empire Test Pilots' School. The establishment was about 2000 strong, a majority of whom were civilian engineers and scientists. All the flying was done by service pilots and armament division was also mainly service manned and headed by an RAF engineer group captain. There were a significant number of servicemen in navigation and radio division, especially graduates of the Spec N course, the navigators' equivalent of the ETPS Course. Facilities on the base included an electromagnetic compatibility (EMC) test facility, a weighbridge hangar which could weigh an aircraft of up to 135 tons accurately, a couple of flying laboratories, a Comet 4 and a Sea King helicopter, both comprehensively instrumented to provide a realistic dynamic environment; a pretty basic telemetry facility; and an environmental test facility for both cold and hot weather testing. Not least, we had a pretty impressive apprentice school with about 100 apprentices.

There were four units in flying division. My old home of 'A' Sqn which undertook the testing of all fighter, trainers and light aircraft; 'B' Sqn which tested heavy aircraft, mainly transport and bombers; 'D' Sqn which tested helicopters for all three services and was manned by a mix of Royal Navy, Army and RAF aircrew; and the Empire Test Pilots' School which trained all test pilots. 'C' Sqn, which had been the Navy test outfit in my earlier days, had been amalgamated into 'A' Sqn and ceased to exist; as had 'E' Sqn which used to test transport aircraft.

The first issue that arose was that of who was in charge. The chief superintendent, Brian Ramsdale, seemed to run everything and the commandant was just a figurehead. Whilst he most definitely had the responsibility for technical probity for flight test and the superintendent of flying, David Bywater, was responsible for the conduct of flight test, it seemed to me that the overall responsibility for running the establishment should lie with the commandant. So, one of my first actions was to take over the chairmanship of the management committee which had long been Brian's responsibility. While it probably did not make a lot of difference, it made me feel better!

The other main issue was to whom the establishment belonged. Being responsible for all the aircraft and equipment clearances for all three services, the major customer being, of course, the Royal Air Force, one would have naturally thought that the RAF would have some say in the operation and output of the place; however that was not the case. As commandant I came under the aegis of the Controller Establishments, Research and Nuclear (CERN) who was a 4* equivalent scientific civil servant. To add to the confusion it was not he but the Controller Aircraft (CA), a 4* RAF officer, who was responsible for the acquisition of RAF equipment who actually issued the clearances to the RAF completed by Boscombe Down. CERN and CA reported to the chief of defence procurement (CDP) although CA was also a member of the Air Force Board. CERN had the responsibility for all UK research and that included the Atomic Weapons Establishment (AWE), the Royal Aircraft Establishment (RAE), the Royal Signals & Radar Establishment (RSRE), the Royal Armament and Research Development Establishment (RARDE), my neighbour at Porton, the Chemical Defence Experimental Establishment (CDEE), plus one or two others that I have either forgotten or never knew about. But there was a difference between all those other establishments and Boscombe Down in that all the others undertook pure research; whilst A&AEE did aircraft and equipment clearances. Being a totally different end product, we had little in common with the other establishments apart from the fact that we were manned by a large majority of the scientific civil service. The current CERN was a pure research man and as far as he was concerned Boscombe Down was a somewhat annoying flea on his back which did not really interest him, so when it came to investment in facilities or budget priorities, it was inevitable that A&AEE was right at the bottom of the list. But in terms of the RAF reporting lines, my reporting officer was DGA2, an RAF 2* man who worked for the controller aircraft. In the first instance DGA2 was AVM Bob Hooks who was replaced by John Porter for most of my time; and John became a life-long friend. You really could not have thought up a more arcane (illogical?) organisational chart if you had tried, and one that led to a certain amount of frustration and confusion.

Apart from being the UK's main flight test centre, Boscombe was also a deployment base for the USAF and, just after I arrived, a whole squadron of F111s descended upon us for three weeks. One might have thought it would disrupt operations quite badly but they seemed to settle in well and disruption to normal operations was minimal. I had a trip in one of their aircraft and whilst the aircraft itself was pretty impressive their idea of an operational profile seemed a bit odd to me. Despite all their sophisticated aids, being in unfamiliar territory, they seemed to rely on 'beacon crawling' in the main.

One minor issue that arose was the local chairmanship of the Royal Aeronautical Society. Brian Ramsdale informed me that it was traditional that the commandant was always the local chairman. The only problem was that I was not and never had been a member. So with undue haste I was proposed, seconded and accepted as a Fellow of the Society. The main duty was to preside at branch meetings and lectures, not particularly arduous except when you had a lecturer like Peter Mariner from GEC whose lecture I did not understand (nor did most of the audience) and my memory of trying to summarise makes me cringe even now. I was invited to give the James Martin Memorial Lecture at the RAeS in London. For that I was able to dig out the files of the flight test of the Martin Baker MB5. The aircraft used wings similar to the MB 3, but had an entirely new steel-tube fuselage. Power came from a Rolls Royce Griffon liquid-cooled V-12 engine, producing 2,340 hp and driving two three-bladed contra-rotating propellers. Armament was four 20 mm Hispano cannon, mounted in the wings outboard of the widely spaced retractable undercarriage. The first flight of the MB 5 prototype took place on 23 May 1944. Performance was considered outstanding by test pilots, and the cockpit layout was praised by everyone. The accessibility of the fuselage for maintenance was excellent, thanks to a system of detachable panels. It was in many ways ahead of its time. Unfortunately the days of the piston engine fighter were numbered in 1945. But it was said, and the files confirmed it, that the MB5 had one of the most outstanding reports ever written by A&AEE. It was almost certainly the ultimate piston engine fighter and certainly made a good subject for a lecture.

My office in the main office complex overlooked the airfield and the main apron. My flying activities were generally restricted to keeping my hand in which meant, in the main, flying the Hawk, the Hunter, the Jaguar, the Basset or a Gazelle helicopter. The Basset was a useful piece of kit and quite a pleasant aircraft to fly although its single engine performance was nothing to write home about. It had been ruined when it was bought by the RAF, nominally as being able to transport a V bomber crew between bases, because someone had insisted that a set of hydraulic steps be put in so that a visiting air officer could climb out of the aircraft with dignity when clutching a sword for ceremonial. The extra weight incurred converted a perfectly good twin transport support aircraft to a marginal one when it came to single engine performance. It did not last that long in RAF service and, as occurred with many aircraft that were past their sell-by date or impossible to support on the front line because they were prototypes, they ended up at Boscombe. We had two of them and used them for transport support, delivering and picking up pilots from contractors and so on. It was useful (to me) because once I had done the quick conversion and got an instrument rating, it was a civilised way of getting around the country. The Hawks, Hunters the Jaguar and the Gazelle belonged to ETPS who were my main source of aviation. Normally I would tend to fly towards the end of the day when I had done all my paperwork and felt that I needed an hour of light relief and, as ETPS was located near my office, it was easy to see what might be available. A quick glance to see what was standing in dispersal and a telephone call used to suffice. Having gone through the usual routine of acquiring the necessary qualifications and instrument ratings—even the commandant had to be seen to stick by the rules—I was able to keep my hand in although I did not seem to have a lot of time to spare for such activities.

Quite apart from trying to get to grips with the various activities of the establishment and other issues, I was kept busy with official visitors, the annual reception to which all the worthies of the local community came, the McKenna Dinner for the graduating pilots from the current ETPS course, the UK, German and Italian Heads of OTC (official test centres) meeting at Manching, the Apprentices Prize Giving Ceremony, and a visit to Patuxent River, our US Navy equivalent establishment in Maryland USA. It was at one of the OTC meetings that took place in Rome that the Italian general made a memorable remark. It was extremely hot, almost unbearably so, and as the host he said just before lunch that the meeting after lunch would reassemble on the beach and he would provide everyone with swimming costumes. I was somewhat horrified as I wanted to get the meeting finished and get back to UK. He saw my look and said, 'You know, meetings like this go on all the time and we never remember them after the event. However, if we continue on the beach, it will be a meeting you will never forget.' He was absolutely right.

One of our more unusual visitors was a delegation from the air force of the Peoples' Republic of China to talk about the possibility of one or two of their pilots joining the next ETPS course. They arrived on 23 November 1983 and stayed for a couple of days. The delegation of six was led by the Chinese air attaché, Wang Guoli, being the only one who spoke any English. We took them out to a local pub for an evening's entertainment playing skittles and organised a visit round Salisbury Cathedral which, for some reason, engendered a certain amount of hilarity with our visitors. As far as I could gather they were looking at some of the more impressive gravestones in the Cathedral and saying that whoever they were they must have been members of the Politburo.

However it very quickly became obvious to both us and the Chinese that their pilots would never be able to cope with the environment or the language. This led to the possibility of ETPS advising the Chinese on setting up their own test pilots' school; which was to be the subject of further discussions.

In January 1984 we lost a Jaguar which caught fire as it was downwind in the circuit to land. The pilot, Sqn Ldr Tim Allen, had not realised quite how serious the problem was until someone shouted at him to bail out— an action he took without hesitation. Unfortunately he was just over the Porton Down Chemical Defence Establishment when he did so and he landed on the roof of one of their laboratories. The incident caught the attention of 'Jak' who was, at the time, the cartoonist of the *Evening Standard*, and he produced a wonderful cartoon of an RAF pilot sitting in the mess with growths coming out of him all over the place saying that it really had not been much bother.

Mid-February and at last the builders moved out of our quarter and we moved in. I have to say that they had done a brilliant job and it was without doubt one of the most comfortable and convenient quarters we have ever lived in. I am glad to be able to say that the renovations had not been very costly but the results were impressive. The only problem was that the rather ancient oil fired boiler, which had not been replaced, was rather akin to something that would have kept the *Queen Mary* going and the oil tank used to empty at an alarming rate. Brian Ramsdale, the chief superintendent, left and was replaced by Brian Childes who I knew from my previous tour at Boscombe. Brian had been the engineer who worked with Robin Hargreaves and Jerry Lee on the Jaguar programme at Istres.

It was at this stage, around April 1984, that we were selected as the establishment to try out a system called responsibility budgets. Prior to this event no one seemed to have any idea who was spending how much on what. We had a budget but no control over how we spent it. In fact this was true of most establishments and RAF Stations in those days. Initially the establishment secretary recommended that I went on a short finance course at Cranfield School of Management. It was entitled Finance for Non-Financial Executives, lasted a week or so and was aimed at board directors who had budgetary responsibility but had little or no financial or accountancy training. It was an excellent course; there were about 15 or so of us from very varied backgrounds and they were all somewhat surprised to find an RAF officer in their midst!

Back to Boscombe and, as a start, I was given control over certain budget items. Some, such as aircraft fuel and manpower, were not within my remit—which was a pity as they were the big spenders, but other running expenses, such as MT, were. So we could make some attempt to rationalise our MT and not run vehicles that had plainly become uneconomic to maintain as was the usual Government habit. The item I remember most vividly was telephones. When we looked at the detail, it turned out that our telephone bill was enormous—even outrageous, so we looked quite closely at it and it turned out that we had been paying line rental on telephone lines around the airfield which had been out of use for years. On closer inspection we also found that our bill for calls overseas, especially to the USA, were out of all proportion to expectation, mainly because our scientists and engineers used to enjoy long conversations with their opposite numbers in the US. The solution to that was to give a fixed telephone budget to each division and then say that whatever they saved from that could be used for buying new equipment. Perhaps the most disturbing thing that came out of the analysis of our phone use was the revelation that someone was running a betting ring on the system; that was closed down! It was the telephone that provided the main savings from the initial efforts, but it did go to show that there were significant savings to be made by giving the responsibility for budgeting to the user. What I did find remarkable was, that when I gave a presentation on the experiment to RAF station commanders at the support command, the reaction was that they really did not want be distracted from their main job, as they saw it, by matters of finance.

As a result of our initial meeting with the Chinese and a number of other meetings in London at their embassy which, I might add, provided some of the best Chinese food I have ever tasted, I was invited to visit their flight test centre in the middle of China at Xian-Yanliang. I decided to take Robin Hargreaves, who ran ETPS at the time, Jim Giles, one of his tutors, and his chief ground instructor, Alan Mattick and, at a meeting at Boscombe, I asked more in hope than expectation if we had anyone who spoke Chinese. A young squadron leader by the name of Peter Rogers at the back of the room put his hand up hesitantly and said that he spoke Mandarin; he had taken a degree in Mandarin at Leeds University and then done six months further language training in Hong Kong. Not only did he speak Mandarin, he was a qualified helicopter pilot who had also, somewhat unusually, completed the Spec N course (primarily for navigators); so I decided to take him along as well.

The security services started to take an interest in our activities and insisted on giving us a briefing before we left. We flew to Hong Kong on 14 May 1984. Ian Keppie, who had been the CO of 'A' Sqn back in 1969 when Robin and I were pilots on the squadron, was now the personnel director for Cathay Pacific and lived in Hong Kong. He had offered to look after our wives whilst we went into the depths of China. So Judy and Paula, Robin's wife, came with us. Having arrived in Hong Kong, we left Judy and Paula with Ian Keppie and his wife and went by train to Guangzhou (Canton). This was at a time when China was only just about emerging from the shadows and we were surprised to find that our hotel, the White Swan, was a recent addition to the city and had everything you would expect from a luxury hotel. In fact it was a very attractive hotel with a most impressive lobby. It was interesting to watch the expression and reaction of the (very) attractive waitresses when they were addressed in Mandarin by a very tall and dark westerner. We were to learn later that Rogers' language ability did have some serious limitations when it came to ordering more than a few beers.

I really have no idea as to why we were delayed but we spent three or four days hanging around Guangzhou. Our PRC Air Force escort kept taking us out to visit various attractions, and failed to explain the delay. But after four days we were suddenly whisked off to the airport and flown to Xian. I have to say that internal flights in the PRC were not quite to western standards at that time—the word 'basic' probably gives an adequate description. On the way to Xian we had to change flights at Guilin which was in a very picturesque and attractive mountainous part of China. Unfortunately the effect was slightly spoilt by the sight of a burnt out Trident aircraft by the side of the runway which had obviously been there for some time and did not actually fill one with confidence. When we got to Guilin, we looked for somewhere to eat or at least get a cup of coffee and a roll as we had been unable to get anything before we left Guangzhou. There was nothing in the terminal building but there was a small restaurant just outside. We sent in Rogers to order the necessary; and that was when we found the limitation to his language abilities. Instead of a coffee (or tea) and a sandwich or whatever, we were faced with a full Chinese banquet and no option but to eat it. We did our best but, at 7 o'clock in the morning, it was just a little too much.

We arrived at Xian and once again put into a hotel and were dragged around museums. In fact one, the Banpo museum, was quite interesting. It housed artefacts from the archaeological site of Banpo. The museum gave access to the excavated buildings, and also had several reconstructed houses designed to resemble the Neolithic settlement, a typical Neolithic matriarchal community of the Yangshao Culture dating back about 6,000 years. However it really did not have much relevance to aviation!

We were then treated to an even more spectacular display when we were taken to a private viewing of the Terracotta Army followed by visits to various emperors' tombs. The Terracotta Army had been discovered in 1974 by accident by some local farmers digging for water. At that time the dig had not received a lot of publicity and it was one of the most amazing sights I have ever seen. It too had little relevance to aviation but it was well worth the time and the journey.

Finally we were taken to the PRC flight test centre; it was two or three hours by car north of Xi'an. The roads were not exactly easy travelling, but the countryside was fascinating. One thing that impressed me is that they did not waste any land, however small; crops were being grown everywhere. But the overwhelming impression was of relative poverty and life at a subsistence level. It was a relief to reach the flight test centre and the first of quite a few surprises; the first being the accommodation. I was shown into a suite of rooms consisting of a lounge, a bathroom, and a bedroom; quite comfortable really except that they had not been updated from the time they were built which, I would guess, had been some time in the early 1930s and obviously for European/Western use. I never did discover for whom or why. While the facilities looked OK, they were spoilt by the fact that water was only available for about an hour a day and even then it was a bit hit or miss and certainly of a colour that did not encourage bathing. There was even a television in the lounge but I never did get it to work—I have a suspicion that it was only capable of transmitting not receiving.

The flight test centre was a very large facility. Off one end of the airfield was the Xi'an Aircraft factory that was building the Chinese variant of the Tu-16 (Badger) bomber. I had been led to understand that they also had a USAF F4 Phantom and a F5 hidden away which they had purloined during the Vietnam War, but naturally that was never discussed. We were hosted by General Wang Ang, a 3 / 4* general in charge of the base—and probably a lot more—with a supporting cast of which I have no idea as to names. One particularly sinister individual was quite obviously the 'political' man who sat quietly watching and listening. At one meeting I inadvertently caused uproar when I asked why he had not got his 'little red book' with him. Everyone, with the exception of the political adviser, seemed to think that that was hilarious.

We were given a detailed tour of the facilities which were impressive and an air display, mainly involving MiG-21s, which was not. They were pretty critical of the Soviet engineering of the MiG-21 which they described as 'dockyard'. That may be so, but it still had a pretty impressive performance for its time and the basic engineering meant that it was fairly simple to maintain. The so-called morning meteorological briefing was like no other that I have ever experienced in aviation. The pilots, about thirty of them, were drawn up in column of threes on the dispersal whilst some individual harangued them for ten minutes and then they were dismissed. I was told that that was the norm and all I can say is that I could not have seen this working in the decadent west. The way they treated their pilots was interesting. They were confined to the base all week and their families lived off base. They were allowed to get together for just one day in the week. I do not think that would have worked in the decadent west either! I gathered, but could not be sure, that this was to ensure that were properly fed and victualed.

The tour of the facilities was extremely interesting, especially when it came to telemetry. We were first of all shown a very basic telemetry facility, Russian in origin, with no more than 20 channels. It even made the Boscombe facility, such as it was, look acceptable. I tried to make some trite remarks about simplicity being best when our guide said the usual 'Pliss to follow'. We were then escorted to another building at the door of which we were asked to don white coats and dust covers for our shoes. We were then shown the most modern telemetry facility that I had ever seen anywhere in the world, including the USA. It had everything, including a TV auto tracking capability, and more. It was quite obvious that it had only been recently installed and that, understandably, they were having some trouble in learning how to use it. We wondered where on earth they had procured such a system and it turned out that it had come from France.

They also showed us their latest project which was, I understood, a development of the Russian Su-9 (Fishpot). From our discussions, it became evident that they were having some difficulty with the intake design which was causing major engine problems. My advice was sought and, not being an aerodynamicist, I had no idea as to what to suggest. However, they appeared to believe that, because I was the head of a flight test establishment, I must have some idea and refused to listen to my protestations of ignorance on the subject. This problem came up at all our formal meetings on the base; and they also wanted me to sign a formal Government to Government Memorandum of Understanding (MOU) for formal links between Boscombe and Xi'an. I tried to explain that military officers in the UK did not sign formal MOUs between governments these days and the last one to do so had probably been Lord Nelson. That cut no ice and they then started to threaten, saying that our air transport to Beijing was becoming very difficult and that the train journey was very uncomfortable, if indeed we could be found any seats. I could see a diplomatic incident rapidly approaching. But suddenly and for some unknown reason, they decided to back down and once again everything became sweetness and light. But I must admit to having a few nervous moments for a time.

The final event was a Chinese version of a guest night. It was in fact a very enjoyable evening and the food was first class. I do remember tasting a dish which I thought was particularly good. And no sooner had I made the remark than another dish of the same appeared at my side. So, to be polite, I ate it all only to discover that it was garlic stems in some sort of sauce the results of which were not entirely lost on me or my colleagues on the following morning. A feature of the evening was the continual toasting with Mao-Tai, a particularly evil beverage. To get our revenge, we introduced them to 'Schooner Racing' with beer and it very quickly became evident that this was a technique that the Chinese could not master. And, somewhat surprisingly, there was another technique that they could not master that was to do with chopsticks. After two weeks in China, we had become quite adept with chopsticks to the extent that we were able to pick up two peanuts simultaneously from the opposite side of the table. Something, it turned out, that they could not do! It was an enjoyable evening and we all ended up on the best of terms despite that fact I had not solved their intake problem or signed an MOU.

Our air transport to Beijing miraculously appeared and I went to the embassy for a debrief. I met with our ambassador and I expressed surprise that we had been left on our own in the middle of China without any local support, especially in the light of events. He apologized profusely and admitted that they had no idea that we were there. I had assumed that because our security people had briefed us before we went that the diplomatic staff would automatically be informed. Sadly, such was not the case. Never assume; always check!

Beijing was just starting to get modernised and new hotels were in the process of being built. We stayed in one of the first such hotels which was only half finished but nevertheless preferable to any alternative. To make up for their omission, the embassy arranged for us to visit the Great Wall and the Forbidden City, both being very fascinating and worthwhile. And then we flew back to Hong Kong to be reunited with our wives, spent a very pleasant evening with the Keppies at one of the best Japanese restaurants I have ever been to before flying back to UK.

Our Chinese saga did not end there as the following February the Chinese came back to Boscombe. They had decided that they would set up their own test pilots' school and looked to ETPS for advice. The delegation was led by General Wang Ang this time and I decided that I would throw a buffet supper in my house for him and his cohorts which again included the air attaché from London, Wang Guoli. It was an interesting evening; first of all my wife agonised over what to feed them. She decided on mainly rice-based dishes followed by fruit salad as she had been advised that the Chinese did not eat dairy based products. She did however produce some dairy based puddings and cheese for the local guests. And just as well, because the Chinese hoovered up just about everything in sight. Either they did not realise what was dairy based or someone had neglected to tell them that they did not touch such stuff. The evening turned out to be a great success. One of our local guests had a Singapore Chinese wife who sang risqué Chinese songs. I have no idea what they were about but the Chinese seemed to appreciate them; and at one stage, my daughter Kim, who was 17 years old at the time, suddenly appeared with her flute and her recorder and we were treated to a duet with the general on the recorder and Kim on the flute. It turned out that this was at the request of the general who obviously understood more English than we had appreciated. It was a very good evening.

Wang Ang moved on, I believe, to some post in the civil ministry of aviation. I last saw him at Farnborough in 1985 when he asked me to join him in London prior to the show; but our association with the Chinese had proved interesting and challenging and I believe they have since formed their own test pilots' school.

I came back from our visit to China to find that the CND had decided to conduct a 'festival of peace' with the aim of setting up a permanent peace camp at Boscombe. For some reason they had always associated Boscombe with nuclear weapons and therefore the base was on their target list. In the event not many turned up and those that did conducted themselves peacefully and relatively inoffensively; but a small handful decided to stay on and became a small thorn in the side, camping on the end of the runway just outside the fence. We left them there for some months in the hope that they would finally get bored and drift away. But they did not and we decided at the beginning of winter that enough was enough and we were going to clear them away. With the collaboration of the local police and our Ministry of Defence police we moved in on them early on a Sunday morning; and I do not think I have seen a sadder sight. Their tents were indescribably filthy—as were they—and the smell was quite horrendous. When they were told to pack their bags and leave, I got the impression that they were somewhat relieved to be told to go away.

Certainly we did not have any objections and the site was cleaned up and they never came back.

It was in the second half of 1984 that we were tasked with the assessment of a new trainer for the RAF. The contenders were the Swiss Pilatus PC9, the Brazilian Embraer Tucano and the British NDN Firecracker. They were all fitted with the Pratt & Whitney PT6 turbo-prop with a fairly impressive performance. Apart from good handling as trainers, and decent engineering for maintenance, the one performance requirement that sticks in my memory was to be able to cruise at 300 kts at low level—the trainers being besotted with the need to teach low flying at a reasonable speed and in multiples of 60 kts. Being two seaters, I flew all three during the tests and there was no doubt which was the most exciting to fly by a country mile; that was the Firecracker, it was very light and by far the most lively of them all. As an experienced pilot, it was also the most fun to fly but it did have one very startling habit; and that was if you put it into an upright spin and just lingered a little too long on the recovery, it would flick straight into an inverted spin. Even for experienced aviators, this could be alarming if not downright confusing—inverted spinning not being a manoeuvre habitually practised. Quite what the inexperienced student would have done, apart from bailing out, is difficult to imagine and I have to say that the engineering of the Firecracker we flew was definitely not in the class of the other two competitors. So the competition was in effect between the Tucano and the PC9. Generally the PC9 was the preferred option—and it could also cruise at 300 kts at low level. Both aircraft were well engineered, there being nothing to separate them. But politics ruled the day and the combination of giving a large contract to a Northern Ireland company and a sop to South America to mend fences for our foray into the South Atlantic became more important than the best solution. The Tucano was in fact a perfectly acceptable solution except that Shorts did not make too good a job of production.

Pilatus supported the PC9 with the single engine Turbo-Porter, an almost legendary aircraft with the most impressive short take-off and landing. It was flown in by Bob Cole, an ex-RAF test pilot who had joined Pilatus. He invited me to fly his Turbo-Porter and, to my amazement talked me through my first landing in the machine. Nothing unusual, you might think; except that my first landing was across the runway at Boscombe rather than in the more conventional direction, much to the surprise of Air Traffic. Admittedly, the Boscombe runway is wider than most at around 50 metres, but it was still pretty impressive—even more so as it was my first landing in the aircraft.

Life went on much as usual with a list of never ending visitors. Robert Key, our local MP became quite a frequent visitor, not surprisingly as we were one of the biggest employers in the Salisbury area. In fact we had good relationships with all the local organisations, political and civic and with the Cathedral, all of which made for a rewarding time. The chairman of Salisbury District Council, the mayor, the mayoress and the chairman of Amesbury Town Council toured the establishment and flew in a Wessex to get an overall picture of their domains from the air. Government ministers, high ranking service officers from all three services and high ranking civil servants descended upon us from all directions. In the main it was a pleasure to show them around and most showed extreme interest in our activities. There were other diversions, such as conducting the annual inspection of Dulwich College CCF, reviewing the Jersey Air Training Corps.

There was one other pleasant duty that fell to me and that was to fly our Sea Fury T20—commandant's perks. It was an aircraft that had been purloined by Boscombe from the Germans for whom it had been a target tug. I am not sure quite why or how it came into our hands. But we had it—and it needed to be flown! It had been refurbished by courtesy of the apprentices and a substantial amount of help from some of our enthusiastic engineers, much of it during their spare time. I had kept current on the Harvard, of which we still had two used primarily for photo chase. The Sea Fury was probably the most powerful and fastest piston engine fighter in the world and the final development of the Tempest and Typhoon. Although conceived during the Second World War as an aircraft for both the RAF and the Navy, the RAF version was cancelled and the Navy version was the only one to enter service. It was the only piston engine aircraft to shoot down a jet in the Korean War in the hands of Lt Cdr Hoagy Carmichael who had been involved in our dive bombing trial of the Hunter back in 1960. It had a Bristol Centaurus sleeve valve engine of about 2500 hp. You were warned to watch the oil pressure like a hawk as, if it started dropping, the engine could easily seize or catch fire (or both). The only other peculiarity was the lack of decent brakes. Being primarily a carrier aircraft, Hawkers had relied more on the hook rather than the brakes for stopping it on the ground. However they were still capable of tipping the aircraft on its nose if you applied them too sharply because of the weight of the engine.

When the time to fly the Sea Fury, I went down to Yeovilton and did a couple of trips with their Sea Fury expert in their two seater; and finally I flew ours, and what an experience. The first thing that struck you was the torque on take-off and you had to be very careful opening up the throttle or you could find yourself very quickly off the side of the runway. But once you were airborne it was a delight to fly with fairly light and responsive controls and a very impressive performance. We had decided that two people would fly the aircraft and my back-up was an experienced test pilot from B Sqn who shall remain nameless. I did two trips in the Sea Fury and my back-up converted to type and on his first trip managed to crash it by tipping the aircraft on its nose on landing. In fact the aircraft ended up on its back in the middle of the runway. The canopy was smashed, the engine probably ruined because of the shock loading and, worst of all, there was a slight crease in the fuselage indicating that all was not well with the frame. The engine could probably have been recovered, but Sea Fury T20 canopies did not exactly grow on trees and the crease in the fuselage indicated the possibility of substantial airframe damage. All in all, it was a write-off, and my views concerning the experienced test pilot from B Sqn—who was totally uninjured—were unprintable. Worst of all, I felt for all the people who had invested a large amount of time and energy rebuilding the aircraft. What a waste and how disappointing.

It was the disposition of our flight test organization within the 'system' that really continued to concern me and the fact that the RAF had little or no control of, or say in what we did and how we went about our work especially as they were in reality the customer. There was a change that occurred half way through my tour which was, in my view, progress. And that was the arrival of the central tactics and trial organisation's operational testing unit. This consisted of a number of Tornados and Harriers which conducted operational flight tests using our facilities but under the control of HQ Strike Command. It was (and still is) my view that basic flight testing and operational flight testing of military aircraft should not necessarily be separate entities. Whereas there is of course a difference between the two, there is always an overlapping area as you move from basic to operational. And it is of course essential that those doing the basic flight test do not lose sight of the ultimate application—which can and has happened. So I am not a proponent of keeping the two apart. Which is why, when CTTO moved their operational testing to Boscombe, I tended to regard it as the start of a sensible trend.

To that end I regarded, as a first essential step, the move of the control of A&AEE from CERN to CA. Although both were part of the MoD procurement executive, at least the controller aircraft was a 4* RAF officer. It required the agreement of CERN, CA and, as the final step, the chief of defence procurement, a certain Mr Peter Levene. I managed to get the agreement of CERN and CA, and as a final step all I needed was CDP's blessing. He decided to come and visit Boscombe to find out what we were about, and then I made a fatal mistake. In an attempt to impress and get the visit off to a good start, I sent a Bassett to pick him up at Northolt. He was not impressed. Whilst to me the Basset was a very reasonable and comfortable form of transport, the trip out to Northolt and then being strapped into what he regarded as a smelly and uncomfortable Basset did not impress. An upmarket helicopter would have been a more suitable choice—but unfortunately I did not have such a beast. Whilst during the visit he was sweetness and light and I was left with the impression that all might be well, it was quite obvious that, after his return to London, we had failed in our mission. I think what got to him was the fact that our two clapped out Bassets which looked the part, were an indulgence too far, and I suspect that he was already plotting 'QinetiQ'. He said nothing to me; but subsequently his decision on the reorganisation was to leave it as was as he had rather more grandiose ideas. So I failed, in my own eyes, at the last hurdle—which after two years of gentle lobbying and persuasion was a great disappointment.

In the latter months of 1985 my tour was coming to an end. Robert Key made another social visit, I attended the AOC in C's annual conference at Support Command, another visit by the new Chinese air attaché, Zhang Lai Gui, the McKenna Dinner at which Admiral Sir Raymond Lygo was the reviewing officer, the annual prize giving for the apprentices and it was all over bar the shouting. Peter Gover arrived to take over the reins; and then there was one last flight. A&AEE had the last single seat Hunter Mk 9 still in service and flying, XE 601, usually referred to as the Raspberry Ripple because of its rather garish paint scheme. So, on 12 December 1985, I strapped into 601, took off and behaved like a hooligan for 40 minutes before coming back to Boscombe at 500 kts with that evocative 'blue' note to break and land to be met by Ron Burrows, the superintendent of flying, with a glass and a bottle of champagne in hand. It seemed appropriate that, after 30 years, my flying career finished where it had all started—in a Hunter. And it was a tribute to the aircraft that it had lasted so long in service.

EPILOGUE

Whitehall

It was, of course, inevitable. After years of enjoying myself in the cockpit, there had to be some form of payback, and it was that the last five years of my life in the Royal Air Force were to be spent in Whitehall. After Boscombe, I was posted in January 1986 to MoD to be a director of operation requirements (DOR(Air)2) in the central staffs. The job involved looking after all the operational requirements for all the equipment that I understood least—namely air defence, electronics, radars and so on. The first priority once again was our domestic arrangements, and we decided to move to Sandwich so that Judy was close to her aged mother, who lived in Broadstairs, so that she could look after her. We also bought a small studio flat in Pimlico so that I became a weekend commuter again.

I was not to know it at the time but my time as DOR 2 was to be of great benefit in the future. I was forced to get familiar with the esoteric world of radar and electronics and I spent the next nine months so doing. My boss as assistant chief of defence staff (OR) air was Mike Adams who I had known from the test world at the time of the transatlantic air race. Indeed it was his demise that led to my participation in the event. It was not long after I had arrived that he asked me to come and see him one morning. I had no idea what it was about but he sat me down and said that he had agreed with the controller aircraft (CA), Air Chief Marshal Sir David Harcourt-Smith, that I could be attached to his staff for a specific task. He did not say what the task was but added that CA would explain it in detail.

So off I went to see CA whose responsibilities included the acquisition of all platforms and equipment for air systems. It was at a time that the Nimrod AEW had run into problems and the company was having difficulty getting the radar to work properly. The platform—the Nimrod—was acceptable if only just adequate in terms of size. CA, instructed I believe by Peter Levene, had decided that it was time to have a showdown with the company and as a first step he wanted a risk assessment of the merits of the Nimrod AEW versus the Boeing E3 and the Grumman E2 and he wanted me to head the team undertaking the task. I was aware of the problems as the programme came under my aegis in OR and I was also aware that the Royal Signals and Radar Establishment at Malvern had a vested interest in the system as they had been responsible for the basic design. So I said I would get together a team but I would not under any circumstances have anyone from RSRE on it as they would almost certainly be biased. Having said that, I knew I was going to have some difficulty finding enough radar specialists to be on the team and, in particular, a man capable and with the street cred to lead the technical aspects of the assessment. CA accepted my provisos—and then I had the problem of finding the people.

My thoughts immediately went back to Boscombe and, in particular, to the head of navigation and radio division, Tom Caldwell. So I rang him and asked him whether he would consider heading a technical team to undertake the risk assessment. Much to my relief, because I could not think of anyone else more suited to the challenge, he accepted the job. Tom decided to base himself in London in an office close to me and together we put together a team. The task was politically highly charged for a number of reasons. RSRE felt that their reputation was at risk; GEC—and in particular Arnold Weinstock—felt that their reputation and their bottom line was at risk and generally, especially politically, there was a bias towards the home grown equipment. On the other hand there were people who were tired of being held to ransom by UK industry and being asked to accept inferior equipment for the sake of 'buying British'. We had a problem persuading Boeing that we were serious about the assessment and they were concerned that they were just going to be used as a whipping boy for GEC. We persuaded them that we were indeed serious; but whatever the outcome it was certainly not going to be a cake-walk.

The weeks went by and it became pretty obvious that the Nimrod was never going to be the equal of the E3 which was, at this time, an in service system with an impressive performance. Even the E2 had a good performance but being a much smaller platform maximised for carrier operations, it was not in the same league as the E3. On the other hand,

GEC were having great difficulty getting their system to work properly. It certainly was not helped when they invited us up to Hawarden to fly in the aircraft and the Nimrod proceeded to dump all its hydraulic fluid all over the dispersal on start-up. Arnold Weinstock wrote to the Prime Minister, Margaret Thatcher, complaining about my behaviour and that of one of my flight lieutenants. The PM just forwarded the letter to me with no comment—and how I wish that I had kept a copy.

The choice of the Nimrod airframe proved to be the wrong one, as it was too small to accommodate the radar, electronics, power generation and cooling systems needed for a system as complex as the one required. At just over 126 ft, the Nimrod was close to 26 ft shorter than the Boeing 707 aircraft that formed the basis of the E3. With the planned all-up weight it was around half that of the American aircraft, but was expected to accommodate sufficient crew and equipment to perform a similar function. Nimrod was designed to have a total of six operator consoles (four for the radar, one for ESM and one for communications), which was less than the nine stations fitted aboard the E-3A. The size of the 707 also meant there was room to increase the number of operators. The choice of computer to integrate the various sensor systems was wrong, as the GEC computer was simply too slow and too underpowered to perform the tasks required of it: by the time of project cancellation, the mission system mean time between failure was around two hours, and it took around two and a half hours to load all the mission data via a tape system. What mission performance there was, was largely due to the IFF which complemented the radar system. With the addition of IFF data, the system could successfully track aircraft carrying IFF transponders, but when the IFF was switched off, radar tracks would rapidly be lost. This meant that the system would successfully track civil and 'friendly' military aircraft, but would not reliably detect hostile aircraft which did not carry a compatible IFF system—detection of which was the whole point of the project. The aircraft also had two scanners, fore and aft and getting the two scanners to synchronise proved difficult, resulting in poor all-round surveillance capability.

Towards the end, we had a meeting with CA, the head of RSRE and a number of other officials on a Sunday evening in MoD. Predictably RSRE took the side of GEC arguing that the Nimrod AEW was the only sensible way forward ignoring, it seemed to me, the fact that the system did not work and was going to cost at least the same again to get any reasonable performance out of it. Even then it could not be guaranteed and it certainly would not have the same potential as the E3 which was an extant system with a superb performance and well capable of being developed further. CA had a major clash with the head of RSRE and, I thought, won the argument. Nevertheless I walked away from that meeting thinking that, having come out in support of trashing the Nimrod and going for the E3, if the final decision went against us, I would have no option but to resign.

It is a matter of history—and much to my relief—that our recommendation to go with the E3 was accepted by all. Eventually, it was recognised that the cost of developing the Nimrod radar system to achieve the required level of performance was prohibitive and the probability of success very uncertain, and in December 1985 it was decided to open up the programme to a competitive bid. The Nimrod programme had cost in the region of £1 billion up to its cancellation, contrasting with manufacturer claims in 1977 that the total cost of the project would be between £200–300 million. It is a matter of record that the E3 was eventually procured and has been a very effective system—and that is probably an understatement.

After all this excitement I was told, to my surprise, that I was going to take over from Mike Adams as ACDS (OR) Air on promotion to Air Vice Marshal. Suddenly my time as DOR 2 made sense, allowing me time to get familiar with a number of unfamiliar systems and technology. I would like to think that it had been done with a certain amount of foresight; however my natural cynicism suspects it was more by luck than judgement.

One of the first things to happen was that I was invited to have lunch with Arnold Weinstock in his eyrie at Stanhope Gate, the GEC head office at the time. Also present at that lunch was Sir Michael Beetham who was GEC's military adviser. I have little doubt that Sir Michael had persuaded Arnold that it would be prudent to try and mend fences with me after the trials and tribulations of the Nimrod AEW affair. In fact it was a very pleasant occasion. Arnold told me that there was one action he regretted during the Nimrod affair and that was the letter he had written to the PM complaining about the behaviour of one of my staff. He thought that was an unforgivable error; no mention of complaining about my behaviour as well as I was obviously fair game. I have to say that I liked the man and I always seemed to get on well with him. Subsequently he never failed to greet me like a long lost friend whenever we met, which was not infrequently, and he never failed to recount some amusing story. He must have turned in his grave when he saw what his successors did to his company.

My post was part of the Central Staffs although the chief of the air staff kept a pretty beady eye on my activities. My 'boss' was a Navy admiral by the name of Sir Jeremy Black, a.k.a. 'The Black Knight'. Despite his natural dark blue bias, I always found him a reasonable man to work for. One of my first tasks as a result of the demise of the Nimrod AEW was to sponsor the requirement for the Boeing E3. The French decided to join in on our coat tails and we asked for eight E3s and the French wanted another four. In the event we ended up with seven aircraft and the Black Knight supported us all the way.

The procurement process was (and probably still is) a painful and long-winded business and because of the process you are almost guaranteed to ensure that the equipment desired is late into service and, by the time it gets there, out of date. It started off with the drafting of a requirement and this would usually go through so many iterations that it would take several years before you could get any form of agreement. Then you would have to get the programme funded and into the long term costings (LTCs). This was a dream sheet of programmes that were usually given minimal costings so that you could justifiably squeeze them into the LTC. You would of course be opposed by the civil servants and the other services who would see that your programme was going to be at the cost of one of their pet projects. The papers being circulated would go round and round with someone always finding fault. Indeed the MoD civil servant would regard such a paper as an challenge to his virility if he could not find some objection, thus demanding a complete rewrite and another six months added to the process. Once you finally got the requirement approved through the equipment committee, you were only part way there. Then the process of acquisition and bidding would take place. Some companies would come in with completely unrealistic bids secure in the knowledge that, once they had won the contract, they could renegotiate the price; not difficult in the circumstances because the procurement had taken so much time that it was inevitable that what was once seen as a solution needed changing because of a change in the threat—and so it went on.

It was interesting to note that when it came to an urgent operational requirement (UOR)—as occurred during the Falklands War—miracles could be performed in very short timescales and at very reasonable cost. Everyone pointed in the same direction, no one tried delaying tactics, and, because there was only so much that a company could charge for work in a relatively short timeframe the whole business became cost effective. Unfortunately you could not operate as for a UOR all the time and, of course, it would not apply to very large acquisition programmes which by their nature took years.

The major programme in my time as ACDS (OR) Air was what is now the Typhoon. After the demise of the Nimrod AEW, it dominated a large percentage of my time. The UK had identified a requirement for a new fighter as early as 1971. Designated AST 403, the specification, issued by the Air Staff in 1972, resulted in a conventional 'tailed' design. While the design would have met our requirements, the UK air industry had reservations as it appeared to be very similar to the FA 18 Hornet which was then well advanced in its development with McDonnell Douglas. It had little potential for future growth, and when it entered production it would secure few exports in a market in which the Hornet would be well established. However, there had been a West German requirement for a new fighter which had led to the development of the TKF-90 concept. This was to be a cranked delta wing design with forward canard controls and artificial stability. Although the British Aerospace designers rejected some of its advanced features such as engine vectoring nozzles, they did agree with the overall concept.

In 1979, Messerschmitt-Bölkow-Blohm (MBB) and British Aerospace (BAe) presented a formal proposal to their respective governments for the European Combat Fighter (ECF). In October of that same year Dassault joined the ECF team for a tri-national study, which then became known as the European Combat Aircraft (ECA).. The separate development of differing national prototypes continued. France produced the ACX. The UK produced two designs; the P.106 was a single-engined 'lightweight' fighter, superficially resembling the JAS 39 Gripen, the P.110 was a twin-engined fighter. The P.106 concept was rejected by the RAF, on the grounds that it had 'half the effectiveness of the two-engined aircraft at two-thirds of the cost' although I think I might have subscribed to 'two-thirds the capability at half the cost'. The ECA project collapsed in 1981 for several reasons including differing requirements, Dassault's insistence on 'design leadership' and the British preference for a new version of the RB199 to power the aircraft versus the French preference for the new Snecma M88.

Consequently the Panavia partners (MBB, BAe and Aeritalia) launched the Agile Combat Aircraft (ACA) programme in April 1982. The ACA was very similar to the BAe P.110, having a cranked delta wing, canards and a twin tail. One major external difference was the replacement of the side-mounted engine intakes with a chin intake. The ACA was to be powered by a modified version of the RB199. The German and Italian governments withdrew funding, and the UK Ministry of Defence agreed to fund 50 per cent of the cost with the remaining 50 per cent to be provided by industry. MBB and Aeritalia signed up with the aim of producing two aircraft, one at Warton and one by MBB. In May 1983, BAe announced a contract with the MoD for the development and production of an ACA demonstrator; and so the Experimental Aircraft Programme (EAP) was born.

In 1983, Italy, Germany, France, the UK and Spain launched the 'Future European Fighter Aircraft' (FEFA) programme. The aircraft was to have short take-off and landing (STOL) and beyond visual range (BVR) capabilities. In 1984 France reiterated its requirement for a carrier-capable version and demanded a, if not the, leading role. Italy, West Germany and the UK opted out and established a new EFA programme. In 1985, West Germany, the UK and Italy agreed to go ahead with the Eurofighter; and confirmed that France, along with Spain, had chosen not to proceed as a member of the project. Despite pressure from France, Spain rejoined the Eurofighter project. France elected to pursue its own ACX project, which was to become the Dassault Rafale.

By 1986 the cost of the programme had reached £180 million. When the EAP programme had started, the cost was supposed to be equally shared by both government and industry, but the West German and Italian governments wavered on the agreement and the three main industrial partners had to provide £100 million to keep the programme from ending. In April 1986, the BAe EAP was rolled out at BAe Warton, by this time partially funded by MBB, BAe and Aeritalia. The aircraft first flew on 6 August 1986. The current Typhoon bears a strong resemblance to the EAP and design work continued over the next five years. Initial requirements for numbers were: UK: 250 aircraft, Germany: 250, Italy: 165 and Spain: 100. The share of the production work was divided among the countries in proportion to their projected procurement— DASA (33 per cent), British Aerospace (33 per cent), Aeritalia (21 per cent), and Construcciones Aeronáuticas SA (CASA) (13 per cent). The Munich-based Eurofighter Jagdflugzeug GmbH was established in 1986 to manage development of the project and EuroJet Turbo GmbH, the alliance of Rolls-Royce, MTU Aero Engines, FiatAvio (now Avio) for development of the engine (EJ200).

I give that brief history of the project just to show how time-consuming, frustrating and wasteful such collaborative programmes can be. The main cause of delays, apart from the French in the early days of the programme, was the Germans who were for ever looking for ways of minimising their commitment whilst maximising their industrial share of the programme. They just kept prevaricating mainly because of budgetary concerns and causing delay after delay. There is no doubt in my mind that the UK could have saved a significant amount of money and time by going it alone once we had made the decision to go ahead with the EAP demonstrator. But then again there is always the argument that once you are involved in a multinational agreement, it is difficult to get out of it and the programme is therefore less likely to be cancelled. Large military programmes are difficult enough; but get politicians and foreign governments involved and the difficulties increase exponentially. As I recollect, I got approval from the Equipment Procurement Committee for the programme in 1988. And it was to be nearly 20 years before we had a squadron of Typhoons declared operational—and coincidentally it was No. 3 (F) Sqn. And if you took it back to the original thoughts about the need for such an aircraft, it was nearly 40 years. Absolutely ridiculous; no wonder it is an outrageously expensive programme because, not least, 'time is money'.

There were two other arguments which dominated discussions. One was the possibility of 'buying off the shelf'; and in this case that meant the F18 or the F16. Certainly McDonnell Douglas was approaching the Prime Minister direct with their proposals and she was willing to listen. The second argument was the issue of stealth technology. Without doubt the F18 or the F16 would have been a cheaper and quicker and probably a more cost-effective solution. But then there was the issue of UK industry, in this case British Aerospace, Rolls Royce and GEC plus sundry other SMEs. Not that I had much say in the issue, but I took the view that the UK industrial lobby was such that to cut them out would be cutting off your nose to spite your face. It seemed to me that if there was a possibility of exporting an aircraft, then it was probably worth pursuing as a national project, and a new fighter aircraft was such a case in point. If the proposal was to develop a national solution that would almost certainly be unique to the UK, then it probably did not make sense. An example of that, which occurred after my time, was the proposed development of the Nimrod MRA 4 based on the remaining Nimrod airframes which were basically almost 50 years old. If you have ever tried to refurbish a vintage car, you just know that it is going to be at least twice as expensive as you thought and that it would never achieve the same performance as a modern motor car. Apply the same theory to an aircraft and the problems would be multiplied, and added to that you had not the slightest chance of exporting the product as there were no more airframes available. So where was the sense in that?

The issue of stealth technology was more difficult. Very few people in UK, in fact only about half a dozen, were aware of the US capabilities with regard to stealth technology and that was including the Prime Minister. I had had the privilege of a guided tour around the US facilities including the wing of F117 Nighthawks, a twin engined stealth attack aircraft, which the public, even in the US, did not know existed. I was well aware that EFA had no stealth technology in its design and, that if the Soviets had such a capability, it could negate its superior airframe performance, but I could not say anything. However I did go to a meeting at Langley with the CIA and DIA in Washington to find out what they knew about Soviet capabilities. It was an interesting meeting if only for the fact that it came to a halt half way through because of some disagreement between the two US organisations. It was not because they were concerned about what they could tell us but because the CIA did not want the DIA to know what they knew. However, it turned out that it was unlikely that the Soviets had advanced very far with stealth technology and that it would not affect the operational capability of EFA.

The culmination of all this was a meeting with Margaret Thatcher in No. 10 to get her blessing before going ahead with the programme. It was quite fascinating to watch her in action. She had all the papers in front of her and it was obvious that she had read every single word—the famous yellow highlighter had been hard at work. Basically she fired questions at us like a machine gun. If you came straight back with an answer, she did not wait to listen to it; she just moved on to the next question. She continued in that mode until you hesitated and then the knife would be in. It was quite an exhausting and demanding cross-examination. Being one of her ministers must have been quite a challenging occupation if she used the same technique on everyone, and I believe she did. Afterwards I had a one-on-one session with her concerning stealth technology about which she was very concerned; the outcome of that meeting was a somewhat reluctant go-ahead.

There was a slightly amusing sequel concerning stealth issues. The US had agreed that we could put an exchange pilot into the programme, but because the knowledge of it was so restricted, the pilot had to be chosen without anyone knowing exactly what it was for. The CAS of the time, who was one of the few who did know about it, took it upon himself to choose the candidate, which he did. He subsequently sent me a note to say who he had chosen and I was horrified to see that it was a pilot I had fired for unsuitability from my Jaguar wing in Germany in 1979. With some trepidation I went upstairs to his office to tell him that I thought it was not a particularly wise choice. I thought that it would not be well received; but much to my relief he just said 'Well you had better choose him then'! So I did.

Fortunately not all programmes were as complex as EFA; but not many were straightforward. British industry always wanted their pound of flesh and the politicians just loved interfering, and then accusing officials of incompetence or waste. Air programmes were usually expensive so the other services would always oppose them as they could see the RAF taking a large slice of the budget. The MoD civil servants also had to have their say and rather than being supportive, they would usually regard it their duty to say why not. They usually regarded it as an intellectual exercise and the needs of the services were usually submerged under a sea of paper, but it all made for an interesting and varied life with never a dull moment. After four years of being a Whitehall warrior, at the end of 1989 I was ready to go elsewhere—but where.

It turned out that there not many options at the time and finally I was asked, much to my surprise, to take over as commandant general of the RAF Regiment and director general of security. It was not something I had expected and indeed I felt somewhat diffident about the prospect. As a Harrier man, I had had a fairly close association with the Regiment and I had always been of the view that to put a GD pilot in the post of commandant was a bit of a slap in the face for the professional Regiment officer. They had a wealth of very capable people and, indeed, there had been several RAF Regiment officers who had made the grade. So just why the RAF continued to put a pilot as commandant general was beyond me and quite wrong. Nevertheless, after some thought, I accepted the post. And having accepted the post, as the Queen was the air commodore in chief of the Regiment, I was summoned to the Palace for an audience with Her Majesty. This occurred in a small drawing room and was, in fact, a very informal and relaxed event.

The Regiment had the good sense to provide me with a first class personal staff officer (PSO). His name was Ian McPhee and I also had an old friend on the staff, Air Cdre Mickey Witherow, whom I had known for years. Between the two of them they would keep me on the straight and narrow. Indeed all of the Regiment staff were very supportive and keen to ensure that their commandant general did not put a foot wrong. The other half of the job was looking after the RAF police who were a slightly strange and secretive bunch and tended to look after themselves. So it was the Regiment that got most of my attention. And a more professional, loyal, disciplined and enthusiastic bunch of people you could not wish to meet. Their values were, I suppose, best described as old fashioned—and none the worse for that—and served as an example to us all. One of the first events I attended was the annual regiment dinner for serving and retired officers. Who should be there but 'Dad' Roberts, by now a retired group captain and a revered figure as far as the Regiment was concerned. So I recalled the event of him marching me off the parade square at Cranwell much to the amusement of the audience. And at the dinner the following year, he came up to me and presented me with a beautiful glass tankard engraved with an outline of the RAF College and cadets on parade—and one being marched off in ignominy. It is one of my treasured possessions.

Fortunately I had throughout the years kept myself reasonably fit as, in all my time in MoD; I used to run two or three miles at least three times a week. So when it came to doing the Regiment fitness test, even though I did not have to, it was not difficult. I snuck off to Uxbridge one morning with my PSO and driver and the three of us completed the test. They were, I think, quite surprised that a superannuated fighter pilot could achieve the standard without a problem. It was during another trip to Uxbridge for a ceremonial parade that an amusing incident occurred. When we left the office in Northumberland Avenue we were advised not to use the front entrance as there was some problem with an unidentified package—this was in the days of IRA bombs—and we went out the back way. We got to Uxbridge and started unloading the car to change into uniform. My PSO, as a Regiment officer, had his 'parade hat and shoes' in a special case and we discovered it was missing. The penny dropped and we realised what the unidentified package had been. I say 'had been' because despite making an urgent phone call back to MoD it was not in time to prevent the bomb squad from blowing up the said hat and shoes. It would not have been such a serious incident if it had not also closed off the whole of Whitehall and prevented Margaret Thatcher from getting back to No. 10! We were not very popular and Ian had to go grovelling to the police to make our apologies.

I enjoyed my time with the RAF Regiment and they made me feel completely at home. I was privileged to watch the Ceremony of the Keys at the Tower when the Regiment were taking their turn of duty and one can only feel pride when watching the Queens Colour Squadron, who usually represent the Royal Air Force at ceremonial events, doing their continuity drill display. I am not sure that the RAF at large appreciates what a superb and professional organisation it is and how lucky they are to have the Regiment looking after base security both on the ground and for close air defence. Their performance in Afghanistan only goes to prove the case. When the chips are down, you can rely on the Regiment. However I still felt slightly uncomfortable that they did not have a home grown commandant and, as there was one waiting in the wings—David Hawkins—I resolved to take early retirement and hand over to him. And after a year as CG, I was asked whether I would consider undertaking a task as an independent consultant for AGARD, a NATO research organisation based in Paris, and that provided me with the opportunity to bow out gracefully. That meant another audience with the Queen and, for the life of me, I cannot remember what was discussed. All I can remember was that both interviews were relaxed and informal events.

So ended my 37 years with the Royal Air Force. I had enjoyed my time flying which had been longer than most, and, much to my surprise, I even enjoyed my last five years in MoD. If I had sat down right at the start of my time in the RAF and sketched out my dream career, I would not have had the nerve to ask for what actually happened. It had been beyond my wildest dreams. It had been challenging, hard work, enjoyable and the Queen even paid me for doing what I enjoyed most—namely flying. In retrospect I do not think I would have changed a thing. Each tour had had unique challenges and it was never the same thing twice although there was, of course, a recurrent theme of aviation. Even the ground tours, the Royal College of Defence Studies and HQRAFG, had been enjoyable in their own peculiar way; although I did find the repetitive nature of RCDS a bit boring towards the end. But it was different and eminently preferable to the grind of MoD. However, having said that, if you are going to have to work in MoD then operational requirements is perhaps one of the most interesting of jobs as the future of the Air Force is in your hands. And finally the RAF Regiment reminded me of old fashioned values and the merits of loyalty, commitment and duty as demonstrated in the way they went about their business. They are an example to us all and a reminder of the things in life that matter.

It had been a 'rhapsody in blue' and it was time to move to pastures new.

Glossary of Terms and Acronyms

A&AEE	The Aeroplane and Armament Experimental Establishment
ACDS(OR)Air	Assistant Chief of Defence Staff (Operational Requirements) Air
ACM	Air Chief Marshal (4*)
AFME	Air Forces Middle East
AM	Air Marshal (3*)
AMSO	Air Member for Supply and Organisation
AP	Air Publication
APC	Armament Practice Camp
AP & R	Alert Posture & Readiness
ATAF	Allied Tactical Air Force
ATC	Air Traffic Control
AUW	All Up Weight
AVM	Air Vice Marshal (2*)
BOQs	Bachelor Officers' Quarters
CAS	Chief of the Air Staff
CBU	Cluster Bomb Unit
CCF	Combined Cadet Force
CFS	Central Flying School
CG (1)	Centre of Gravity
CG (2)	Commandant General
CinC	Commander in Chief
Clutch Stations	Wildenrath, Brüggen and Laarbruch (RAF bases in Germany)

COC	Combat Operations Centre
COMAAFCE	Commander Allied Air Forces, Central Europe
CRDF	Cathode Ray Direction Finding—a transmission from the aircraft would bring up a bearing on the CR display
DFLS	Day Fighter Leaders' School
DME	Distance Measuring Equipment (displays the distance from a beacon)
Dual capable	Units capable of nuclear and conventional attack missions
DUS(Air)	Deputy Under Secretary (Air)
Dutch Roll	A combination of yawing and rolling which is difficult to control
ENT	Ear Nose & Throat
EOKA	A Greek acronym for the National Organisation of Cypriot Fighters
ESM	Electronic Support Measures
ETPS	Empire Test Pilots; School
FAA	Fleet Air Arm
FAC	Forward Air Controller
FLIR	Forward Looking Infra Red
FR	Fighter Reconnaissance
FRA	Federal Regular Army—an Arab/Adeni force with British officers
FRG	Federal Republic of Germany
GAF	German Air Force
GCA	Ground Controlled Approach (by radar operator)
HE	High Explosive
HUD	Head Up Display
IAF	Italian Air Force
IFF	Identification Friend or Foe—an ATC system used to track and identify aircraft
IN	Inertial Navigation
INAS	Inertial and Navigation Attack System (Harrier)
IRE	Instrument Rating Examiner
IRT	Instrument Rating Test
JPT	Jet Pipe Temperature
JSF	Joint Strike Fighter, the Lockheed Martin F35
LGB	Laser Guided Bomb—a guided bomb that uses semi-active laser guidance to strike a designated target

LTCs	Long Term Costings—the method by which MoD attempts to budget for future expenditure
MADGE	Microwave Aircraft Digital Guidance Equipment—a portable tactical instrument approach and landing system
Maple Flag	A Canadian variant of Red Flag
MEXE	Military Experimental Engineering Establishment—who developed the landing pad for the Harrier
MPC	Missile Practice Camp
MT	Motor Transport
MTI	Moving Target Indicator
MRAF	Marshal of the Royal Air Force (5*)
NAVWASS	Navigation and Weapon Aiming Sub-System (Jaguar)
NBC	Nuclear, Biological & Chemical
nms	Nautical miles
OAS	Organisation de l'armée secrete—a French far right paramilitary organisation during the Algerian war
OC	Officer Commanding
OCU	Operational Conversion Unit
OQs	Officer Qualities
ORTF	Operational Reliability Trials Flying
PPL	Private Pilot's Licence
PRC	Peoples' Republic of China
PSI	Public Service Institute—a non-public fund which organises activities of a welfare nature on an RAF station
QFI	Qualified Flying Instructor
QRA	Quick Reaction Alert
RAE	Royal Aircraft Establishment (Farnborough)
RAFA	Royal Air Forces Association—a charity providing welfare support for serving and ex-serving RAF personnel
RCT	Royal Corps of Transport (Truck!)
RDAF	Royal Danish Air Force
RNLAF	Royal Netherlands Air Force
RSO	Range Safety Officer
R&R	Rest and Recuperation
SACEUR	Supreme Allied Commander Europe

Salmond Trophy	A tactical navigation and bombing competition between the RAF Germany squadrons
SAM	Surface to Air Missile
SAP	Semi Armour Piercing
SASO	Senior Air Staff Officer—the senior staff officer in a HQ responsible for air operations
SME	Small and Medium size Enterprises
SMO	Senior Medical Officer
SNEB	SNEB refers to the name of the manufacturer—it is a 68 mm air to ground rocket with 18 rockets in each pod
SOAF	Sultan of Oman's Air Force
SSAFA	Soldiers Sailors Airmen and Families Association
STO	Short Take Off
TACAN	Tactical Air Navigation—provides a bearing and distance from a ground beacon
USMC	United States Marine Corps
USN	United States Navy
VCDS	Vice Chief of Defence Staff
VL	Vertical Landing
VTO	Vertical Take Off
WO	Warrant Officer
WSO	Weapons System Operator

APPENDIX

List of Aircraft Flown

Aircraft Flown (as Captain)

Gliders
Sedbergh
Olympia

Piston
DH82a Tiger Moth
Provost T1 and T52
Chipmunk
Harvard 2b
Beaver AL Mk1
Beagle Pup
Devon C Mk1 & 2
Twin Pioneer
SE5a
Basset
Sea Fury T20

Helicopter
Gazelle HT3

Turbo Prop
Viscount 744
Pilatus PC9
Tucano

Jet
Vampire FB9 & T11
Meteor T7, F8 & NF14
Jet Provost 3, 4 ,5 & 5a
Hunter F4, F6, T66, T7, T7a, T8, FGA9 & FR10
Seahawk 6
Javelin Mk 2/7 & 9
Canberra B2 & T4
Lightning DB/1. 2, 2a, 2½, 3, T4, T5, F6, 52
Sea Vixen FAW2
Scimitar F1
Short SB5
P 1127
Harrier DB, GR1, T2, GR3, T4
Phantom F4k prototype, FG1, FGR2
Jaguar A, GR1 & T2
Buccaneer S2
Gnat
Hawk T1

Aircraft Flown but not as Captain

Piston
Aero Commander
Cessna Titan
Piper Chieftain
Trago-Mills SAH1

Helos
Scout
Whirlwind
Wessex
Puma
Sioux
Chinook

Turbo Prop
Firecracker
Turbo Porter
C130 Hercules
Argosy
Andover

Jet
T33
T38
F104D
F100F
CF5B
F15B
F18
F111D
Alphajet
BAC1-11
VC10 K2